P9-DNR-065

REASONS FOR HOPE

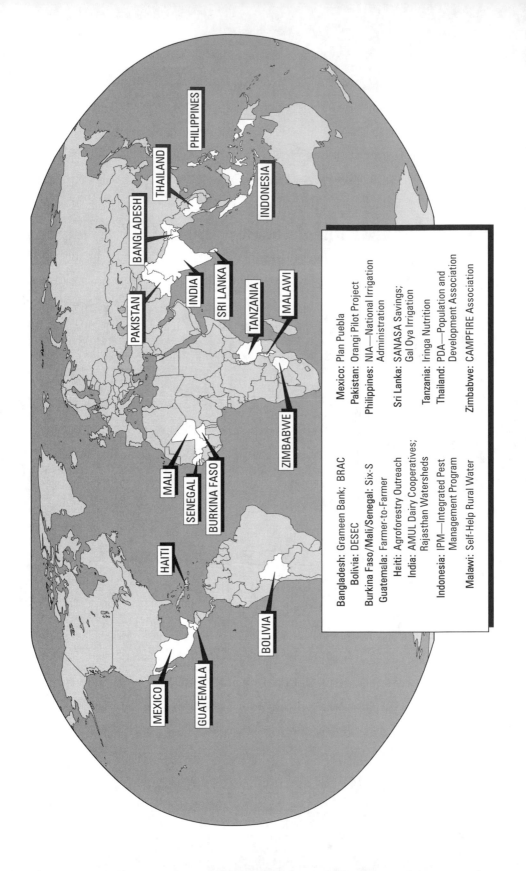

Bangladesh: Grameen Bank; BRAC
Bolivia: DESEC
Burkina Faso/Mali/Senegal: Six-S
Guatemala: Farmer-to-Farmer
    Haiti: Agroforestry Outreach
    India: AMUL Dairy Cooperatives;
        Rajasthan Watersheds
Indonesia: IPM—Integrated Pest
        Management Program
    Malawi: Self-Help Rural Water

Mexico: Plan Puebla
Pakistan: Orangi Pilot Project
Philippines: NIA—National Irrigation
        Administration

Sri Lanka: SANASA Savings;
        Gal Oya Irrigation

Tanzania: Iringa Nutrition
Thailand: PDA—Population and
        Development Association

Zimbabwe: CAMPFIRE Association

REASONS FOR HOPE

INSTRUCTIVE EXPERIENCES
IN RURAL DEVELOPMENT

editors
ANIRUDH KRISHNA
NORMAN UPHOFF
MILTON J. ESMAN

Kumarian Press

Reasons for Hope: Instructive Experiences in Rural Development.

Published 1997 in the United States of America by Kumarian Press, Inc.,
14 Oakwood Avenue, West Hartford, Connecticut 06119-2127 USA.

Copyright © 1997 Kumarian Press, Inc. All rights reserved.

No part of this book may be reproduced or transmitted in any form
or by any means, electronic or mechanical, including photocopy, recording, or
information storage and retrieval system, without prior permission of the publisher.

Production supervised by Jenna Dixon
Copyedited by Beth Richards   Typeset by Corinne Girouard
Text design by Jenna Dixon   Proofread by Ann Flanders
Map by Christopher L. Brest

The text of this book is set in 10.8/13 Sabon;
the display type is Rockwell Condensed.

Printed in Canada on recycled acid-free paper by Best Book Manufacturers.
Text printed with soy based ink.

Library of Congress Cataloging-in-Publication Data
Reasons for hope : instructive experiences in rural development / editors Anirudh
    Krishna, Norman Uphoff, Milton J. Esman.
        p.   cm. — (Kumarian Press books on international development)
    Includes bibliographical references and index.
    ISBN 1-56549-064-9 (alk. paper). — ISBN 1-56549-063-0 (pbk. : alk. paper)
    1. Rural development—Developing countries. 2. Agricultural development
projects—Developing countries. 3. Human services—Developing countries.
4. Natural resources—Developing countries—Management. I. Krishna, Anirudh,
1958–   . II. Uphoff, Norman Thomas. III. Esman, Milton J. (Milton Jacob),
1918–   . IV. Series.
HN981.C6R43   1996
307.1'412'091722—dc20   96-26552

06 05 04 03   10 9 8 7 6 5   1st Printing 1997

Contents

SOCIAL SERVICES: HEALTH, NUTRITION, FAMILY PLANNING, AND WATER SUPPLY   201

NATURAL RESOURCES: AGROFORESTRY, WATERSHED, AND WILDLIFE MANAGEMENT   239

Illustrations

Instructive Engagements in Rural Development

Two contrasting trends in Africa, Asia and Latin America have imprinted themselves on the public mind. We see growing poverty and misery in many countries, accompanied and often caused by environmental degradation—soil erosion, deforestation, water and air pollution. Millions of people are still unable to produce enough for their subsistence needs and suffer from ill health, illiteracy and other debilitations. We also see the rapid growth of third-world urban centers, which are doubling their size every twelve to fifteen years. This population increase is accelerated both by the push of rural poverty and the pull of expanding industrial and service sectors.

It would be fortuitous if urban growth could provide the solution to rural underdevelopment. But the more disparity there is between rural and urban sectors in incomes and quality of life, the more people are drawn into cities and towns, desperately searching for the better lives denied them in villages and on farms. This depresses wages and urban living conditions and overtaxes already strained urban services such as housing, water supply, electricity and waste disposal. It also makes maintaining orderly and safe urban society nearly impossible. Moreover, long-term economic progress depends heavily on having a more productive agricultural sector that is able to feed the growing urban population, provide markets for their goods and services and release surplus labor for more productive opportunities in cities, not a depressed and stagnant sector that expels wretched refugees.

There are some remarkably divergent views of the future for the Third World. One scenario emphasizes urbanization and industrial growth potentials, adapted to the electronic information age, that hold out the possibility that more countries will follow the path of the "tigers" in East and Southeast Asia (see World Bank 1993; and critique by Amsden 1994). This scenario presupposes that macroeconomic policies installing liberalization, marketization and export orientation will produce a take-off into technology-driven, trade-dependent economic growth. A contrasting, more despairing view foresees many, if not all, Third World countries slipping into despondency and dissolution due to growing populations, environmental collapse and civil disorder (Kaplan 1994; Connelly and Kennedy 1994).

1

The second scenario is probably more likely than the first, although we are not yet ready to accept either. We have studied rural development for the past twenty-five years and have been engaged with planning and implementing programs in West Africa, South Asia and Southeast Asia. Looking at a variety of experiences around the world, we see reasons for hope that rural—and, ultimately, national—collapse is not preordained, and that we need not pin all our expectations on the urban sector. Of course, the cities and towns of Asia, Africa and Latin America will continue to grow. We are not "rural fundamentalists" who think this process can or should be stopped. But we believe that the future of both rural and urban populations depends on finding ways to make rural life both more productive and more attractive, so that urban societies and economies are surrounded and supported by vigorous, progressive rural communities and regions.

We are acquainted with numerous instructive examples of how life for millions of rural households has been improved by purposeful initiatives over the past several decades. Some of these have been initiated by government agencies and some by nongovernmental organizations. (Fortunately, government programs are not necessarily doomed to failure, as is argued so often these days.) Some had effective external donor assistance, while others progressed with few outside resources. Some were conceived and promoted by remarkable individuals; others were the product of team efforts or institutional initiatives. In all the cases, however, success depended on sets of persons who saw acutely both needs and solutions, and who persevered as they innovated, bringing into being major programs that have benefited large numbers of their fellow human beings. Many, if not all, programs have become institutionalized, involving both local and external resources and personnel in appropriate, yet changing, combinations and roles.

These cases speak for themselves—eloquently, movingly, persuasively. They show us that approaches to rural development that respect the inherent capabilities, intelligence and responsibility of rural people and that systematically build on experience have a reasonable chance of making significant advances in improving those people's lives. A critical success factor is creating organizational capabilities at local levels that can mobilize and manage resources effectively for the benefit of the many rather than just the few.

These advances are not just idiosyncratic, even if the successful formulas were improvised case by case, and even if the institutional mechanisms evolved are quite varied. There are important commonalities among these experiences which, we believe, should be more widely recognized and adapted (not simply adopted) in similar efforts elsewhere. External assistance can be beneficial if given at times and in ways that are "pump-priming," that is, positive-sum. Too often, however, the way assistance has been given displaces or even discourages local resource contributions, resulting in outside aid that is zero-sum, or worse, negative-sum. The critical elements for success have been novel ideas and strong value commitments that outside resources could support and make more productive, once a significant learning process (Korten 1980) is initiated and carried through. This learning process establishes appropriate forms of organization and technology that complement and support each other.

We know a number of the people who have been instrumental in initiating large-scale programs to promote rural development in different ways, and others who could help us enlist the cooperation of these protagonists of rural development in our undertaking. Because we have been personally involved in two of the cases included in this volume, we know them from the inside, which gives us a greater appreciation of what is required to make others' efforts succeed.

Now more than ever, it is important to reaffirm that significant advances are attainable for the hundreds of millions of households who constitute "the rural poor." They are a potential source of great wealth and creativity who, under present institutional, cultural and policy conditions, must seek first and foremost their own survival. Their poverty deprives not only them but also the rest of us of the greater value they could produce under more conducive circumstances. The people who pioneered the various programs recounted in this volume recognized this potential and sought to evoke it.

The cases in this volume illustrate how inspired leaders, thoughtful planners and creative managers have put together effective combinations of participatory and administrative organizations that utilize appropriate technologies and effective incentives. In addition to the widely recognized cases, we include some lesser-known programs that have accomplished remarkable improvements for their members or beneficiaries. We hope that they will be influential in ongoing efforts to broaden the base of rural development, in their own countries and beyond.

We started with a list of almost thirty cases from Asia, Africa and Latin America, having followed the literature on rural development on a worldwide basis for years. We wanted to be able to learn from "insider" perspectives on what is needed and what is feasible for bringing about large-scale improvements in rural quality of life. In anthropology, a distinction is made between *emic* and *etic* views of reality, in an analogy to the difference in linguistics between *phonemics* and *phonetics* (Headland, Pike and Harris 1990). The first refers to people's subjective perspective about what they are doing, saying or believing, while the second attempts to reconstruct, from an outside or objective perspective, what is being done, said or believed.

Considering how best to present and learn from the various cases, we saw value in having both the *emic* and *etic* treatments of the respective experiences. We wanted to see from the inside how these programs got started, how they evolved, their difficulties and results. We also wanted to compare features such as the adaptation of technology, the role of participant organizations, the nature and impact of institutionalization and the use of external resources by looking at the experiences within a common framework. The scope of the project we had in mind quickly became greater than could reasonably be encompassed within one book, so we decided to divide the project into two parts. This meant preparing two volumes, one presenting the experiences *emically*, as understood by those who "made things happen," and another considering these and other cases *etically* to construct an analysis of what is required to achieve success in rural development across different environments.

This volume, *Reasons for Hope*, shares with readers a remarkable set of rural development success stories from the *emic* perspective across various sectors in fifteen countries. A companion volume, *Reasons for Success*, offers an *etic* assessment of the factors that contributed to these and other programs' ability to alter positively and sustainably the lives of large numbers of rural households. The selection of programs presented here was constrained by our ability to enlist the cooperation of some very busy people.[1]

We would have liked to include a dozen more, but these eighteen cases are among the most important and impressive examples of scaled-up, sustainable rural development. We doubt that there are eighteen other cases in Asia, Africa and Latin America that, taken together, would be as broadly significant as these. There are more cases from Asia than from other parts of the Third World—seven are from South Asia and three from Southeast Asia, with four each from Africa and from Latin America. This reflects the larger relative numbers of people living in Asia and also the stronger traditions there of large-scale collective self-help.

One of the debates in donor circles these days is whether external agencies can have widespread and beneficial impact through direct investment in development programs such as these, or whether more can be accomplished by trying to change the policy environment. We are glad to see donors having doubts whether the "project" mode of assistance is cost-effective. We have previously analyzed the long-term effectiveness of donor-aided projects and found that conventional projects, especially megaprojects, seldom produce sustainable and equitable benefits commensurate with their cost (Uphoff 1990).

Some of the cases included here, such as the farmer organization effort in Sri Lanka and the agroforestry initiative in Haiti, were indeed "projects." But as can be seen from reading their history, these were conceived and implemented quite differently from the way that most donor projects are carried out. Nothing is wrong with projects as purposeful initiatives to bring about economic and social change. Rather, it is the predilection of donor and government agencies to design and implement detailed interventions in a "blueprint" mode that is at fault. Such a rigid plan constrains them from making appropriate modifications and adaptations as the work proceeds and as more is learned about the task and the task environment. We also find dubious the concept of a terminal date for a project. To be successful, change has to be continuous, sustained and locally grounded. Sporadic bursts of effort seldom produce results that survive.

The case studies here give evidence of the importance of the policy environment for development initiatives, but they also show how well-conceived and flexibly implemented initiatives can *change* that environment in desirable ways. Change needs to come simultaneously from above and below. Too often, however, "policy dialogue" is limited to making adjustments at the top levels, with the hope that these will somehow percolate and, in due course, benefit the large and ever-increasing fringe. There is no simple sequence, however, where one first changes policy, then implements an appropriate program. Rather, the process of policy change involves more experimentation and iteration than implied by the language of "policy dialogue"—a "big bang" theory of development.

Some economists suggest that projects are not important because more can be accomplished through macroeconomic policy changes, by "getting the prices right," to use a popular phrase, or by some other manipulation of market incentives. This approach to rural development is no better, in our view, than attempts to "push projects" and "move money." The macro-economic recommendations commonly incorporated in "structural adjustment" packages have little positive impact on the rural poor and do little or nothing to create local- and intermediate-level organizational capabilities to plan, monitor and manage various other improvements in people's lives and livelihoods. As the following case studies show, once greater capacities for local management are in place, they are available to introduce other innovations that raise productivity and enhance the quality of life. Such externalities mean that most investments in organizational capability (costs) have multiple payoffs (benefits).

We have adopted a hybrid *emic–etic* approach to this subject, trying to maintain a degree of scholarly detachment from the subject while also being personally engaged with it. We think that this is an extremely important subject, one that has major implications for the world that all of our children, in rich as well as poor countries, will inherit. We draw inspiration as well as ideas from the accomplishments of those who have blazed new paths for rural development in Africa, Asia and Latin America. We admire them and the thousands of other persons in these and similar programs who shared the vision and hopes of the founders and guides. Many unnamed and unheralded people contributed to the successes reported here, and those who initiated these efforts express their appreciation in this book to the many others who helped them give life and force to the ideals that animated their efforts.

We find throughout these cases that reductionist approaches are part of the problem—trying to explain success as due *only* to the prominent leader, or *only* to the incentives employed or *only* to the technology used. In contrast, these cases convey a sense of the complexity and interdependence of social change. Many contingent factors are merged to produce robust, innovative methods for improving agriculture, health, water supply or soil conservation. While the world is indeed complex, we see that constraining "circles," even if they are not always "vicious," can be broken by initiatives that are well thought out but adaptable, conceived by leadership that persisted and shared credit widely, by melding so-called traditional and modern features into new and attractive combinations. No formulas or recipes for rural development are proposed by these cases. Rather, many techniques, approaches and principles are presented that, when suitably combined and reinforced, offer the promise of change that is transformative, not just incremental.

We thank the contributors for their input to this project and for their generous cooperation. The cases are presented without editorial introduction or elaboration. The editors offer some concluding observations at the end of this volume but reserve most of our own thoughts on this subject for the companion volume *Reasons for Success*. We thank also the Cornell International Institute for Food, Agriculture and Development (CIIFAD) for its support of this undertaking to clarify requirements for building local management capabilities.

NOTE

1. We regret that there are no women contributors to this volume. We invited Ela Bhatt, founder of the Self-Employed Women's Association (SEWA), which has improved the lives of tens of thousands of very poor women in Ahmedabad, India (Rose 1992); Sithembiso Nyoni, executive director of the Organization of Rural Organizations for Progress (ORAP), a grassroots NGO with nearly one million members in Zimbabwe; and Nafsiah Mboi, first national president of the PKK, a women's organization in Indonesia that supports a national network of village-level health posts (Posyandus) to improve health, nutrition and family planning of women and children. Unfortunately, given heavy demands on their time, they were not able to participate in this project. Some of the lessons from their programs' success will be incorporated in the companion volume.

MULTISECTORAL DEVELOPMENT

1 The Grameen Bank Story: Rural Credit in Bangladesh

Muhammad Yunus

Bangladesh became an independent country in December 1971 at the end of the war of liberation. In 1972, I returned from the United States where I taught economics, and joined Chittagong University as head of the economics department. At that time, in the first flush of independence, everyone believed that things would start moving. It was thought that the misery of the common people would soon come to an end. Instead of moving up, the country started sliding down very rapidly. I became aware that there was much that could not be solved by following the teachings of development economics. I decided to go out among the common folk in the countryside to see for myself.

Chittagong University is located among the villages. I could just walk out of the campus and see the poverty for myself. I began my work in the village of Jobra. I talked to a lot of village people and learned many things. The story told by one woman touched me so deeply I decided to do something immediately. This woman, Sophia Khatoon, made bamboo stools for a living. She had the skills and worked very hard, but her daily earnings amounted to the equivalent of only two U.S. cents. I found that there was a simple reason for her poverty: she did not have working capital. Twenty cents was all she needed to buy a bamboo from which to make stools, but she was so poor that she had to borrow the money from a trader. In Bangladesh, as in many other countries, private moneylenders charge exorbitant rates of interest, up to 10 percent per day. The trader also forced her to sell the finished product back to him at well below the market price. I was struck by the simplicity of the solution that her situation required. If only credit was made available to her, she could work her way out of poverty.

I took a student of mine and we went around the village to see if there were more people who were borrowing from traders. In a week's time, we came up with a list of forty-two people. The total working capital required by all forty-two of them was only thirty dollars. I was ashamed of myself for being part of a society that was unable to provide thirty dollars to forty-two able, hard-working, skilled people. I lost faith in all my fancy development theories.

9

I started by lending thirty dollars of my own money to free these forty-two people from unfair business deals. I found that even this small amount made a big difference to their condition. I wanted to help more poor people, but how long could I keep doing this with my own money, and how many people could I help?

The banks are supposed to make credit available. I set about trying to establish a link between the bank and the poor people in that village. I talked to the local bank manager, but the banks, I came to realize, have real difficulties in working with poor people. The banks are tied to their procedures, and they will advance loans only to those who can furnish collateral. The bank officials laughed at me when I suggested that banks should lend to poor people because they would repay the loans. I talked to more senior bank officials and received the same answer—without collateral, without guarantees, the banks would not make loans. I was beginning to lose hope when somebody gave me an idea—if I could find a guarantor, someone who would offer collateral on behalf of the poor, the banks would give the loan.

So, I went to the banks and offered myself as the guarantor. They told me that, with my personal guarantee, they could provide loans up to $300. After all these discussions, the banks still took six months to process the case. Finally, in 1976, I succeeded in getting a few loans and passing them on to the poor people in the village. Thus was born the *Jobra Grameen Bank Prakalpa* (Jobra Rural Bank Project), organized as part of the Rural Economics Program of Chittagong University. We attempted to test, through action-research, the hypothesis that if credit, with reasonable terms and conditions, can be made available to the poor, they have the skills and ability to haul themselves out of poverty.

Because the banks were convinced that poor people would not repay loans, I felt challenged to develop procedures to ensure that people would pay back. And they did. So I gave more loans. At this point, having shown that the system could work very well, I asked the banks to take on the job themselves. "No," they said, "this is a special case in one village; this is not big enough." So I expanded my work and took it to more villages.

THE GRAMEEN BANK STARTS IN 1983

Credit is a kind of key, a passport to explore the potential of a person. The moment you lay your hands on credit, your mind starts ticking. You find out that you are a capable person. With each loan cycle, I could see our borrowers moving to ever-higher levels of creativity and self-expression. I knew then that credit was the real missing link between people and their creative potential. I wanted to make credit available to more and more poor people to give them the chance of a better future.

My efforts were not going unnoticed. In 1978, I was invited to speak at a seminar organized by the Bangladesh Bank, the central bank of Bangladesh. One banker in the audience challenged me to show that my system could work on a district-wide scale. I told the assembled bankers that if I got cooperation from all of them, I would show that the system could work not only in one district but throughout Bangladesh. When the deputy governor of the Bangladesh Bank found that I was serious about the enterprise, he convened a meeting of managing directors of all state-owned banks and asked me to present my proposals. They were accepted, and I was given two years' time in which to prove that lending money to the poor could be made to work at the district level.

I began work in Tangail district. I worked hard and the system did well. International agencies began to take notice of our work, and we began to receive grants from the Ford Foundation. In 1982, the International Fund for Agriculture Development (IFAD) gave us a low-interest loan of $3.4 million to help us expand our activities to three other districts—Dhaka, Patuakhali and Rangpur.

During these years, we had continued to show that poor people can borrow and pay back with excellent rates of repayment. Compared to the average rate of repayment for banks in Bangladesh (27 percent), our repayment rate was far higher (98 percent). Still, the banks maintained that the poor were not creditworthy. They continued to make huge numbers of loans to the rich. The same people who were given loans to start industries—which they drove into the ground—were given fresh loans to revive "sick" industries.

Something is wrong with the way the entire banking system is run. The poor and the unlettered are denied access by the condition of collateral and by all the documents and forms they are required to fill out. Collateral and documents are defended on the grounds that banks are the custodians of other people's money, and, therefore, they have to take all precautions while giving out loans. But have the banks taken these same precautions while lending to industrialists? What has been the impact of all their precautions when they cannot recover even one-third of their loans? What is the logic of collateral when, at election time in Bangladesh, the bulk of agricultural loans given to farmers are written off? No, collateral is not the only way for a bank to protect its money. The banks are neither able nor willing to help the poor. They are unwilling to change their procedures and their thinking. They are unwilling to step out of their offices, as we are doing, to take banking to the poor.

Finally, I asked myself, why am I running after the bankers? Why don't I set up a bank that will work only for the poor? In 1983, after a lot of running around, I received permission from the government to set up a bank. Thus the Grameen (rural) Bank was born as an independent financial institution. Today this bank serves two million borrowers and works in 34,000 villages, half of the 68,000 villages of Bangladesh. We have 1,041 branches and over 11,000 staff members.

A BANK OF THE POOR

Every human being has enormous capacity, enormous potential. Many people never get a chance to discover what capacity they have and how far they can go. This is not the fault of the poor person—he or she has to exert great effort and develop skills merely to survive. The fault lies instead with the societal arrangements that we have made, with the institutional designs we have introduced. No one seems to recognize that poor people are the ones most in need of credit. Only if they get credit on reasonable terms can poor people generate incomes for themselves and their families. And only if they generate incomes can they establish their right to food, to shelter, to clothing and to a decent and humane existence. I have seen bowed and subdued people transformed into proud and creative entrepreneurs when credit has come in to change their lives.

Credit is of fundamental importance if we are to build a just society where all human beings can live with dignity. I am convinced that credit is a basic human right. All other basic rights—food, shelter, education, health—are denied when a person is poor. Credit unlocks the door.

In Grameen, we lend only to the poorest of the poor. All our borrowers are rural people who own no more than half an acre of land. More than 45 percent of the population of Bangladesh falls into this category. Yet there is no element of charity in our operations. We charge an interest rate of 20 percent on our loans, which is 5 percent more than the official commercial rate. Still, people borrow with enthusiasm and with their ingenuity and talent, they change their own lives.

Ninety percent of the shares of Grameen are owned by its borrowers. They become shareholders by buying one share in the bank for US$2.50. Ten percent of the shares are owned by government. Grameen Bank's board of directors consists of thirteen members, nine of whom are borrower-shareholders elected every three years by the other borrower-shareholders. Three members are appointed by the government, and one is appointed by the board.

Members are free to use their loan for any productive economic activity they wish. Borrowers use their loans primarily for individual agriculture-based and rural nonfarm enterprises. Over 450 types of such activities have been financed, including milk-cow raising, paddy husking, cattle fattening, grocery shops, handlooms, bookbinding, perfume making and a variety of other productive microenterprises. Since 1982, we have been making loans to groups for collective enterprises, such as irrigation pump sets, shallow tubewells, rice hullers and oil mills. Loans are also made for leasing marketplaces in townships that traditionally were the preserve of the powerful and rich, for leasing land for cooperative farming, to take advantage of modern farming techniques, and for other group enterprises.

We have changed the lives of millions of poor people. The poorest of the poor have been transformed into self-employed entrepreneurs and have emerged as microengines of capitalist growth in rural areas. This is not a greedy or cut-throat capitalism. No one is exploited by anyone else. Social conciousness, along with a vision of individual well being, is the driving force.

SYSTEMS AND PROCEDURES

Because of the difficulties I initially faced in persuading the banks to lend money to the poor, I paid a lot of attention to the procedures and rules that we devised. I wanted to show the banks that their fears were unfounded: that the poor would repay because they had a strong sense of dignity. More than anything else, four elements of the Grameen strategy have been responsible for our success. These elements are group-based lending, taking the bank to the poor rather than having the poor come to the bank, a focus on women and a system of regular weekly installments for loan repayment.

Group-Based Lending

When a person wants to borrow from Grameen Bank, we ask him or her to form a group of five persons by finding four other friends of similar economic situation. The persons of the group must not be related to one another. We lend only to those who are landless or near-landless, that is, they must own less than half an acre of land. Only one member from any family, preferably a woman, can receive loans from Grameen. The group elects a chairperson and a secretary who hold office for one year only. The same persons cannot be reelected until other members of the group have had their chance. The chairperson is responsible for the discipline of the group and it is through her or him that the group conducts its business with the bank.

When a new group is formed, it is observed by a bank staff member for one month. If group members conform to the discipline of the Grameen Bank, the loan process starts. We do not give loans to all five persons in the group at the same time. The group chooses the two people who are neediest, and they receive loans first. The group is asked to monitor that these first two loans are used correctly and that repayments are made on time. If the first two members have repaid their installments on time for a month or two, the next two members become eligible to receive loans. The group secretary and chairperson are usually the last in the group to get loans.

The first loans are usually small. As members develop confidence, they ask for larger amounts. A member qualifies for a second loan after he or she has fully repaid the first loan. In each case, the group has to agree on the amount of the loan. Currently we are lending the equivalent of about one and one-half million dollars every working day. The average loan size is around 100 dollars.

The group has the power to discipline individual members. If a member does not attend the weekly meeting or pay the installments on time, the group can, by unanimous decision, impose a fine. It can also expel any member for chronic lack of discipline. A member who leaves the group must repay the full amount of any loan outstanding. If a member leaves without repaying the amount owed, the group must repay the balance. A new member may join the group if the group agrees unanimously about admitting him or her *and* if he or she meets the bank's eligibility criteria.

During this lending process, a kind of group support builds up. Each member is responsible to the group for her or his actions; in turn, the members help each other overcome problems. There is no need for Grameen to ask for collateral or guarantors. The groups themselves ensure that no individual borrower takes actions that prejudice the chances of any other member. Social collateral replaces material collateral. Individual greed is suppressed by collective responsibility. Each member of a group becomes a social-consciousness–driven entrepreneur.

Besides being a lending institution, Grameen also requires its borrowers to save. Each week each borrower saves at least one taka (2.5 cents), which is deposited at the weekly group meeting. In addition, 5 percent of each loan received is levied for the "group fund," and for loans larger than 1,000 taka another 0.5 percent of the loan amount is charged for the emergency fund. The group fund is managed by the group. Members can borrow from it in times of severe need, on terms fixed by the group; they can also invest the amount in any activity of their choosing. The emergency fund is managed by the bank and is used as a life insurance program. The total savings of Grameen borrowers now exceeds $70 million.

Several groups get together and form a center, and in each village there may be one or two centers. A center chief and a deputy center chief are elected by the respective group chairpersons from among themselves. All bank business is transacted at weekly meetings, which are held on designated days of the week for each center.

Taking the Bank to the Poor

Our whole operation is based on trust and on mutuality. In contrast, traditional banking is based on distrust and makes a person feel helpless and dependent. The poor feel bewildered and weak when they go to a bank and are asked to go from this window to that window, to furnish this document and that surety. In particular, people who are illiterate feel very intimidated.

In the Grameen system, we do not ask the borrower to come to the bank; instead, the bank goes to the borrowers' doorstep. Our staff go on a designated day of the week to each of the centers in all of the 34,000 villages. They meet personally with our two million borrowers. Each staff member is assigned a fixed number of centers, which often means he or she has to walk or cycle several miles to reach the centers. All the business of the bank is conducted openly in front of all the members, who know what is happening and can assess their situation with respect to all the other members. This helps to develop the mutual trust among the members of the groups and centers and acts as a disincentive against indiscipline by any member.

Coupled with this openness is a simple system of accounts. Each member is given a loan passbook in which all transactions are recorded. When a loan is fully repaid, a repayment certificate is issued, which enables a borrower to get a fresh loan. Bank staff members maintain ledgers for each of their centers. Accounts and audits are designed to facilitate operations. Once again, the starting point is trust, not mistrust.

Women

In Bangladesh, as in much of the developing world, the poor woman has the toughest time of all. She is confined first to her father's house, then to her husband's house—and has very little security in either place. She wants to do something about her plight, but the doors of opportunity are closed to her by social custom, by tradition and by what passes as religion in our villages. The prejudices against women are so deeply rooted that even some of our professional people cannot conceive that women can make a future for themselves and for their families. Commercial banks in

Bangladesh do not want to lend to women. If a woman wants to borrow from a bank, the manager will ask her to bring her husband along to discuss the business.

When I started giving loans, I wanted to make sure that at least 50 percent of our borrowers were women. Giving money to women was not easy. We faced opposition from husbands and from religious leaders. The village *mullahs*, in particular, were a potent source of opposition. They told the women that if they took loans from the Grameen Bank, they would be violating religion, they could not be assured of a decent burial and would face eternal condemnation. It was very difficult to work in these circumstances. But we started quietly in one corner. A few women, desperate to improve their lives, took loans. Their lives improved. Others saw them and followed. In this way, the movement gradually spread.

Not surprisingly, we also faced opposition from the regulatory agency, the Bangladesh Bank. To them, this was a completely new way of doing business. At one stage, they sent us a letter: "We notice a very high percentage of women among your borrowers. We cannot see the reason behind it. Please send your explanation." I wrote back that I would be happy to give an explanation, but I would first like to know if the regulators had ever sent a letter to any other bank asking why they had such a high percentage of male borrowers. I also told them that if they considered all the borrowers in Bangladesh, not more than 1 percent of them would be women, and that something must be wrong with their system.

When we achieved the 50 percent goal, we noticed some significant results, which convinced me that I had been right in my insistence. Loans made to women bring more benefits to the household, as women tend to be more farsighted and more concerned for the long-term security of the household. A woman gives first priority to her children; her second priority is the household. A man has different priorities; he does not give the family top position. Why then should we try to help poor households by giving our loans to men? We realized that by addressing the mothers we will be building a better future for the children. So we gradually focused more and more on women. Today, as a result of this policy, 94 percent of Grameen's borrowers are women.

Weekly Repayments

The system of regular repayments of installment has been very important in our ability to show a consistent loan recovery rate of over 98 percent. When I began this program, I saw all the banks—even the cooperatives—making loans which were to be repaid at the end of a very long period. When the repayment time comes six months later, or one year later, the borrower tries to find reasons for not paying back. People have a psychological aversion to paying back large sums of money all at once. If they can find a way, they will try to avoid repayment. This tendency was strengthened when the government started periodically writing off agricultural loans. At the time of election campaigns, for example, all political parties would announce that, if elected, they would write off all loans up to 5,000 taka. Since then, people have been even more reluctant to repay their loans from commercial banks.

In 1976, I was trying to understand what would make people repay without hesitation. I saw that if we could make payments very small, the psychological barrier would not come into play. So the first rule I made when we started was that loans would have to be repaid in small daily installments. If someone borrows 1,000 taka, I asked them to pay back 3 taka per day. She thinks, "Oh, this 3 taka is nothing! I can pay each day." As the borrower earned, she paid back her loan. She did not have to wait to accumulate a large sum of money. Poor people find it difficult to accumulate money, as there are a lot of pressing reasons to spend money. A daily or weekly payment routine makes it easy for them to repay. As our operations expanded, it became very complicated to collect money every day. Now we follow a weekly schedule.

The systems that were devised at the initial stages have, with minor modifications, stood the test of time. We never go to the courts, to lawyers or to the police. Lending is our business, and if we know how to do it, we should not have to go to the courts or to the police. Each month we lend out more than $30 million in tiny loans, and a similar amount comes back to us in repayments. In the entire system there is no legal instrument. This would be just a cumbersome piece of paper, unintelligible to our borrowers. Our business is with people, not with papers. We build on our relationship with people: We have trust in them, and they have trust in us.

THE ORGANIZATION AND ITS PEOPLE

Our greatest asset is the dedicated and committed cadre of staff that we have built up over the years. To gain employment with the Grameen Bank, people must first complete intensive training in the field, for a period of six months. While exposing them to the life histories of the poor and their economic and social realities, this training also makes them familiar with the physical hardships of the job. Those who experience the psychological rewards of working with the poor remain in the job; the rest leave. We have a staff training institute to meet continuing training needs.

All our staff are encouraged to think creatively and to make independent decisions in the field. They face a high degree of social pressure as they have to make all financial decisions openly in front of all the members present at the center meetings. Within the organization, too, information is not kept secret. All staff members are involved and are actively kept informed of what is going on. Since the organization has grown through a process of learning through action, bona fide mistakes made by any staff member do not invite severe penalties.

The image of Grameen is one of "bankers on bikes." However, Grameen staff receive salaries and benefits on the same terms and with the same conditions as staff of government banks. There are regular performance reviews and opportunities for promotion. Our total of 11,000 staff operate within a multitiered organizational structure that begins with village-level groups and centers and which enables field staff to be effective. The branch office, the lowest administrative unit, serves a maximum of fifty to sixty centers, roughly twelve to twenty-four villages. Each staff member attached to a branch office is responsible for five to ten centers. Almost 90 percent of the staff work at the branch level, so the organization is "bottom-heavy." Each branch is regarded as an independent profit center, and up to 10 percent of branch profit is awarded to branch workers as an incentive.

Area offices are located in small towns, and their staff supervise ten to fifteen branch offices. Zonal offices are the next higher unit of administration. Located in the district capitals and serving the whole district, these offices generally act autonomously and serve ten area offices. The head office in Dhaka coordinates overall operations and liaises with the government, with the Bangladesh Bank, and with international donors. Most matters are discussed by a high-level committee and most policy decisions are decided by consensus. They are not decided by any single individual by virtue of his or her power or status.

GOING BEYOND CREDIT: SOCIAL AND ECONOMIC PROGRAMS

At a national workshop held in March 1984, one hundred women delegates representing the five zones were in attendance. The delegates developed a social program consisting of Sixteen Decisions (see Table 1.1), which reflect the social aspirations of Grameen borrowers. Among them is the decision not to give or take dowry at the time of marriage of a daughter or son. Other decisions encourage members to grow vegetables, an important source of vitamins and nutrition for poor rural people; to keep their houses in good repair and to construct new houses at the earliest

Table 1.1 The Sixteen Decisions

1. We shall follow and advance the four principles of the Grameen Bank—Discipline, Unity, Courage, and Hard Work—in all walks of our lives.
2. Prosperity we shall bring to our families.
3. We shall not live in dilapidated houses. We shall repair our houses and work towards constructing new houses at the earliest opportunity.
4. We shall grow vegetables all the year round. We shall eat plenty of them and sell the surplus.
5. During the plantation season [for trees], we shall plant as many seedlings as possible.
6. We shall plan to keep our families small. We shall minimize our expenditures. We shall look after our health.
7. We shall educate our children and ensure that we can earn to pay for their education.
8. We shall always keep our children and the environment clean.
9. We shall build and use pit latrines.
10. We shall drink water from tubewells. If it is not available, we shall boil water or use alum.
11. We shall not take any dowry at our sons' weddings, neither shall we give any dowry at our daughters' weddings. We shall keep the Center free from the curse of dowry. We shall not practice child marriage.
12. We shall not inflict injustice on anyone, nor shall we allow anyone to do so.
13. We shall collectively undertake bigger investments for higher incomes.
14. We shall always be ready to help each other. If anyone is in difficulty, we shall all help him or her.
15. If we come to know of any breach of discipline in any Center, we shall all go there and help restore discipline.
16. We shall ensure discipline in all our Centers. We shall take part in all social activities collectively.

opportunity; to plant as many tree seedlings as possible during the planting season; to educate their children; to build and use pit latrines and keep the environment clean; and to act collectively in the interests of the group. Each center tries to ensure that all its members are guided by the Sixteen Decisions in their daily lives.

The Grameen Bank has also expanded its scope of activities to help its borrowers turn their visions into reality. Credit enables a poor person to live with dignity, to eat two meals a day instead of one. I have seen some of our borrowers who had only one set of clothes and they could not come out to meet me when I went to their houses, because they had just washed these clothes. I have also seen the pride appear on these peoples' faces as they earned the money to feed and clothe themselves and their families.

Housing Loans

Housing is another basic need, and our borrowers gave this high priority among the Sixteen Decisions. An opportunity to add housing loans to our lending activities came in 1984, when the Bangladesh Bank announced a new scheme for rural housing. Banks could borrow from it at 2 percent interest and lend this money for house construction at 5 percent interest. We applied to the Bangladesh Bank, requesting provisions so that we could introduce a housing scheme for our borrowers. Since our borrowers could not afford to repay the standard loan of $2,500 provided in the new scheme, we asked to make individual loans of only $300. The Bangladesh Bank experts objected to this. They said that nothing could be built with $300 that could qualify as a house and thus constitute adequate collateral. Once again, the banks were out of tune with the needs of the poor.

Only after I intervened with the governor of the Bangladesh Bank were we given a chance to begin in a small way. Today, more than 260,000 houses with tin roofs and sanitary latrines have been built with Grameen loans. There is almost 100 percent repayment through weekly installments. In 1989, Grameen's housing program received the Aga Khan International Award for Architecture.

Health Care

Bangladesh has a system of free health care for all. Perhaps because of the vast spread of the system, it is of uneven or indifferent quality. Generally, the rich and the privileged avail themselves of superior services while the poor receive less or lower quality care. Grameen has started its pilot health care program through Grameen Trust, another member of the Grameen family of companies. Grameen borrowers who avail themselves of the service are required to pay $1.25 per family per year toward health insurance. Each visit to the doctor costs a nominal amount, two cents. Laboratory tests also require a small fee; medicines are available at cost. Village people who are not Grameen borrowers can also subscribe to the system although they pay a slightly higher rate. The system is expanding quite rapidly to cover larger areas.

Education and Training

Among the Sixteen Decisions adopted by Grameen's members is their commitment to education for their children. Members of many centers have opened nursery schools, which also provide day care. Over 16,000 such center-operated schools are functioning today, with more being opened each year. Grameen also organizes workshops to train our members on various topics including health and nutrition, livestock and poultry operations, and other social issues. A comprehensive training program educates women about maternal health, nutrition and child care.

Fisheries

From time to time, the Grameen Bank has been asked by the government to take on additional activities. In 1986, we were asked to take over a fisheries project that had constructed nearly 800 ponds with a combined surface area of 1,000 hectares. The government had started a project to grow fish in these ponds but had given up. Grameen began by organizing the poor people living around these ponds into groups, to become partners in pond management. Grameen provided the capital and know-how; the groups provided the labor and the vigilance. The harvest would be shared on a fifty-fifty basis. From a low of 50 tons being harvested when we took over management, the annual catch rose to 805 tons in 1993. Encouraged by these results, we have created a new nonprofit subsidiary called Grameen Fisheries Foundation. This company is going to expand rapidly, since Bangladesh has over two million ponds with food- and income-generation potential that has barely been touched.

Agriculture

In 1992, a subsidiary company called the Grameen Agriculture Foundation was registered. This foundation seeks to enter into partnership with any willing farmer to bring new technology, crops and inputs; search out new markets; and supply essential inputs, advice and marketing to the farmers— free of cost. In turn, the foundation will get a small share of the harvest.

To support the people's decision to plant trees, Grameen provides millions of seedlings for planting. We have become one of the largest seedling sellers in the country. To help people grow vegetables, we provide vegetable seed to all of the villages where we do business. Between July 1992 and June 1993, about five million packets of seed and two million seedlings were distributed by Grameen Bank.

Textiles

There are a half-million weavers in Bangladesh operating more than a million handlooms. These weavers are extremely poor, and there is hardly any market for their product. About three years ago, we saw an opportunity to help them. The country was importing $80 million worth of handloom fabric, which was used to make garments to be exported to the West. No one had considered that fabric of the desired quality could be produced by our weavers. Grameen undertook the task of showing that it could be done. We had samples made, and we displayed them. We started to accept orders and assured that we would be responsible for quality and delivery date. The business has grown and provided more work for our weavers. Another subsidiary has been formed, Grameen Enterprise, which is branching out into new areas of rural industry.

INSTITUTIONAL RELATIONS

Grameen Bank has also had an effect, albeit an indirect one, on the mainstream banking establishment in Bangladesh. Grameen is a specialized development finance institution; however, various reviews from the financial sector have not really considered it a "bank." This may be because it was not founded under the Banking Act but under a special ordinance called the Grameen Bank Ordinance of 1983, which permits it to lend to the rural poor without requiring collateral.

Our work has presented a challenge to other banks by proving that the poor are bankable, that banking with the poor is profitable (or at least financially viable) and that it is possible to obtain a repayment rate of 98 percent while disbursing an average of over $30 million a month. In a country where mainstream banks are suffering from excess liquidity and are unable to ensure loan utilization and repayment, the Grameen experience points to something fundamentally wrong with their objectives, approach, management and procedures. Grameen Bank is becoming an increasingly large client for loans from the central bank and commercial banks, and we are now issuing bonds that are being purchased by the banks. Grameen is not competing with them in the sense that they do not lend to Grameen's clientele; rather, we have expanded the concept of what development banking should do and can accomplish.

In the past, Grameen Bank has steered clear of both national and local politics, which was relatively easy since, for a long time, political parties virtually ignored the bank. Except for the relevant government departments with which we deal, we also stayed away from the government, to protect ourselves from government interference. However, as Grameen has grown, it has become more visible and has had to be recognized as an important actor in the development field. It has raised many policy issues and also participated in policymaking at the national level. This was systematically done on behalf of the poor.

Politicians have not been able to discover how to get political mileage out of Grameen Bank. Their manifestos and programs do not go beyond rhetoric—they do not touch the realities of poverty eradication. Grameen borrowers, however, are having progressively more influence on local elections. As the conditions of participating in elections and voting have improved, larger numbers of borrowers are voting, and larger numbers of borrowers and their family members are standing for office in local elections. In the last round of local balloting, over 300 Grameen members were elected to office. We encourage borrowers to exercise their rights as citizens in selecting their representatives and also to demand accountability from the representatives who are voted in. Formal national endorsements would only attract political ire and fire, but informal local endorsements, after interviewing the prospective candidates, are increasingly giving the poor some weight in local politics.

REFLECTIONS

The strategy developed in the Grameen Bank is not the only route to solving the problems of poverty; nevertheless, it is of value to many developing and developed countries. As Grameen Bank has grown, many bilateral and multilateral donors have come in to provide assistance. In doing so, they have given us some useful suggestions, and they have also carried our strategy to other countries.

This is not to say that our strategy is perfect. One of the major criticisms that has been levied against us relates to our administrative costs, that the way we do business, by processing large numbers of tiny loans, involves too high a cost of administering loan operations. However, we believe that the issue is not how much it costs; the issue is whether we can cover the costs. We do. With the 20 percent interest that we charge on our loans, we are a sustainable financial institution.

For me, an important question is how does the money spent on Grameen's operations compare with other methods of poverty alleviation? When we speak of poverty alleviation, many immediately think of employment-generation schemes. But, how long will it take to open enough factories to employ half the poor people of Bangladesh? How much money will be required to create each job? Wage employment is not the solution to the problems of the poor. They should not have to wait around until someone else comes along to lift them out of poverty. That time may never come, and the poor will continue to live in their misery. Country after country has tried this route and failed.

Because of the traditional focus on wage employment, people do not see that one simple solution—credit—can help solve these problems. Each tiny loan creates self-employment, and the borrower does not have to leave home for this employment. He or she does not have to go to some over-crowded city to live in a slum and perhaps accept charity until work is found. With credit, *a process of building a person's self-esteem begins that is more important than the money itself.* Thus, the right solution lies in helping people to create their own jobs. When people have a job and an income, they can also have decent levels of food, clothing, shelter, education and health. Credit is the most basic of all human rights; it is the key to all the other human rights.

The poor should be provided equal opportunity to find expression for their capacities, their talents and their energy. We have to support them in their claim to a just and secure livelihood. We have to build the institutions that will provide support for self-help. As long as countries and donors are willing to spend money on alleviating poverty, I can think of no better way of spending it.

We have to build a network of social-consciousness–driven entrepreneurs through building supportive institutional arrangements, state policies, education systems and incentive structures and through creating international support systems. The role of the social-consciousness–driven entrepreneur will become more important than the role of greed-driven entrepreneurs in the newly configured capitalist world. This network will help to build a world of cooperation, mutual support and human dignity rather than a world of aggression, cutthroat competition and human and environmental destruction. There are already many small efforts in this direction in different parts of the world. The Grameen Bank is one.

2 The Orangi Pilot Project: Uplifting a Periurban Settlement near Karachi, Pakistan

Akhter Hameed Khan

In 1980, at the age of 66, I was in semiretirement after having spent my life working among the poor of my country. From doing action research in the Comilla project in Bangladesh (then East Pakistan), followed by teaching and research in Pakistan and at Michigan State University, and finally acting as an adviser to rural development projects in Daudzai and to other programs in the country, I felt I had done my share to contribute to knowledge about the possibilities for rural development. I was therefore unprepared when the Bank of Credit and Commerce International (BCCI) Foundation invited me to start a new project, this time in Orangi.

Orangi is the country's biggest *katchi abadi* (unauthorized urban settlement). It is not an inner-city slum, but a huge suburban settlement located 12 kilometers from the center of Karachi, the largest metropolitan center in Pakistan. With a population of six million people, Karachi is the industrial, commercial and financial hub of the country and thus is a natural magnet for migrants and displaced persons from all over the country. Surrounding Karachi there are over 400 *katchi abadis*, which have a total population of over three and one-half million people.

Orangi is the largest of these. It began to be settled in 1965 and grew rapidly after 1972, with the influx of refugees from newly independent Bangladesh. At present, it is spread over approximately 7,000 acres and still growing. Its population is estimated to be about one million, consisting of *mohajirs* (long-established immigrants from India), Biharis (more recent immigrants from Bangladesh), Pathans (immigrants from Pakistan's Northern Areas), Punjabis and local Sindhis and Baluchis. Although seen as an adjunct to Karachi, Orangi is large enough to qualify as a city by itself. Indeed, its area and population compare with those of Colombo or Amsterdam. With its diverse ethnic composition, Orangi represents a microcosm of Pakistan. Most Orangi residents belong to the middle- and lower-income classes, and monthly income for an average household is between 1,000 and 1,500 rupees. With an exchange rate of about thirty rupees for one U.S. dollar, this means a family of five or more would have an income between thirty and fifty dollars per month.

The particular reason for taking up a pilot project in Orangi was to test and develop an approach for developing *katchi abadis*, which flourish around Karachi and other urban centers, but for which no institutional solutions have been found within the framework of government-run municipal services and official development agencies. These settlements are poorly served by government agencies because they are irregular, that is, they are outside the city's official master plan. Being economically and politically weak, the residents of these settlements—mostly poor migrants from rural areas—are unable to wrest a share of official development expenditure. Official agencies turn a blind eye to the filth and squalor that prevail in these settlements.

As rural poverty drives ever larger numbers of people to these settlements, human misery will grow unless new institutional models are developed—with the active participation of residents. This is not just a Pakistani or even a South Asian phenomenon. Throughout the developing world, burgeoning squatter settlements, unrecognized and therefore unassisted by official agencies, can be observed wherever deepening rural poverty, civil strife, land degradation and population pressures have forced the rural poor to migrate to urban areas.

In developing a pilot project for Orangi, I started slowly; I did not go in with any preconceived set of program activities, based on prior notions of what the people of the settlement needed, or what was good for them. Instead, the entire effort consisted first of learning, and then teaching. Over the last fifteen years, the project has become intimately involved in the lives of the people. We have programs that deal with sanitation and health, with education and training, with house construction, social forestry and income-generation activities. In spite of their social segregation and low educational levels, women have been active participants in each of these programs. In fact, with assistance from the program, a large number of women have set themselves up as self-employed entrepreneurs.

The approach we took to each activity was developed gradually, with the continuous and active involvement of local residents. We are still learning and we are still conducting research through the actions that we take. In each activity, however, a basic strategy was followed:

1. To develop, in consultation with area residents, an appropriate and affordable solution that is technically sound and also culturally acceptable;

2. To help in the development of suitable social organizations that build upon existing political, social and commercial networks, and that can implement the suggested solutions;

3. To support the formation of autonomous local institutions to deal with each program activity. As these autonomous institutions have come into being, the project has gradually withdrawn from its direct involvement in these activities. These institutions work under the project umbrella but are autonomous in their day-to-day functioning.

Through the years, we have held to our belief that genuine development can not take place by subsidizing the costs of any activity; people themselves should be prepared to pay for what they want. We have spread out from our initial base in Orangi to take on work in other *katchi abadis* and also in the rural areas that surround Karachi. During the last four years, UNICEF and the World Bank have examined and accepted our development approach. UNICEF is adopting the Orangi approach in its sanitation and health program in the cities of Sukkhur, Shikarpur and Larkana, and the World Bank in Hyderabad. Both agencies have appointed our project as consultant for their projects. NGOs and official agencies are also taking a keen interest and have been sending their staff to the Orangi Pilot Project for training.

THE BEGINNINGS

In many respects, the Orangi Pilot Project (OPP) was very different from what I had previously experienced as director of the government Academy for Rural Development in Comilla, in what is now Bangladesh. OPP was a small private body, dependent for its resources on another nongovernment organization (NGO). Compared to official agencies, OPP possessed no authority, no sanctions and, initially, no legitimacy. It could observe and investigate, but it could only advise, not enforce. It could organize people but only on a voluntary basis. We could not compete with government departments or contend with elected representatives.

To begin with, as director of OPP I had no staff, no office, no connections and no contacts even among the people that we had set out to serve. In addition, I had never lived in Karachi before, so I was a newcomer. I set out to educate myself. For several months I wandered around Orangi, looking at the settlements, talking with the people, officials, councillors, lobbyists and the chairmen of associations and clubs. I could afford to go slowly; I was a free agent, not sent by a boss with plans and targets to achieve. Gradually, I learned what sorts of people were living in Orangi, what their problems were, what was being done for them and what they were doing for themselves.

I found that there were local associations everywhere, which were aware of their vote power and their street power, and which ceaselessly petitioned government for civic amenities. However, the official agencies had neither the resources nor the authorization (nor the incentive) to satisfy their demands. The facilities that had, so far, been provided by government were grossly inadequate. Much more had been done by residents through their own private initiative. For example, 95,000 houses had been built without any help from official agencies; 509 private schools and hundreds of small clinics had been set up (compared to just 76 government schools and two dispensaries). Transport was almost entirely under private management, and thousands of workshops and family enterprises were creating employment. However, a peculiar leadership structure and an unsavory relationship with official agencies had resulted from this pattern of development.

Land on which to build houses had been obtained by most residents from middlemen who illegally occupied vast stretches of public land, often in collusion with officials and other powerful persons. After carving out plots and selling them at huge profits, these middlemen then set themselves up as leaders of neighborhood associations, promising to obtain sewerage and other amenities by virtue of their influence with the authorities. Under pressure from the more influential of these leaders, the Karachi Municipal Corporation (KMC), a public-sector body, had constructed a few roads and some stormwater drainage lines. Kickbacks and profiteering—shared among the engineers, contractors and these self-styled Orangi leaders—resulted in high construction costs, lapses in supervision and the use of poor quality materials. Most of these projects collapsed after a year or two.

This activity was irregular—it was outside the master plan and was undertaken by KMC as a special political favor—and it was tiny in scope. However, it enabled the self-styled leaders of Orangi to perpetuate the belief among residents that construction of sewerage facilities was KMC's responsibility, and that only they (the leaders) could get such projects sanctioned. Since sewerage and water supply were of the highest priority for Orangi residents, they continued to fund these leaders to support their lobbying efforts. Meanwhile, open drains and stagnant sewage pools abounded, and human and animal refuse flowed down the streets and pathways. As a result, morbidity and infant mortality remained high, and the already poor inhabitants spent large amounts of money on doctors and on medicines.

The leaders' self-interest had helped perpetuate a myth. When I met with KMC officials, I was informed of the official position: no water supply or sewerage facilities could be provided in any residential area, unless the residents had deposited the requisite development charges. Depending on the locality, development charges were calculated at the rate of 75 to 200 rupees per square yard of plot area. Given that an average Orangi resident had built his house on 60–100 square yards, spending a total of 15 to 20 thousand rupees, spread over three to four years, he would not be able to afford five to seven thousand rupees to pay for water and sanitation facilities.

KMC officials suggested that I should frame a proposal for international assistance. This might have brought more money to the KMC budget, but I was sure that, for the Orangi people, it would only result in a debt trap that they could never get themselves out of. It was certainly not the route that a pilot project ought to follow. Instead, a new strategy for development that relied on the strengths and resources of residents needed to be developed. First of all, however, residents would have to be convinced of the need to act for themselves, and of their ability to do so successfully.

DEVELOPING LOW-COST SANITATION

When the program began, most residents used bucket latrines that a scavenger would empty every fourth or fifth day, often into the unpaved lanes. More affluent persons constructed soak-pits (at unit costs of 1,800 to 3,000 rupees), but these filled up after a few months and had to be emptied at great cost, or new ones constructed. Some people had laid sewerage lines from their houses to the nearest *nallah*, or natural drain. However, such lines were few, usually defective, often clogged and, as there was no joint community effort, there were often multiple, parallel lines in one lane. We felt that if an effective lane organization could be developed and supported with the right kind of technical designs, and backed up with training and tools, then an underground drainage system could be constructed to solve the most pressing problem faced by the residents. A four-step process was developed to activate this strategy:

1. Social motivators, employed by OPP held meetings with lane residents, typically in the evenings after residents had returned from work. Using slides, posters and pamphlets, these motivators explained that it was futile to keep on waiting for KMC to lay sewerage lines, that they could not afford KMC's charges. Instead, residents were told that if they formed an organization in which the entire lane participated, OPP would give them technical assistance. Acting on their own, they could construct the system at a fraction of the cost charged by KMC, not only because they could choose the most appropriate level of service and technical standards, but also because they could eliminate overheads and corruption.

I recruited the first social motivators from among the people I had met in my wanderings through Orangi. These were obvious natural leaders who were active in their neighborhood organizations, had superior communications skills and commanded respect among lane residents. Since the social organizers also needed to be familiar with the technical aspects of the work, we trained them to use new low-cost technology and taught them simple engineering concepts and surveying techniques.

The lane was chosen as the appropriate unit of organization not only because sewers needed to be constructed starting with the lane as unit, but also because we felt that the entrenched leadership at the sector (encompassing about fifty lanes) and circle (averaging about seven sectors) levels would not feel greatly threatened by any group that was organized only at the lane level. Of the thirteen councillors elected from Orangi to the KMC in 1979, only a few cooperated with us at the start, so it was in their areas, and with their involvement, that the work was commenced. Whenever the social motivators organized a lane meeting, they contacted the concerned neighborhood organization. At the beginning, we aimed at inviting the least antagonism and thus worked toward creating minimal disruption in the social and political life of Orangi.

2. In the second stage, the lane formed its organization and choose its lane manager. There was no prescribed structure for lane organizations, and they varied considerably from lane to lane. The lane manager, speaking for the lane, formally asked OPP for technical assistance. It was clearly understood that there would be no subsidies. OPP staff does not handle construction money at any stage, restricting themselves instead to giving technical advice and supervision, and providing tools and scaffolding.

3. OPP technical staff surveyed the lane, established benchmarks, prepared plans and estimates, then handed over these data to the lane manager. A lane meeting was called, and very active discussion resulted about the costs and likely benefits. OPP staff were called upon to defend their designs, and at times they revised designs and estimates after gaining a better understanding of problems and solutions from the lane meetings. Since people were to pay all the costs, they were free to accept or reject the technician's proposals. In the process, OPP had to upgrade and improve the technical options.

4. The lane manager collected money from the people. Most lane managers were selected by the people because they were known to be honest and because they could spare time for this work. They obtained tools from OPP, apportioned costs among residents and arranged for carrying out the work. Each lane organization was free to devise its own arrangements. Typically, poorer residents were allowed to pay a reduced amount, or through installments. Work arrangements have also varied: some lane

organizations contracted out the work to local masons, others organized voluntary labor and purchased material from the local *thallawala* (building components manufacturer). OPP provided general supervision, but it only guided people, not enforced compliance. To help maintain a high standard of construction, we trained a large number of local masons and artisans in the new technology. We gave designs and prototypes to many *thallawalas* to help them develop the materials, for example, manhole covers, included among the low-cost techniques. A list of such masons and *thallawalas* was provided to the lane manager.

The search for a relevant technology and its acceptance by local organizations has been marked by mistakes, which are milestones in our learning process. We carried out periodic evaluations, and an evaluation conducted by us in September 1982, with criticisms provided by a visiting team from the United Nations led to changes in the initial design.

TECHNOLOGY AND COSTS

A critical element in convincing people that they could construct the sewerage system on their own was the development of cheap technology that was easily understood by lane residents. This had two components: first, research to iteratively develop a cheap and relatively simple system; second, training and education to upgrade local skills and public awareness of problems and solutions. Over time, we have developed a technology that costs less than one-fourth of the traditional KMC pattern, even without accounting for kickbacks and overhead.

One advantage of starting slowly was that mistakes could be identified, and solutions developed and then monitored for feasibility. Our own evaluation in 1982 revealed that some work was of poor quality; crooked lines, inferior quality of concrete and insufficient curing were frequently observed defects. Research was carried out to identify causes and potential solutions, but since people were themselves financing and managing the work, education and persuasion were the only means for rectification. We held hundreds of meetings, explaining the problem with the help of pamphlets and posters and discussing the results of research. People learned the proper way to mix concrete, how to make inverts into manholes, and how to align drains correctly. At the same time, OPP staff were further refining the techniques to make them easier to handle and cheaper to construct.

I will not go into a detailed discussion here of the various techniques that OPP has developed; interested readers can write to us for designs and estimates. This technology is not the exclusive preserve of our dedicated and innovative technical staff. They have trained a large number of residents in the use of this technology and have developed prototypes that can easily be used by local people, without any need for sophisticated engineering education. One major investment that we made was in acquiring and making available tools, instruments and scaffolding that could be used by the lane and neighborhood managers during construction, thus eliminating the need for contractors.

As a result of these ongoing efforts, a low-cost sanitation system has been achieved without compromising engineering standards or system quality. This was accomplished through innovative technical solutions, not by using substandard or inferior materials and techniques. Each component has been thoroughly analyzed and tested before its installation, and training has resulted in highly professional workmanship.

However, there are limits to what a people can do for themselves. There are four major constituents of any sanitation system:

- inside the house: the sanitary pour-flush latrine,

- in the lane: underground sewer lines, manholes and house connections,

- secondary or collector drains, and

- main drains and treatment plant.

In Orangi, the house owners have been willing to accept the responsibility for the first three levels, which constitute 80–90 percent of system costs. The main drains and treatment plants, like main roads and water lines, must remain the responsibility of a central planning and implementing authority. Progress from the household level to the lane, secondary drain and main drain levels has been slow but sure.

Initially, only those lanes were selected that could drain their sewerage into adjoining *nallahs*. However, we realized that not only were we leaving out a large number of lanes, we were simply transporting the problem of the lane to the *nallahs*, which were inhabited on both sides. Thus, both for sociological and technical considerations, we needed to go into the construction of secondary sewers. This required that lane organizations be grouped together to form neighborhood associations. It also required a higher level of surveying and designing skills.

A physical survey of Orangi was carried out with the help of final-year students of the architecture and engineering colleges. The constituency of each elected councillor (that is, the circle) was selected as the unit of survey. After thirty to forty students moved through Orangi, conducting measurements and talking to the people, a new awareness of sanitation problems emerged among Orangi residents. The veil of mystery and technical sophistication was removed. In turn, the students understood the idea of socially relevant engineering and carried it back to their campuses. A few of these students, after graduation, formed a consultancy organization called Human Engineering Services.

As a result of this survey, people and their representatives became more active. Several lanes got together to form neighborhood organizations, building up from the structure of lane organizations. More councillors became involved in the work of sanitation. In 1984, one of them petitioned KMC to construct a main drain with some of the funds that were available for development work in his constituency. This marked a change in the relationship between OPP, the councillors and KMC. The secretary of KMC, the chief engineer and some staff visited Orangi for the first time. Impressed by what they saw, they agreed that the work done by OPP could be integrated into the master plan of the city.

Over time, people acting through their elected councillors have been able to persuade KMC to lay some secondary drains and main (trunk) sewers. The contractors employed by KMC have used the techniques developed by OPP. Their work has been informally supervised by residents, who have acquired a deep awareness of sanitation through their personal involvement in the program. As a result, construction quality and costs incurred by contractors are monitored by area residents.

There has also been a subtle change in Orangi's leadership pattern. Social organizers and lane managers are wooed by all political parties at election time. A few of these "people's leaders" have contested elections, and some have been elected to public office. With their new-found power, people no longer have to present themselves as supplicants before public agencies.

By early 1994, over 97 percent of the lanes in the OPP area were being served by underground sewerage; 1,281,468 running feet of primary sewers had been laid by lane organizations at a total cost of US$600,000. Over 90 percent of the people had constructed sanitary latrines in their houses, at a total cost of US$1.3 million, and 391 secondary drains with a total cost of US$58,000 had been laid. All of this money, almost 60 million rupees, or US$2 million, came through voluntary contributions from Orangi residents. Total OPP expenditures for staff to handle social organization and technical advice and for provision of tools and implements came to only about 6 percent of this amount. Thus, *every rupee given to us by donors was multiplied seventeenfold by the people of Orangi.*

Furthermore, these people succeeded in installing efficient and functional systems at a cost they could afford. The cost of the sanitation system for the first three levels (the sanitary latrine in the house, the underground pipeline in the lane and the underground secondary concrete drain) came to less than 1,000 rupees per house (US$33). If you compare this with what the municipal authorities would have charged (at least five to seven times more per house), you can see a potent reason for the level of people's involvement in the program.

Besides the technology, several other reasons enabled the sanitation program to go on rapidly. First, due to the efforts of the social organizers, people gained a better appreciation of the relationship between sanitation and health. The economic benefits of good health became apparent: fewer doctor's fees, less money spent on medicines and fewer lost wages. Second, property values started going up in the lanes where sewerage had been installed. This provided a major incentive; since Orangi people have little capital apart from their houses, they are very concerned about property value. Third, by late 1983, large areas in Orangi began to receive regular water supplies from municipal standposts. In neighborhoods without adequate sewerage and drainage the introduction of large quantities of waste water resulted in flooding and waterlogging. Many houses had to be vacated as waste-water stood ankle-deep in the street. The presence of a visible and affordable solution was a powerful demonstration in these circumstances.

When we started, it took us over three months to convince residents of just one lane that our system could work. As the benefits of the work began to be obvious, residents began to organize themselves into lane associations and to approach OPP for help. Within three years, this became the dominant trend, as people gained confidence to act on their own behalf and OPP gained the expertise to assist them. People have also formed maintenance committees to keep their systems in good repair. As in much of the social organization in OPP, there are no formal or written rules. People manage efficiently based on mutual understanding; they contribute money and labor whenever these are required.

In 1988, the planning commission of the government of Pakistan evaluated the sanitation model and recommended that OPP be recognized as a research and training institute. This resulted in the registration of OPP-RTI as the first of many independent institutions formed under the OPP umbrella. OPP-RTI has taken over the sanitation (and housing) function within Orangi, and increasingly in other areas. UNICEF, the World Bank, KMC and other municipal bodies have engaged OPP-RTI as a consultant to adapt the Orangi sanitation model to other *katchi abadis* in the country. NGOs from Pakistan and abroad are sending their staff to learn from OPP's experience.

At the same time, the range of OPP activities has expanded as our association with Orangi's people has led us into newer areas of assisting community-based development. Our other programs include:

- Women's Work Centers (from 1984)

- Health and Family Welfare (from 1985)

- Education Program (from 1986)

- Economic Program for Family Enterprise (from 1987)

- Low-Cost Housing (from 1988)

A Social Forestry Program started in 1990 and a Rural Pilot Project begun in 1992 are not discussed here as they are focused outside Orangi. Most recently, in 1994, a new pilot project for rural water supply was introduced. The approach followed in each of these programs is similar to that described above. Through action research, a set of solutions was devised and grounded in community-based organizations. We provide technical help and, in some instances, credit, but none of the activities is subsidized. From 1989, each program has been made autonomous, with its own separate managing body, budgets and accounts. The OPP Society Council functions as the central funding agency, receiving funds from donors and distributing them according to the budgets of the programs. In addition to the BCCI Foundation, at one time or another we have received funds from the Swiss Development Corporation, the World Bank, UNICEF, the Rockefeller and Winrock Foundations, the Aga Khan Foundation, the Government of Pakistan, U.S. Agency for International Development, the United Nations Development Program and others.

WOMEN'S WORK CENTERS

OPP has been helping accelerate the process of women's development since 1984. As with all our other activities, we entered this area after carrying out studies to understand the prevailing situation and to find out the scope for assistance. We found that Orangi was the biggest pool of cheap female and child labor in Karachi. We realized that instead of trying to introduce new crafts ourselves, we would achieve much more if we worked toward upgrading skills and forming cooperative associations. We started with the largest category of women, those who were tailoring clothes on piece-rate contracts. Exporters had engaged middlemen-contractors who, in turn, passed on this work to the Orangi women. These contractors not only paid unjustly low wages to these helpless women, they often cheated them, and sometimes harassed them sexually.

We decided to replace the contractors with a more socially conscious institution. The seamstresses were organized into a number of work centers, each of which was located at the home of one of the members. A central support organization was set up, with the responsibility for obtaining orders directly from exporters, arranging for tools and machinery, providing training and supervision and coordinating among the work centers.

By 1989, thirteen work centers were operating, with more than 800 members. The women managers of these centers had organized themselves into a cooperative society and were dealing directly with the exporters. A well-knit cadre of managers, supervisors and competent workers had been developed. OPP's support organization had worked itself out of a job and was therefore disbanded in June 1989. No support budget is now provided by OPP for women's work centers.

The growth of these family enterprises is leading to the emergence of women as active economic partners. Stepping out of their traditional role of subservience and dependence, women have not only begun to work alongside their men, they have also taken on entrepreneurial roles of their own accord. Women have played a very active role in educating Orangi children as part of a program started in 1986. A 1990 survey conducted by OPP showed that out of 1,818 teachers employed by 585 schools, 74 percent were women. Most of these schools (87 percent) were run privately, without any government support, and 87 percent were coeducational. Out of 80,600 students enrolled in schools, 36,300 students (45 percent) were female. OPP has been assisting Orangi schools through teacher training, development of educational aids, and by providing loans for upgrading of facilities and buildings.

HEALTH AND FAMILY WELFARE

OPP's research revealed two main reasons for the high incidence of disease in Orangi: the absence of sanitation, and ignorance of modern hygiene. In 1985, after the sanitation program was established, we started a health program for teaching hygiene and disease prevention to the housewives of Orangi. By tradition, women have been confined to their homes and kept segregated from society. In Orangi, they were largely illiterate or had very little education. Thus, mobile teams had to be organized to go into the lanes and speak to the women. Even though a large number of clinics and dispensaries had been set up in Orangi, the need for preventive medicine was poorly understood.

We began with one mobile team organized under the leadership of a woman doctor. A grant from the Population Welfare Division of the government of Pakistan helped us assemble a second team. We received additional assistance from other donors; eventually four mobile teams were functioning. Lane managers recommended women activists to join these health teams. Training courses of six months' duration were organized by the health teams at the houses of these activists. Ten to twenty housewives from neighboring houses attended these sessions, where they received advice about nutrition, child care and kitchen gardening.

The health teams also immunized children and introduced family planning. The latter was controversial and had to be approached delicately, but after six months, the housewives began to talk openly about it. The response to the health program was quite encouraging: over 90 percent of the children were immunized, and over 95 percent of Orangi families adopted modern hygiene in their homes. Compared to the national average of around 10 percent, 44 percent of Orangi families adopted birth control. We supply contraceptives through female sales agents and area pharmacists.

People's expenditure on treating illness has also been considerably reduced—by as much as 80 percent according to some estimates. The program has been very cost-effective, with per family annual costs of less than 125 rupees (US$4). In 1989, we registered an autonomous institution, the Karachi Health and Social Development Association (KHASDA), to carry out the health sector programs started by OPP.

The success of these programs and the awareness generated by them has forced us to reconsider and reduce our role. From November 1993, KHASDA ended its daily neighborhood meetings. Instead, schools, private clinics and family enterprise units serve as the institutional base for the program. Teachers and managers of clinics and family enterprises are being trained to offer the same services that were provided by our mobile teams. KHASDA will maintain just one center at the OPP office in Orangi to guide and support these people and to make supplies available to them.

ECONOMIC PROGRAM FOR FAMILY ENTERPRISE

Hundreds of family enterprises were operating out of the homes of Orangi residents, with more being set up each day. These represented the people's response to the empty promises of jobs and opportunities that are made, but seldom fulfilled, by political leaders. After careful observation, OPP concluded that expanding these enterprises was the quickest way to increase employment and family incomes. There was almost unlimited demand in the Karachi market for their products and services, and because they employed cheap, family labor and had low overheads, these units were quite competitive. The only bottleneck was capital, because commercial banks were not prepared to advance credit to these unregistered, informal, microenterprises.

To provide credit to them, we formed the Orangi Charitable Trust (OCT) and registered it in 1987. The success of this endeavor helped many people in their struggle for a life of dignity and self-help. More than that, it convinced me that such enterprises represent the best way out of our present widespread unemployment and poverty. It was clear that working class families possessed an abundant entrepreneurial spirit. Even some college graduates came forward to set up such enterprises, forsaking the hope of the cushy office jobs that such persons usually aspired to and willing to take on the hardships and the risks. What these promising entrepreneurs, educated and uneducated, lacked was credit.

OCT functioned by borrowing from the commercial banks at regular rates of interest, then lending to family units with a small mark-up to cover our costs. (We have also received trust funds from a number of donors—the BCCI Foundation, the World Bank, the Swiss Embassy, and others.) From our borrowers, we did not ask for collateral or mortgage, only for two guarantors. We were fully aware that prevailing standards of integrity were low, but we hoped that with proper selection and supervision the percentage of bad debts would be low. In the first two years, we made many mistakes; 21 percent of the loans we gave out in the first year had to be written off as bad debts. Nevertheless, we did not lose faith. We believed that if we behaved honestly and faithfully and took greater care in the selection of debtors and guarantors, our business would improve. Now, there is a growing circle of loyal clients and a clearer understanding of the causes of bad debt. Today, over 300 loyal clients stand ready to admonish tardy debtors, creating a social pressure to repay OCT loans.

As the amount of annual lending has gone up from 1.2 million rupees (US$40,000) in 1987–88 to 11.1 million rupees (US$370,000) in 1993–94, the percentage of bad debt has steadily fallen to below 2 percent. Although our circle of honest and reliable clients is widening, the risk of loss cannot be altogether eliminated. We have learned to identify three main causes for bad debts: dishonesty, incompetence and misfortune (death, severe illness). Defaults are scrutinized every quarter, and there is no delay in writing off bad debts. As of early 1994, out of a total lending of 35 million rupees to 2,945 units, only 3.9 percent of this (1.37 million rupees) involving 197 units had to be written off. Of this, 2 percent was due to dishonesty, 1 percent due to incompetence and the remainder due to misfortune. Every year, the percentage of bad debt (in particular due to dishonesty) has been coming down. Considering the fact that OCT deals with poor people and their microenterprises, this level of risk seems unavoidable and worthwhile. Our surveys reveal that out of our 1,361 current clients, only 180 (13 percent) have to be reminded to pay their installments; the rest come regularly to the OCT office. Consequently, our operational costs are quite low, and we employ only eight people for this program. Our overhead costs have come down from 12 percent of those loans made in 1987–88 to 4.5 percent in 1993–94. Since 1990, we have been covering all our costs and continue to do so.

Our 2,500 borrowers fall into fifty-five different professional categories. Among the largest categories are consumer stores, small production units, dairy cattle, *thallawala*, fishery, schools, clinics, medicine stores and taxis. Women entrepreneurs are a growing subgroup of our borrowers. Up to now, over 350 women entrepreneurs have borrowed almost 5.5 million rupees. They use these funds to finance operations in thirty-five types of family enterprises, with tailoring units forming the largest category.

LOW-COST HOUSING

All the houses in Orangi—over 90,000—were constructed by residents with their own resources, with no technical or financial support from any government agency. Houses were constructed in stages, as people's finances allowed. Materials were purchased from the local *thallawala*, who also provided advice and rented out tools. Local masons were hired for more complex construction.

Although such house construction was cheap, a survey conducted by students of the architecture college revealed that the quality of construction suffered from several defects. Almost all houses were constructed with concrete blocks fabricated by the *thallawalas*. These blocks were found to be brittle, with substandard load-bearing capacity. Sturdier blocks were required for more durable construction and to allow for the addition of an upper floor. A more durable roofing design also needed to be developed to facilitate vertical expansion. With the tin roofs and substandard blocks that were being used, people needed to tear down existing structures before they could add another floor; given the small size of their plots, they could only expand vertically.

After several months of research, OPP engineers developed a small-scale process for mechanizing concrete block production. With research targeted at producing machines appropriate for adoption by Orangi's *thallawalas*, the total cost of converting to the mechanized process was only 75,000 rupees (US$2,500). OPP did not set up its own manufacturing facility, as we thought it wiser to work through existing commercial networks. In 1987, four private *thallawalas* converted to this new process with the help of OPP loans and technical supervision. Almost all the others have since converted. Orangi *thallawalas* have multiplied their production and incomes severalfold and are sending more than 70 percent of their production out of Orangi. Consumers have benefited as the new blocks are four times stronger than before. And the blocks sell at the same price: mechanization trebled daily production, so there was no justification for any increase in price.

Similarly, an improved roofing process, relying on precast battens, tiles and slabs, was researched, developed and delivered to the local *thallawalas*. A precast slab staircase was also developed to further simplify vertical expansion. In addition to being easier to work with than reinforced concrete, the newly designed roofs and staircases were also about half the cost of earlier models.

Another large component of the housing program is training. Much time and money have been spent in training local masons in improved construction techniques. The improved housebuilding technology has now passed fully to the people of Orangi and to those—masons and *thallawalas*—who assist them in this activity.

REFLECTIONS

I can sum up in a few words what I have learned from my experience in Orangi and all the other programs that I have dealt with earlier. The common people in Orangi and other places—villagers or slum dwellers, farmers or workers—are living in a difficult period of transition, of impotent institutions. These people are hardly passive or fatalistic. On the contrary, they are striving very hard merely to survive; they are, in fact, masters of the art of survival under very harsh conditions. Their efforts to tackle these problems, however, become much more fruitful when they are given social and technical guidance and material support.

In most cases, the development agency has to fulfil this need—to devise appropriate technical solutions, help create participatory social organizations and develop people's confidence in their own ability. Usually, the infrastructure—roads, communications, market linkages—are already existing. There is no need to subsidize development activities. Small entrepreneurs can increase their production and incomes if they are provided credit, without red tape and corruption. Whenever they also have faith that the development agency—government or NGO—is a responsive and responsible partner, the common people readily accept the invitation to join development projects. However, as our experience with Orangi demonstrates, this requires that the development agency is willing to go out among the people, to listen and learn, and only then to teach and advise.

3 The Bangladesh Rural Advancement Committee: How BRAC Learned to Meet Rural People's Needs Through Local Action

F. H. Abed with A. M. R. Chowdhury

> BRAC works with people whose lives are dominated by extreme poverty, illiteracy, disease and malnutrition, especially women and children. Their economic and social empowerment is the primary focus of all BRAC activities. Our success is defined by the positive changes we help people to make in their own lives. Although the emphasis of BRAC's work is at the personal and village levels, the sustenance of development depends heavily on a pro-development policy environment. BRAC is committed to playing a role at this level through its research and advocacy work. BRAC works in partnership with like-minded organizations, governmental institutions and donors to achieve its ends.
>
> BRAC believes that development is a complex process requiring a strong dedication to learning and to the sharing of knowledge. Our work is based, therefore, on the services of highly committed, competent and serious professionals.
>
> —*BRAC Mission Statement* (1994)

In 1972, we set up BRAC—originally the Bangladesh Rehabilitation Assistance Committee, now called the Bangladesh Rural Advancement Committee. Its original purpose was to provide emergency relief to people of a small area in northeast Bangladesh. The country had been devastated by a cyclone, one of the worst in our history, in November 1970. The destruction wrought by the cyclone was made worse by the war of independence that followed almost immediately. In March 1971, the Pakistan army cracked down on the citizens of Bangladesh (then East Pakistan) after declaring invalid the results of a general election. Ten million people, uprooted from their homes, sought refuge in neighboring India. In December 1971, after a short but terrible war that ravaged the countryside, the Pakistan army surrendered and Bangladesh became independent. The refugees returned to their homes, only to find a barren place, their homes destroyed or burned down and their belongings looted.

The new government of independent Bangladesh was overwhelmed by the huge task that it faced and had difficulty mounting the massive relief operation that was urgently needed. The situation was particularly bad for people who lived in inaccessible areas such as Sulla in what is now Sylhet district. A group of us—some of whom came from that part of the country and had worked together during the 1970 cyclone relief operations—got together again to provide relief to the people of Sulla. Thus, BRAC was formed, and, served by a core group of young university graduates, it started carrying out relief and rehabilitation work in 200 villages. Over 14,400 houses were rebuilt. Tools such as looms, wheels, hammers, saws and chisels were given to craftspeople to help rehabilitate them in their trades.

We thought that this effort would be needed for two to three years, at most, in which time the situation would normalize, and the national government would start carrying out the urgently needed development functions. But as we worked among the rural areas of Sulla, we realized increasingly that early withdrawal of BRAC was a premature and too-hopeful expectation. The tasks of development were huge, and government agencies were not sufficiently motivated or equipped to perform these tasks. Supplementary efforts by NGOs continued to be required.

In Sulla, we began to see the everyday evidence of poverty and to feel people's helplessness in the face of it. We realized that relief measures were fine as short-term goals, but that providing such assistance was not an answer to the longer-term needs of poor people. Different forms of assistance and a different style of working were called for if we were to make any sustainable impact on living conditions. We felt sure that self-reliance among the poor was the only abiding answer to their problems. Developing such an orientation, paradoxically, required the sustained involvement of a development agency over a number of years.

BRAC needed to change its focus, but we were not quite sure how best to go about building up self-reliant village institutions. Initially, we made many mistakes. We saw each mistake as a learning opportunity, not without cost perhaps, but in the long run producing huge gains in knowledge that we have relied upon continually as we have improved our strategy and program content. Perhaps the most important lesson we learned is there is no fix-all strategy for development. Only through constant learning and adaptation can any agency develop its ability to serve the poor.

Turning our attention from coping with an acute crisis to dealing with persistent crisis meant over four years (1973–77) adopting an integrated, inclusive, community-wide approach (Lovell 1992). Most of these early programs were adapted from other development experiences both in Bangladesh and elsewhere, most notably the Comilla model of cooperative development and the barefoot doctors scheme of China.

Many of our earlier programs had disappointing results, due to our mistaken belief that entire village communities, regardless of social and economic differences, could come together in a combined effort for mutual self-help. The reality was that the richer sections of the community used these early cooperatives to their exclusive advantage. They derived maximum benefit from agricultural extension and our other programs, while the poor remained on the fringes. Our experiments with a health insurance scheme also went awry. To obtain insurance coverage, participants were required to pay five kilos of paddy (rice) per person at the time of harvest. Although operations went smoothly and about 30 percent of the costs were recovered from the paddy premium, our evaluations revealed that the program was not reaching poor households, who found it hard to put away so much paddy.

There were also other lapses in program design and management. A health program was set up that relied upon paramedics who were supported and supervised by regular doctors. Once trained, however, the paramedics resisted any supervision, either by BRAC or its doctors, and least of all by village cooperatives. Many of them set themselves up as self-styled doctors, seeing patients and charging fees, often with disastrous consequences to the patient. BRAC was faced by virtual revolt when we attempted to regulate the activities of these quacks.

The evaluations and research studies we undertook convinced us that it was counterproductive to work with entire village communities. Closer and more cohesive communities could be built out of the affinitive links that existed among groups of the poor. Although these links were at best latent, suppressed by the dependency relationships that each poor household had with some particular patron in the village, they could nevertheless be revitalized.

VILLAGE ORGANIZATIONS

This realization led BRAC in 1977 to adopt a target-group approach. We decided to concentrate our efforts on households owning less than half an acre of land that also sell manual labor for survival—more than half of Bangladesh's 112 million people. We go into communities to form village organizations (VOs) from among this category of people. Our program officers (POs) go into villages that lie within their areas and spend time talking to each poor household separately, inviting them to join a new VO and convincing them to break from their dependency relations with rich patrons. Economic assistance is made available to these groups, but it is not advanced immediately. Instead VOs must go through a six-month period of education and conscientization before they become eligible for credit.

During this time, VO members must deposit regular weekly savings in a bank account operated by the group. They also must attend a set of thirty lessons, averaging three hours each, that are designed to raise their awareness of their social and political environment and to acquaint them with the opportunities available within this environment. About half the members of any VO go on to take a second, optional part of the training that is devoted to literacy and numeracy. Though the curriculum has been designed by BRAC specialists, the training is participatory (following the methodologies made famous by the Brazilian educator, Paulo Freire). Trainers are chosen from among villagers having a high school education; they are then required to attend specialized training courses run by BRAC's Training and Resource Centers, or TARCs.

Separate VOs are formed for men and women. In any village, a women's VO must be formed before a men's group can begin functioning. This recent measure seeks to rectify the gender imbalances that are so prevalent in the countryside. In 1979, only about 10 percent of VO members were female; the proportion has now reached 80 percent. Enabling women to emerge from their social and economic isolation, one of our most important objectives, has never been an easy task. Hiding behind the mask of Islam, some people have attacked BRAC property and personnel. They are motivated by the threat that BRAC poses to the traditional, exploitative and oppressive power structure rather than by genuine religious sentiment. Over fifty of our schools were burned down, thousands of trees planted by poor women were cut down, and many BRAC participants and workers were harassed or threatened. But with their new-found solidarity and with the support of BRAC and its dense network of POs and village workers, members have been able to resist retaliatory threats and have persuaded landlords and moneylenders to improve their terms of exchange. Through the credit and other services that flow through their VOs they have helped build a better life for themselves.

However, credit provision to VO members is not the mainstay of our program. Credit can enable the poor to take advantage of existing opportunities, but it cannot by itself expand upon the range of opportunities. To increase the opportunities for self-advancement, credit must be supplemented by a program of institutional support that provides technical assistance and builds helpful links with markets and with the sector programs of government agencies. BRAC has made considerable headway, opening new avenues for members to employ profitably the credit and training that are made available to them.

INSTITUTIONAL STRUCTURE

Many traditional and government institutions exist at the village and national levels, but none of these helps voice the needs or the opinions of the poor. BRAC has tried to close this gap by creating institutions that are controlled firmly by the poor. Links are established with higher-level institutions, allowing the poor to connect more favorably with market opportunities. The area of institutional intermediation includes liaising with government agencies to reorient, redirect or otherwise improve the services and amenities that are already being offered. We have collaborated with the government in the health and education sectors, for example, mounting a national program for Oral Rehydration Therapy that has reduced infant mortality in the entire country.

With any new program, our effort has been to develop appropriate institutional responses to problems, as voiced by our members. In each intervention, technical or institutional, the approach has first been tested in a small area. The Manikganj area, the Jamalpur area and the original Sulla area have, over the years, become our major experimental areas. Many of our current programs were first developed in these learning laboratories. Learning has not, however, stopped at the stage of expansion. Staff in each area are free to experiment and devise more locally appropriate variations on the general theme.

We have expanded both our regional scope and our range of programs over the past twenty years, most rapidly since 1989. In 1990, we were working in about 4,000 villages, with an annual budget of about $20 million. We now work in 35,000 of the 68,000 villages of Bangladesh and have a budget of more than $86 million. Table 3.1 gives more indicators of our current status.

BRAC's programs include our core activities, the rural credit and small enterprise development operations and many other interventions that deal with education, health care, nutrition, legal aid, and other areas that have emerged in response to people's ideas and requests. Our Non-Formal Primary Education Program (NFPE), for instance, was developed when VO members who had taken part in the compulsory functional education programs asked why BRAC did not conduct literacy classes for their children. NFPE is now being conducted in 35,000 schools, with more villages being covered every year. Other programs are also expanding rapidly. Although we believe that it is better to start each new program in a small way, we also believe that program processes, once sufficiently well developed, should be expanded rapidly to cover as many poor people as possible. In the context of Bangladesh and many other developing countries, small is beautiful, but large is necessary.

BRAC's structure reflects the high value we attach to flexibility and to field-level innovation. Even with more than 16,000 staff, our headquarters staff is very small, keeping the field as the primary focus of operations. For each program, the regional manager is the only level between the area

Table 3.1   Scope of BRAC Programs, December 1995

Full-time staff	16,083 (18% women)
Part-time staff	31,676 (96% women)
Participants in credit programs	1.5 million (80% women)
Amount of loans disbursed to the poor	US$239.5 million
Amount of savings by the poor	US$19.7 million
Villages with BRAC programs	over 35,000
Primary schools	35,175
Students enrolled	1.1 million (70% girls)
Total budget (annual)	US$86 million

offices and the program coordinator at the center. For conducting our programs, the area office, headed by an area manager and staffed by a core group of program officers, is the focus of planning and action. Each PO is assigned a separate territory, within which he (or, increasingly she: women currently constitute 40 percent of our POs) is assisted by local workers recruited from among participating villagers. Villagers with special abilities or commitment are selected and trained as specialist paraprofessionals or as general purpose *gram sheboks* (village workers). POs are responsible not only for their respective areas, but are members of the area office's decisionmaking team. Staff members of each area office live and eat together, spending many hours in dialogue about village problems and about the suitability of available BRAC responses.

The area offices, in addition to being implementation agencies, are the units that formulate operational policy. Being at the cutting edge, the area offices must continually adapt programs to address diverse and changing circumstances. Within a framework they themselves help to determine, every staff member, regardless of seniority, participates in decisionmaking. They are assisted in this by specialist trainers and by a small cadre of headquarters staff who handle monitoring and evaluation, research and program development, and who provide guidance whenever area offices request it.

RESEARCH, EVALUATION AND TRAINING

Research and evaluation is increasingly important as the organization grows. The Research and Evaluation Division (RED), an independent unit with more than 100 staff, carries out specific studies, both independently and as called for by program managers. Studies are also conducted by outsiders such as academic institutions, the government and donor agencies.

The results are disseminated through seminars, which are held both at BRAC headquarters in Dhaka and in the field. Bangla versions of reports are prepared for circulation to field staff. Each of BRAC's programs also has its own management information system that allows quick and regular feedback on day-to-day management.

BRAC has invested heavily in developing the capacity of program participants and its own staff. Training courses are regularly organized to cover social awareness education, leadership, organization and management and to teach various skills to POs and paraprofessionals. These courses are provided by BRAC's sixteen Training and Resource Centers (TARCs) located around the country. Staff members also regularly receive on-the-job and refresher training. More promising staff members are also sent overseas for training. During 1990–93, over forty BRAC staff received graduate education in various foreign universities.

As in most other aspects of BRAC's work, training has a strong market orientation. TARCs are designed to be self-financing, and program managers must pay to have their staff and participants trained. As the scale of programs has increased, most area offices cater to training needs within their respective areas. POs and *gram sheboks* themselves conduct a large part of the training, sometimes calling in experts for support. TARC training courses have increasingly focused on training the trainers themselves, with training needs and curricula identified through consultation with program managers and area offices.

THE RURAL DEVELOPMENT AND RURAL CREDIT PROGRAMS

In 1979 we began experimenting with two different types of VO support programs. One was run without credit, relying on people's own resources and on the support they could get from ongoing government programs; the other was similar but included a credit component. Five years of parallel experiments convinced us that although self-help efforts by VO members are essential, it was important that people's initiatives not be held up or their motivation eroded due to lack of credit. On the other hand, credit should not be made available to groups as soon as they are formed. It should be preceded for at least three to six months by a period of education and savings and by building group solidarity. Otherwise, expectations of quick economic gains become the primary motive, driving out concerns for group solidarity and preventing the growth of purpose and self-discipline. By 1985, the two programs were merged into a single program, called the Rural Development Program (RDP). These experiments also showed us that complicated rate schedules and repayment conditions create problems; simple rules are easiest to understand and follow. We decided to reduce alternative rate structures to the minimum. Credit, however, was to be made available on commercial terms, with strict loaning and repayment conditions.

Another important lesson emerging from the mistakes we made during this initial phase was understanding the best route for credit to take from BRAC to an individual borrower. Earlier, we advanced funds to the VOs, which deposited the money in a bank account and operated the accounts with little BRAC involvement. Our mistake lay in expecting VOs to develop, overnight, the required maturity and financial skills. Initially, VO elected officials had little accountability either to BRAC or, more important, to their own membership. Some unscrupulous VO leaders even made off with VO funds.

A more suitable strategy lay in focusing the credit program on small, self-governing groups of five to seven members who, assisted by a BRAC staff member, keep accounts and effect repayments. This small group oversees loan approval and utilization. Loans are rotated among group members, and no one can take out a second loan until all others have received their first. Another condition for eligibility is that the borrower must establish his or her capacity for repayment by first saving at least 5 percent of the requested loan amount with the VO before the first loan is advanced; savings deposits must equal or exceed 10 percent of the requested amount for a second loan and 15 percent for the third loan.

Timely repayments are managed through peer control. Since not more than three loans can be outstanding for any one group, repayment by one member becomes a condition for loans being made to other members. Repayments are made weekly, in small, affordable amounts and begin soon after any loan is advanced. All members must also save at least 2 taka every week (about 5 cents).

Although the small groups oversee the credit program, all loans are sanctioned in full VO meetings. To facilitate greater VO accountability, the secretaries of the small groups form a VO management committee on a rotating basis. VOs must have at least twenty members. On average they have thirty-five to forty members, and only one member is allowed from any household. VOs and small groups hold regular weekly and monthly meetings on predetermined days to administer the credit program. The amounts advanced to village groups are banked with BRAC itself. To facilitate this step, we started our own banking project in 1989, called the Rural Credit Program (RCP). As described later in this section, RCP has been taking over banking operations from the Rural Development Program in areas where the latter has been functioning for four or more years and where mature VOs have emerged.

Three types of credit are disbursed, for: (a) traditional activities such as rural trading, transport (boat and rickshaw) and rice processing; (b) nontraditional activities such as grocery shops, rural restaurants, or technology-based undertakings such as poultry, silk culture or mechanized irrigation (these loans are available only to women to compensate for men's previous dominance); and (c) housing loans. The interest rate for housing loans is 10 percent and 25 percent for the other types. Housing loans can, however, be taken only after any member has become more financially well-off through investing in income-generating activities; without this financial base, it becomes difficult to pay off the weekly installments.

Disbursing credit, however, is not enough. The purposes for which this credit is used must yield incomes sufficient to bring the poor out of their low-level equilibrium. Technical and institutional intermediation thus becomes important. BRAC's Rural Enterprise Project (REP), its technical research and design wing, has been working since the mid-1980s to improve technological options for use in BRAC-sponsored, income-generating activities.

The technology developed by REP is both relevant and realistic. It has to address itself to a felt need and an available opportunity; it also has to be accessible by the poor, that is, it must be relatively cheap and locally usable by village residents. Examples of such technology developed by REP include breed improvement and vaccination, hatchery-construction and rearing techniques for poultry; artificial insemination for livestock; deep-tubewell construction for irrigation; and improved varieties of mulberry trees, quality production of silk cocoons and modern reeling facilities for sericulture (silk production). About 30 percent of our existing credit portfolio is invested in these technology-intensive activities. Following are examples of three such activities to make clear our process of development.

Poultry. BRAC starts by training women to rear high-yielding breeds of chicken. Loans are given to female members of VOs to operate low-cost hatcheries that supply day-old chicks to other village women. These women rear the chicks until they start laying eggs, which are sold to the hatchery and also directly to consumers. Other VO members receive loans and training to become feed suppliers and egg sellers.

One of the major problems of poultry rearing in Bangladesh is high mortality among the birds. The government livestock department keeps stocks of vaccines, but these depots are far away and not accessible to most villagers. BRAC has trained village women, VO members, on how to vaccinate poultry, and then linked them with the local government livestock department, to get a free supply of vaccines. The women receive the vaccine and then inoculate chicks in their own villages for a small fee. The women increase their own income and, at the same time, ensure survival of their neighbors' chicks. By 1994 over 500,000 members, primarily women, were deriving monthly incomes of between 150 and 700 taka through investing their loans in poultry activities.

Sericulture. Similar links have been established for programs such as sericulture, a home-based, labor-intensive activity that, with little investment and low risk, can increase the incomes of women who work only part time. The demand for silk in Bangladesh is high, and despite the government's efforts, through its sericulture board, to promote domestic production, much of the silk sold in the country is imported. Beginning in the early 1980s, we studied this sector intensively. A major constraint, we found, lay in the availability of leaf fodder for silkworms from mulberry trees. Another constraint was the lack of a distribution network to link the sericulture board's silkworm egg production unit with the village silkworm rearers, and the village silkworm rearers with reeling and production units. Again, we used the combination of credit and training to help a number of village women set themselves up as village-level silkworm rearers.

To ensure a good supply of mulberry leaves, large numbers of the trees were planted along village roads, on pond embankments and on any other unused lands that VOs identified. Government food-for-work funds were used to pay women members who planted and cared for these trees. Other VO members were assisted in setting up village-level nurseries for mulberry saplings, often on land leased from other villagers. Close cooperation with the sericulture board has also reduced bottlenecks in the supply of silkworm eggs.

With the assistance of its sister organization, the Ayesha Abed Foundation, BRAC has established a marketing outlet for producers by setting up a chain of reeling and production facilities linked to its network of *Aarong* shops based in major cities. Currently there are eight *Aarong* branches, six in Bangladesh and two abroad (London and Vancouver). The *Aarong* production centers, in addition to helping village rearers of silk cocoons, are also providing direct employment to over 10,000 women. Women's associations attached to each center manage all its affairs, obtaining credit from RDP, designs from specialist consultants, and training from TARCs or, more often, at the production center. By 1995, over 15,000 women were earning up to 1,000 taka per month from sericulture and related activities.

Deep Tubewells. Groups of landless people have received loans for setting up deep tubewells that supply water on a commercial basis to farmers in the vicinity. Individual VO members purchase shares in a prospective tubewell, and the shareholders elect a management committee from among themselves. They also hire some among them to receive technical training, both in tubewell operations and maintenance as well as in agriculture extension. To complement their efforts, other villagers are trained more extensively in tubewell maintenance and repairs.

The irrigation group signs up farmers who purchase water, often paying between one-quarter and one-third of their crop at harvest, in return for irrigation and extension advice. Subsidies under a now-disbanded government program financed part of the initial cost of the tubewells. Before BRAC's program started, these subsidies were all going to the richest farmers. Now, landless persons are not only able to gain some share of government assistance, they are also gaining control over a precious resource. This has, at least partly, reversed the earlier dependency relations between rich farmers and landless peasants.

An important feature of the Rural Development Program is its design to become self-sustaining. After a few years of operation in any area, the interest received from loans is expected to cover the operating costs of the corresponding area office. The step toward self-financing areas has been advanced since 1989 with the launching of the Rural Credit Program (RCP). The idea behind RCP is to take over from the Rural Development Program all the area offices—complete with buildings, equipment and, most important, the loan portfolio—where VOs have been in operation for four years or more and whose loan portfolio is sizable. These mature VOs have derived considerable support from their long-standing association with BRAC, and they should now be able to stand on their own, dealing with commercial organizations and purchasing whatever services they need. Technical and managerial assistance will, however, continue to be provided by RCP personnel, although most often it will have to be paid for.

RCP functions like a bank and is managed through branches similar to the RDP area offices. A typical branch includes about 150 VOs or 6,000 members in 70 to 80 villages. At the present rate of expenditures, a branch with outstanding loans of 9 million taka (US$225,000) or more is regarded as likely to be self-sustaining.

In 1989, its first year of operation, RCP bought out ten area offices, which became its first ten branches. In 1991, twenty more branches were similarly constituted. By the turn of the century it is expected that almost two million members in 52,000 VOs will be associated with RCP branches. To effect the transfer of RDP area offices to RCP, fifty million dollars in funds were made available to BRAC by a consortium of donors headed by the Dutch NGO, NOVIB. Funds made available to RDP in the process will be used to expand its programs to newer areas and to underwrite assistance to the more vulnerable sections of society.

REACHING THE UNREACHED

BRAC's stated goal is poverty alleviation and empowerment of the poor. However, certain aspects of our target group approach militate against the participation of the poorest 10 to 15 percent of the rural population, a group that is dominated by single women households, widows and deserted or abandoned women. They find it difficult to meet all the requirements of our standard approach—attendance at weekly meetings, depositing weekly savings and, at a later stage, paying for services and advice. Unless something special is done, we realized, they remain outside the reach of BRAC programs.

An Income Generation for the Vulnerable Group Development Program has been designed, as a collaborative venture with the government, to meet the needs of these vulnerable women. Since the 1970s, the government has been providing a monthly ration of 31 kilograms of wheat to distressed women in rural areas. This ration is given to any person for two years, after which a new group is chosen and past recipients are left to fend for themselves.

BRAC has been working with the government to improve the longer-term impacts of this program. We provide these women with training in poultry raising during the period they receive the free wheat. With the help of government, we also provide easy credit to them to purchase and rear poultry. The idea is that when the ration is withdrawn after two years, the women can continue to earn an income. By January 1995, nearly 325,000 women have been participating in this program, in 74 out of a total of 460 subdistricts in Bangladesh. Other programs to help especially vulnerable groups are also being considered.

PROGRAMS IN THE EDUCATION SECTOR

As in most other sectors, the public sector's performance record in education in Bangladesh is also dismally poor. Major problems have been low enrollment and high dropout rates. Although enrollment has improved in recent times, the primary school dropout rate is still an alarmingly high 80 percent. Since 1985, BRAC has been experimenting with a new nonformal school system. Catering to the needs of dropouts and those who were never enrolled, the Non-Formal Primary Education Program offers a three-year education to two groups of children, between eight and ten years old and between eleven and sixteen years old.

NFPE began in response to demands from VO members who wanted for their children an alternative to the formal government school system. BRAC assembled a small group of educators who piloted a new approach, working for two years in a small group of twenty-two experimental schools.

They developed curriculum, teaching materials and methods for recruiting and training teachers that could effectively reach out to the children who had been bypassed by the formal system.

BRAC schools are open only to the children of the poorest, those who are members of VOs. Close parental involvement is an important reason for the success that NFPE has enjoyed. Parents hold monthly meetings at which they set school schedules, discuss attendance records and decide other matters related to the day-to-day operation of the schools. Teachers and POs regularly consult with parent groups.

The same teacher takes a group of students through all three years of their education. Children attend for three hours a day, six days a week, without any long vacation. Each school group has thirty-three children per class, 70 percent of whom are girls. Teachers are recruited from among villagers who have had more than nine years of formal education. Women account for more than 75 percent of all teachers in our schools, compared to less than 20 percent in government-run schools. Once recruited, teachers are trained in one of our residential training facilities, and one day each month, continuing training is given to groups of NFPE teachers assembled from adjoining schools. In their three years of education, children are taught a carefully structured curriculum that helps them achieve basic levels of literacy, numeracy and social awareness. All books and other materials are developed by BRAC and are supplied to the children free of cost.

The program has been quite successful with dropout rates of 10 percent or less during the three-year cycle. Most striking has been the number of NFPE students who have gone on to enroll in the formal system: nine of every ten such students have continued their education. This result showed that, contrary to many popular perceptions, the poor do wish to have their children educated; once they have experienced a relevant curricula, delivered in a congenial environment by dedicated teachers who inspire confidence and expect success, children and their parents want to continue with school education.

Beginning in 1990, there was a sharp scaling-up of the system, and BRAC now runs over 35,000 such schools, attended by 1.1 million students all over the country. Not only the children attending the NFPE benefit; the program is putting pressure for improved performance on the public school system. BRAC educators have also begun working directly with the government to help improve the effectiveness of the formal system.

PROGRAMS IN THE HEALTH SECTOR

Our first experiments with paramedics and health insurance were disastrous, but the results of our initial work on family planning proved more successful. Village women were trained to work as family planning organizers, motivating people to use contraceptives and providing them a free supply of oral pills and condoms. Independent studies found a contraceptive prevalence rate of 20 percent, with over 50 percent of pill users continuing usage for more than eighteen months, a distinct achievement at that time in Bangladesh. Based on our experience during this period, we changed our approach to health care. Instead of selecting potential paramedics ourselves, we asked each newly formed VO to select one woman member to be trained as a village health worker. After undergoing training, these women are supplied with a few basic drugs, and they charge a small fee for their services. Since they are selected by the VO and since they live in the villages, they remain accountable to the villagers.

Our early interventions in the health sector taught us two other important lessons. First, the health status of any group depends on developments in other areas, especially literacy, status of women and income levels. Second, it is difficult for any NGO to go it alone. The most useful route involves working in collaboration with government, attempting to improve the effectiveness of its programs and to open its vast health infrastructure to the poorest groups.

Our ten-year National Oral Rehydration Therapy (ORT) Program was our first major effort to work closely with government agencies. Experiments in the Sulla area had proven the efficacy of a simple, homemade remedy—a pinch of salt and a handful of sugar, mixed with a half-liter of water—to combat dehydration among children, a cause of many infant deaths. In 1980, we launched a nationwide effort to teach this simple technique to village women. A core management team was assembled from among people who had gained experience in Sulla and in Manikganj, another pilot area. ORT teachers, who were recruited from among the women in each participating village, were trained by BRAC and then paid to teach ORT to the rest of the women in the village. The work was monitored by a team of BRAC supervisors, who followed the ORT program as it spread from village to village. By 1990, every single village had been covered by this program. Recent studies have documented that the ORT message has been retained in most households, and the widespread practice of ORT is recognized as an important factor behind the recent drop in infant and child mortality in Bangladesh.

BRAC assists also public-sector programs of child immunization and family planning in those districts where government programs are performing poorly. BRAC also pilots innovative methods for delivering health services, particularly those related to women's health, nutrition, tuberculosis prevention and cure and treatment of acute respiratory infections.

FINANCES

BRAC's budget is now around US$86 million. About 60 percent of the expenses comes from overseas donors and international agencies, mostly in the form of grants. Our major donors over the years have been NOVIB (Holland), ODA (U.K.), SIDA (Sweden), CIDA (Canada), KFW (Germany), NORAD (Norway), DANIDA (Denmark), SDC (Switzerland), UNICEF, the Aga Khan Foundation and the Ford Foundation. To avoid dependence on any single donor, BRAC accepts no more than one-third of its annual requirements from any one donor.

In 1990, in response to our plans to scale-up rapidly, NOVIB took the lead in putting together a consortium of nine donor agencies that together could advance the fifty million dollars required for the new thrust (including the new Rural Credit Program). Consortium funding has been helpful both to BRAC and to the individual donor agencies by reducing paperwork and duplication and improving the quality of dialogue and oversight.

LESSONS LEARNED

All BRAC professional staff, except for technical specialists, are recruited as entry-level POs, hired from among recent university graduates and chosen through open examinations. They grow with the organization. Their training includes a year of probation at a field office. The new recruits quickly experience the rigors of this life. About half of all new recruits leave during this period to take up easier jobs elsewhere; those who remain are quite committed, and continuing training sharpens their skills. Currently we spend about 7 percent of our budget on staff development. All program managers are promoted from among the most promising POs.

Staff must also have the authority to experiment and to adapt programs as they feel best suits local situations. Our management system actively encourages innovation and flexibility, which are key to learning. Mistakes will occur, but they are the only route to discovering the correct path. Fear of making mistakes prevents many public-sector organizations from letting their staff's creativity flower. We use monitoring and field research, however, as an early warning system, to avoid the worst excesses that can result from a policy of embracing error and risk. BRAC's Research and Evaluation Division has been doing innovative research in various fields of development, with many of its outputs appreciated beyond Bangladesh.

Ever since BRAC's inception, continuous learning has been its mode of policy planning. This learning has resulted in a number of lessons that guide our work:

- Every person is capable of improving his/her destiny if he/she is given the right opportunity; participation of the poor, especially of women, is necessary;

- Conscientization is essential before economic programs are undertaken;

- There is no one "fix-all" approach; the program strategy needs to be flexible to cope with diverse situations and changing circumstances;

- Small is beautiful, but large is necessary;

- Self-reliance among the poor is the ultimate goal; appropriate institutions need to be developed that undergird self-reliance;

In BRAC's view, a development organization should never become a patron. It must adopt a withdrawal strategy after assisting in the development of suitable institutions that are accountable to the poor themselves and responsive to their needs. Those institutions are most sustainable that bring to life the entrepreneurial spirit latent among all people, and that are guided by a market perspective. Developing such institutions is the real test of any agency's success. Most of all, success in development depends upon the dedication and capability of the agency's staff, who constitute its principal resource. A person who acts only on instructions cannot work in development. What is required is a cadre of persons who think for themselves and act on their own, with a firm commitment to the agency's values and objectives.

4 SANASA: The Savings and Credit Cooperative Movement in Sri Lanka

P. A. Kiriwandeniya

Sri Lankan savings and credit cooperatives—known collectively and individually by the Sinhala acronym, SANASA—have grown into a people's movement that has had a considerable impact on the rural poor. This movement is not a nongovernmental organization, or NGO with a group of leaders running the organization for the sake of beneficiaries. Rather, SANASA operates according to cooperative principles, which means that its members are simultaneously its owners, beneficiaries and decisionmakers, with leaders expected to carry out the decisions of the membership.

SANASA's basic purpose is to provide financial services to the rural community. Societies of 50 to 150 members collect savings from members and disburse these savings as loans. The policies and leadership of these primary societies are democratically determined by members at monthly meetings. Although SANASA's activities are primarily financial, its overall aim is to build a social order based on cooperative principles. Underlying this is the realization that all financial institutions have an impact on the social structure in which they operate and that this social impact must be considered. The cooperative has the important beneficial effects of giving people power to control their resources and allowing them to come together in a democratic forum to create a more harmonious society.

HISTORY AND BACKGROUND

The SANASA movement has seen huge growth since 1978. As of 1995, it had 726,000 members in 7,992 societies. Whereas savings from local societies throughout the country amounted to only 18 million rupees (US$1.16 million) in 1978, by 1995 they totalled 2,037 million rupees (US$40 million), of which 1,677 million rupees (US$32 million) was disbursed in loans. Furthermore, primary societies, in addition to providing financial benefits, have started a range of community development programs that contribute to people's welfare. This rapid growth followed the movement's rejuvenation and creation of a three-tiered organizational structure in 1978. The success of the movement is based on the design of the primary society. Yet without rejuvenation, the societies would never have reached their potential.

Credit cooperatives, established as independent bodies based on the European Raifeisen model, were first set up by the colonial administration in 1906, as a response to indebtedness within the rural community. By 1940 there were 1,302 cooperative societies; most members were middle-income villagers and people on salaries. During World War II, a second system of cooperatives was established to ensure equitable food distribution. Following independence in 1948, as in many other countries, the government took a keen interest in these state-created cooperatives, and in 1957 a nation-wide network of multi-purpose cooperative societies (MPCSs) was established. These societies aimed to cover all the needs of rural communities, including consumer, marketing and financial needs.

MPCSs offered a wide range of services, heavily subsidized loans and a state-subsidized rice ration. This drew membership away from SANASA and other cooperatives that were not supported by the state. The number of independent cooperative societies—those not registered with and regulated by the government—dropped from 4,026 in 1964 to 1,300 in 1978. During this time, the government merged many MPCSs to form societies that appeared to be more efficient but that were too large to be responsive to members' needs.

By 1978, the SANASA movement had stagnated. It had not changed since its inception, and events had overtaken it. The societies were weak for a number of reasons. The government ignored them (although this meant at least they had not been subverted for political gain). Their leadership was not dynamic and rarely tried to expand membership or promote new activities. SANASAs were seen as simple savings clubs rather than as financial institutions. Their membership was largely old, male and elite.

There was no national body to promote the movement. Isolated societies were unable to acquire external funds or gain support from other societies. There was no cooperative education, and members were unaware of their societies' potential. The movement also had little experience with real financial management. Few societies offered interest rates high enough to attract poor savers or to enable them to build reserves. Overall, the movement was seen as dependable but staid and unimportant.

In 1978, having considerable experience in the voluntary sector, I became interested in the SANASA movement. I began by working for over a year with my local primary society in Walgama, talking with members and leaders and testing to see if the societies could be made more effective. Over the course of a year, the society was invigorated. Before, only a small group of older men were members. By the end of the year, all households in the community were represented. The society had also built its own permanent premises and was serving as a local bank.

Throughout this process the members gave suggestions for improving their society and were intimately involved in the evolution of the new model savings and loan society. By the end of the year, the model had proven itself successful. The Walgama society was a test case in which a better primary society structure was evolved and which could be replicated.

Members of neighboring societies, government and banking officials were invited to come and see what had been achieved in Walgama. The first Walgama seminar explained the success of the society to other leaders and allowed them to comment on and improve the model. These society leaders then took these ideas and similarly rejuvenated their societies. The process of rejuvenating the Walgama society could be seen as learning to be effective and learning to be efficient, according to Korten's learning process model (Kiriwandeniya 1992). The SANASA movement was now in a position to grow.

THE OPERATION OF THE PRIMARY SOCIETY

The SANASA movement has been successful because of the strength of its primary societies, which are made up of members of the community coming together to organize cooperative banking activities. The average number of members per society is 100, although it can vary from 20 to 300. Almost all societies are in rural areas. Membership is not restricted to any specific group in the community, such as those with low incomes; all are welcome to join as long as they accept cooperative ideals.

Members of the primary societies purchase shares and deposit savings with their society, for which they receive market rates of interest. This money is then used to make loans to members, again at market rates. The margin between the different rates for savings and loans produces income for the societies.

Members are expected to attend the monthly meetings where policies are decided on a one-member, one-vote basis. They can lose their membership if absent too often. Members annually elect a voluntary (unpaid) committee that handles the society's day-to-day management. These societies are regulated by cooperative legislation, but they are free to determine their own financial policies, interest rates and membership regulations as independent decisionmaking units. Primary societies have been successful for five reasons.

They meet many felt needs of the community. The primary societies supply services that are in great demand in the community, both financial and nonfinancial. Savings and credit services are becoming important to Sri Lankans as rural areas become increasingly monetarized. Savings provide a buffer for the poor against unexpected expenses, such as for medicine or social commitments, and they can cover periods when households have no income, such as at the beginning of the crop cycle or during illness. Without savings, households are forced to choose between taking loans or selling assets, cutting themselves off from future earnings and starting the "ratchet into poverty" (Chambers 1983). Once inside the vicious circle of low production, low investment and exploitation, poor people often find it impossible to escape.

Although the rural poor wish and need to save, existing banks do not like to serve them. Transaction costs, increased by bureaucratic procedures, make it unprofitable for banks to take on many small accounts. Also, it is expensive for the poor to travel to formal banking institutions. Perhaps the greatest block, however, is that the poor do not feel welcome in an urban environment where unfamiliar formal-legal methods are used.

For these reasons, few rural people take out credit from banks. The informal sector will supply credit, but moneylenders charge very high interest rates, often over 100 percent per year, while friends and relatives are unable to meet the full demand for credit (Fernando 1986). In 1989, 54 percent of rural households in Sri Lanka were severely indebted, 70 percent of these to noninstitutional sources. But the situation is even worse when no credit is available. Membership in a SANASA society automatically gives the member the right to credit.

Two types of credit are offered: long-term productive loans and short-term consumption loans, such as for funeral expenses or food in emergency situations. The long-term loans are used for agriculture (26 percent), animal husbandry (6 percent), small-scale industry (18 percent) and housing (36 percent), with 15 percent for other purposes. Small industry investment, particularly popular with women, provides employment and allows diversification of income.

Although the core activities of SANASA are financial, the societies also provide other benefits. Some have begun to act as commercial agents for their members, marketing their produce and keeping the profits from production within the members' community. Many societies have set up village shops that sell household items, including products made in the community, again stemming the flow of cash out of rural areas. Over 300 preschools have been established by the primary societies, imparting principles of self-reliance and cooperative development to the young (and their parents). Environmental programs to preserve land and promote sustainable farming practices have also been developed.

Many rural people lament a lack of community unity and cooperation; many feel society is increasingly fragmented due to increased monetarization and changing roles in the community. Disputes and jealousies are linked to this lack of community spirit. SANASA societies give community members an opportunity to come together on equal terms and work together. The society is a forum for discussing problems and resolving conflicts. Members gain an understanding of each other's situation and needs, which breaks down animosity. Harmony and understanding are built up as age and caste barriers are broken down. One outcome is social and cultural events that the societies organize, ranging from traditional festivals to children's drama.

Group meetings also give ignored members of the population a voice. Women and the poor have traditionally had little opportunity to express their needs and ideas, but they are welcomed into the society as equals. By placing power in the hands of members, the cooperative contributes to more positive attitudes and confidence. In one survey, only 13 percent of members said that they planned their future before joining SANASA, while 87 percent said they did so after joining. Such community spirit, independent thinking and awareness constitutes empowerment and is an important consequence of becoming a SANASA member, thus giving more than financial benefits.

A second reason for success: SANASA is simple. The procedures and organization of SANASA societies are simple and easily understood. Membership is open to all, and leaders are elected by simple vote. Financial transactions are completed with a minimum of bureaucracy; all members are able to save, and all are entitled to get loans. Staff are local and known to members.

This makes SANASA societies very efficient. Usually, high repayment rates require high administrative expenditures. But SANASA has a 96 percent repayment rate with low administration costs, usually less than 3.5 percent of the value of credit disbursed. This compares very favorably with other banking institutions and allows SANASA to take on small savings and loans. Moreover, SANASA societies are understandable and transparent. The poor are rightly wary of investing money in institutions they do not understand.

SANASA is also successful because it is controlled by the local population, in the community. The decisionmaking unit in SANASA is its members, who vote on all major decisions and elect their own leaders, whose job it is to carry out the wishes of the members. Societies are not seen as an outside institution, separate from the village; instead, SANASA leaders are known to members personally and are culturally similar. Existing members who sponsor new members communicate an understanding of the society's activities, making joining easy.

Members feel they own their society, which builds support for its policies within the community. The most evident form of this support is the peer pressure that members put on other members of their society to repay loans, a major reason that SANASA societies have an average repayment rate of over 95 percent. However, SANASA sees membership control as more than the means to an end. Giving the rural poor the opportunity to design their own projects and work for their own development is an end in itself. Leaders who are part of the community are more accountable to—and better understand the needs and ideas of—the members. Members can question leaders at monthly meetings about unpopular or unfair decisions. Making leaders fully accountable to the membership builds trust in the leadership and thus in the institution.

A fourth reason for success is that SANASA societies use the communities' available resources. SANASA makes the most of underused assets. One of a rural community's most valuable resources is its money, yet this money is rarely saved or used for investment, since there are no institutions to take it. When saved in a formal bank, the money is usually used for urban loans, creating a flow of resources out of the rural areas. The rural population has huge amounts of money to invest, as seen from the massive accumulated savings. High repayment rates for loans also show that money can be used productively in the rural areas.

SANASA's primary societies are now fully self-funding. By increasingly mobilizing more and more local funds, the societies demonstrate opportunities for growth without relying on external inputs of capital. Since societies are working with members' own money, they make sure the money is not wasted or lost. Traditionally, no link has been made between savings and loans in Sri Lankan culture. SANASA makes this link by requiring that members borrowing money have in their savings account at least one-third of the value of any loan they receive.

The SANASA movement also mobilizes the community's human resources, including all strata of the rural population. By being heterogeneous rather than restricted to a homogeneous target group, societies can use the resources of richer members, to be drawn on by the poor. Wide membership participation also means that many members gain experience in management, accountancy and leadership. These individuals get recognized as an important asset and are elected to office, enabling the society to manage its own affairs more efficiently.

If SANASA membership were restricted to the poorest, there would be less available managerial capacity. It would be harder for societies to manage themselves, and they would become more readily controlled by outside forces. There is also a danger that influential community members, if excluded from SANASA, would work against it either openly or tacitly, as they would not fully understand it or would see it as antagonistic.

Primary society leaders are often retired professionals and are often considerably wealthier than the average member. But this is an advantage, since few other members could afford to give up the time that leadership requires. More important, it does not work against the prevailing social structure of the community and so attracts no opposition. Vertical allegiances such as patron-client and kin relationships are common in developing countries, especially in Sri Lanka where there is a tradition of voluntary service for community benefit.

Of course it is possible that exploitative relationships and abuses of power will be perpetuated within a heterogeneous organization. However, SANASA avoids entrenching such people in top positions by keeping leaders fully accountable to members. SANASA societies install an alternative to the traditional elite, an accountable and elected alternative that reduces the possibility of exploitation.

Finally, SANASA is successful because it is self-strengthening. SANASA activities create the right environment for continued success of the movement. As members' financial positions become stronger, they have more need for SANASA services. SANASA provides them with experience in financial management and thrift, which makes them more reliable as members. Members are then able to graduate to larger loans, making the societies more profitable for all.

Members also learn the importance to their communities of the cooperative ideology, which stresses the usefulness of working together. As members develop their community, this creates need for more financial services. It also means the community is better suited to follow cooperative ideals. SANASA thus supports an ideology within the community that helps the cooperative structure flourish. Future leaders gain experience with societies' operations through membership participation and by working with other leaders in committees. The SANASA education program also builds their technical capacity. All of these factors strengthen SANASA's position so that it becomes increasingly important to the rural community.

EFFECTS OF FORMING A FEDERATION

The creation of district unions and a national federation have been essential for the development of the primary societies, which were not an active force for rural development before 1978. The societies were isolated and small-scale, usually seen merely as savings clubs. The leadership did little to mobilize money or ideas to invigorate the societies. Since the Walgama seminar in 1978, however, the number of societies in the movement has jumped from 1,302 to almost 8,000, while savings have risen almost thirty-five times. SANASA has been transformed from a collection of village societies into a people's organization.

Following the 1978 seminar in Walgama, representatives from primary societies in Kegalle decided to form a district union to represent the interests of SANASA societies within their area. The district union was composed of a general assembly made up of primary society members and an elected board of directors. By the time a second seminar was held in 1979, five district unions had been formed. These five district unions formed a national federation of SANASA societies, with a general assembly made up of seven representatives from each district union and an elected board. By the mid-1980s, there were twenty-four district unions, representing most of the country.

With the growth in the number of societies, some district unions found that their link with the primary societies was too weak. To bridge this gap, an intermediate level of divisions was formed, still legally part of the district union. The cluster, a group of five to ten societies represented by an elected committee and a paid cluster officer, is a recent addition to this structure. Currently, 8,000 societies are being supported by about 900 cluster offices. (The latter figure is expected to grow to 1,400.) In many areas these clusters are supported by divisions, many of which are served by permanent staff. There are now twenty-seven district unions, all of which are affiliated with the federation.

This multitiered structure allows a top-down influence to complement the bottom-up character of the movement. The decisionmaking body of each level, however, is still made up of primary society leaders, so control remains with the members. The movement has gained four significant benefits from this structure.

Motivation and Education

Motivation of existing societies was an important part of SANASA's rejuvenation after 1978, and the upper levels of the movement have had a role in motivating and educating societies ever since. Before 1978, local officebearers and members did not realize their societies' potential as a force for rural development; after 1978, SANASA motivators set out to change this. Using techniques adapted from methods of Buddhist teaching, first attempted at Walgama, voluntary leaders and staff from the young district unions travelled around the country to discuss the nature and potential of primary societies with members.

Societies were encouraged to consider how the resources of their community could be better used, and members analyzed why some societies succeeded while so many other societies had failed. The results were dramatic. Confidence in cooperative principles and in self-help grew rapidly. Members became motivated to develop their societies into a dynamic local force for development.

SANASA education programs developed naturally. As district unions expanded, they took on responsibility for education. Today, education officers in every district union coordinate a range of education programs. It is vital that members, especially new ones, understand the cooperative principles upon which the movement is founded. Members also need to know about the various services available to them. In turn, leaders need to understand the importance of promoting membership expansion and cooperative ideology. The content of education programs has been learned from outside the movement but, more important, has developed from the experience of SANASA societies. In addition, lateral links formed among the societies have allowed the experience of one society to be used in other societies.

In 1988, 8,336 education programs were conducted at village level, attended by 179,000 people for an average cost of less than thirty cents per person. At division and district levels, 2,302 programs were conducted involving 111,000 members at an average cost of less than one dollar per person. The cost of these programs is kept low by extensive use of volunteer trainers who teach in their local setting.

In 1985, a national training campus was established in Kegalle to support the training program. This SANASA Campus for Cooperative and Development Studies now conducts up to forty one-week residential training courses each year. Participants from district unions and clusters learn cooperative principles and technical skills, such as financial management, banking procedures, leadership techniques and gender analysis. This knowledge is then shared with members at lower levels in the organization. There are plans to expand the campus into a center for cooperative and rural development studies for South Asia, to conduct longer residential courses for advanced students.

The federation publishes a monthly newsletter to educate and motivate members. This is a cost-effective way of reaching members and reflects SANASA's commitment to open dialogue with its membership. Education will remain centrally important for SANASA as the movement is still constrained by limited understanding and professionalism among members. To maintain a loyal and effective membership committed to cooperative ideals, awareness and motivation must be constantly reinforced.

Financial Policies

A second major function of the multitiered structure is that it acts as a central bank for the primary societies. This has changed the role of the district unions and federation from being service providers to acting as financial institutions. Interlending occurs at two levels. Primary societies deposit excess funds with district unions, which are then able to give loans to other primary societies. District unions, in turn, deposit funds with the federation, which makes loans to other district unions.

Interlending carries a number of benefits. Most obviously, it allows more of the movement's resources to be used productively, allowing a high percentage of its deposits to be disbursed as loans. It also halts the flow of resources out of rural areas that occurs when primary societies deposit their money in commercial banks. Poorer societies tend to have a greater demand for credit, while richer societies have larger savings. Thus interlending creates a downward flow of resources, making them available to poorer members.

Interlending has further allowed the movement to pull in external resources. Government and international agencies supply the federation with resources, which are then passed on to members as subsidized loans. A further benefit is that interlending creates income for the district unions and federation. On average, for 1988–91, the difference in interest rates between savings and loans made up 60 percent of district income and 56 percent of federation income. This income could be increased if district unions and primary societies made all their deposits available for interlending.

Primary societies' financial policies have also changed. Before 1978, many primary societies paid interest rates less than the rate of inflation on deposits (negative interest) and offered only a narrow range of services. This kept both savings and surpluses low. As experience was shared throughout the network, societies changed their financial policies. Interest rates were raised to market levels, insuring long-term financial viability. Nonsubsidized interest rates on loans are not a deterrent for the poor, since their only other option is usurious private loans. Freely available loans at market rates represent a valuable service for the poor.

In the mid-1980s, SANASA found it was not able to mobilize sufficient savings, so different kinds of savings accounts were introduced. In addition to ordinary savings and shares, compulsory savings, fixed deposits, children's deposits and nonmember deposits were introduced. SANASA has also diversified the types of credit offered as societies have matured, with many societies now offering up to ten different types of loans.

Membership Diversification

Before 1978, the SANASA movement was largely middle-class and male. This is a common problem for South Asian cooperatives, and studies have shown how larger farmers often capture control of a cooperative and entrench their own position of status. An important effect of SANASA's rejuvenation was the expansion of its membership toward poorer, younger and women members.

A major barrier to membership for the poor was cost. The total cost of entry, including purchase of shares, for opening a savings account and compulsory savings is usually around 300 rupees (about US$6). Members are allowed to spread this cost over a number of months. Since daily wages for a laborer are 50 to 100 rupees per day, this cost is not prohibitive. The federation also started a project to lend a portion of its funds to low-income groups. The poorest members of each society are given subsidized loans and meet regularly to discuss problems.

Although these practical changes are important, the main reason for SANASA's reorientation toward the poor was the change of attitude in society leaders. Before 1978 the movement was seen as a service provider for those with money. Motivation and education sessions organized by the district unions and federation have led societies to try to attract the poor. The societies have also educated nonmembers and have become more visible within communities, creating a snowball effect as poorer members join, they influence the society and support new poorer members.

The influence of the three-tier structure has facilitated formation of new societies in poorer areas. District unions and clusters have actively sought to start new societies, using the experience gained from older societies. This downward expansion means that the primary society membership now reflects the socioeconomic composition of the surrounding society. Over half of SANASA members (52 percent) have annual incomes below the poverty line (2100 rupees) compared to the Food and Agriculture Organization's estimate of 46 percent for the rural population as a whole (Hulme et al. 1994). SANASA is thus not incorporating and serving just the better-off rural strata.

Women, who were badly underrepresented in SANASA prior to its rejuvenation, have also been attracted to the movement after the creation of the multitiered structure. The federation has formed national women's committees; all district unions have women's committees; and over 3,000 women's societies and 4,550 women's clubs have been formed in primary societies. This change in membership is due mainly to a change in attitude among leaders. Half of SANASA members (49 percent) are now female, whereas other rural banking initiatives in Sri Lanka have not successfully reached the female population. SANASA has particular benefits for women. Control of savings and access to credit in Sri Lanka is traditionally a male preserve. Surveys show that women's spending patterns change more after joining SANASA and that women take out more productive loans than men.

Including disadvantaged groups in SANASA's membership has benefited the community as well as the individual. SANASA gives the poor and women a voice, so they are able to express their needs and problems in an open forum. That everyone has equal status within SANASA raises the status of the disadvantaged. SANASA is also increasingly attracting young people. Its youth clubs, children's societies and even preschools are raising a generation with an awareness of cooperative ideals.

Diversification of Activities

SANASA's primary activity is banking. Yet consolidating organizational capacity can include diversifying supporting activities. Without such diversification, there will be little reduction in overall poverty. The cooperative structure encourages spontaneous community development initiatives. The movement's structure supports these initiatives in two major ways. First, cluster officers act as a focal point for societies' nonfinancial activities, organizing larger-scale projects across several societies to gain economies of scale. For example, clusters have started marketing local produce and have opened shops selling local goods. They have also decreased their reliance on urban traders by purchasing agricultural inputs in bulk and buying paddy mills. Second, the federation plans to set up national-level programs to promote nonfinancial ventures. A marketing program has been started that buys produce from district unions in one area of the country and sells it to unions in other areas, ensuring a fair price for both farmers and consumers. Other initiatives are planned in environmental protection, promotion of national unity and income-generation activities.

National Advocacy

The national federation plays a significant role in lobbying to create an environment conducive to the development of SANASA. It promotes the values of cooperative development, protecting the SANASA culture and financial discipline and preventing or minimizing the effects of harmful measures taken by the government or other parties. The federation has successfully lobbied the government to change bylaws governing cooperatives, and there is now agreement, in principle, to make the cooperative law more consistent with the needs of democratic, autonomous organizations.

The federation lobbies political leaders and the bureaucracy to safeguard SANASA's independence, the academic community to get support for expanded educational efforts and the banking establishment to change its rigid posture vis-à-vis SANASA and the poor. Through partners and other friendly organizations, it has worked to get its case heard within donor agencies when they supported government activities that threatened the integrity of the movement. A case in point is the Janasaviya Trust Fund, referred to later in this chapter.

ACCESS TO RESOURCES

The formation of regional and national bodies allows the movement to attract external resources, both technical expertise and financial resources. Technical advice has been used by different levels of the organization. Primary society leaders are encouraged to invite government officials to their villages, exposing them to the grassroots and linking government technical advice with credit availability. Suggestions received by the federation from occasional overseas advisors have permeated down through the organization to benefit primary societies.

SANASA exposes other organizations to its experience. It holds an annual consortium of partners meeting to share its experience and discuss future plans. These partners are international and national organizations working with SANASA or involved with rural development in Sri Lanka. The consortium reflects SANASA's commitment to the belief that development agencies need to operate in a "global village" network. SANASA also organizes meetings for cooperative leaders in South Asia, to discuss the future of cooperatives.

SANASA is strongly committed to the notion of partnership within development. Indeed, the movement is a network of partnerships. Members form partnerships to create a primary society; a district union is a partnership among societies. However, SANASA has had mixed experience with partnerships with funding agencies. For any successful partnership, certain basic requirements must be met. Unfortunately, the primary society members meet these requirements more often than do the international agencies.

1. Partners must respect the working methods and ideals of the movement, especially those of cooperative management and democracy.

2. There should be a positive benefit to all members of the partnership.

3. The partnership must embody free and open communication between both parties.

4. Partners work toward common goals. They must not undermine each other.

Relations with the government have been particularly complex for SANASA, and it strives to avoid potential difficulties. As mentioned earlier, a common problem for cooperatives is "capture" by political interests. Cooperatives' large membership, the fact that they provide services similar to those of government and the existence of a national body has led some political parties to try to take over cooperatives. At local levels, certain political leaders and wealthy groups often try to take over management, wresting control away from the members.

Prior to 1978, political capture was not a problem for SANASA, since isolated societies were too small to be useful to politicians. After 1978, however, the existence of district and national bodies opened up the danger of political influence and takeover, a danger SANASA is alert to. For this reason, SANASA has an organizational norm that individuals active in party politics can not hold office in the movement. The leadership also tries to avoid contact with political interests and maintains strict political neutrality. This makes SANASA almost unique among development organizations in Sri Lanka.

SANASA has not ignored the government, however. Ever since the first Walgama seminar, which government officials attended, SANASA has cooperated with and educated government officials about SANASA's policies. This balance of neutrality and cooperation has led to a working relationship with the government's cooperative department that is based on mutual respect. Government officials claim to be proud of their policy of nonintervention with the movement.

It has not always been possible to maintain this nonalignment. In the past, one case of government intervention resulted in disaster, and another potential problem looms in the future. In 1985, under considerable political pressure, SANASA agreed to participate in a "Million Housing Program" (MHP). It was financed by the U.S. Agency for International Development (USAID), heavily promoted by the then prime minister, and administered by the National Housing Development Authority. The program was designed to allow low-income households to build low-cost housing, using credit. An evaluation in 1984 found the program's credit recovery rate was very low, around 60 percent, and USAID suggested that SANASA, which had very high repayment rates and a network of grassroot societies, should be enlisted to implement the scheme. This was practically forced on the movement, at a time when the prime minister's power was ascendent.

The money that flowed in from the MHP gave SANASA a very different character. Previously, its funds had come from members' savings, making societies very careful about their loan policies and ensuring high repayment. The new money, however, was "easy credit," which undermined repayment discipline. New societies rapidly formed, and new members joined who were not interested in cooperative ideals, thus polluting the spirit of the movement.

Between 1985 and 1988, SANASA membership more than doubled. In some districts, up to 88 percent of loans were for housing. Along with implementation of a government program, however, came interference from local and national politicians who wanted special privileges; SANASA staff received threats from the JVP (Janata Vimukti Peramuna), a radical insurrection movement, for working with the government. Despite all these problems, SANASA managed to keep the default rate on its loans below 10 percent.

But worse was to come. In 1988, USAID, still frustrated by overall low repayment rates, refused to renegotiate its loan for the MHP. Then, shortly before national elections in 1989, the government announced that "poor people" would not need to repay their housing loans. This showed a complete lack of respect for SANASA's autonomy and undermined its central principle of never writing off loans. Predictably, overall repayment rates in 1990 dropped drastically, to 80 percent, and repayment of housing credit was much lower. Low repayment rates threatened the whole movement, although the slide has been contained. Luckily the MHP loan write-off has not contaminated other loans, and the government has not pressed for repayment of housing loans. Still, the experience left SANASA more wary than ever of political intervention.

Another potential problem has developed, which could undermine the organization, again due to the government's not respecting SANASA's ideology and methods of operation. One component of a World Bank-funded program, the Janasaviya Trust Fund (JTF), provides credit to low-income groups. This highly politicized program wants to use SANASA's organizational network to disburse 25 percent of its credit. Rather than working with the federation, however, JTF administrators have worked directly with district unions, which causes internal conflict. At issue is JTF's unwillingness to pay a commission to cover some share of the costs of the educational activities that have undergirded SANASA success. This problem has not yet been resolved.

A number of international agencies, governmental and nongovernmental, have approached SANASA, wishing to form partnerships. However,

SANASA is not willing to form partnerships with agencies unless they meet the requirements outlined above. Commonly, NGOs do not fully understand cooperative principles and ideals. They expect to be able to shape policy and design programs, which contradicts SANASA's policy of membership control. SANASA has avoided these partnerships.

If SANASA becomes involved in too many partnerships, this can become a problem by taking up managerial time. Completing progress reports and educating partners to the movement already takes up a considerable amount of time. However SANASA has established long-term relationships with a number of people's organizations and organizations that have developed along similar cooperative ideals. In particular, the Canadian Cooperative Alliance and Australia's Community Aid Abroad, which supported SANASA after the failure of the MHP, as well as HIVOS in the Netherlands and the World Council of Credit Unions have gained a deep understanding of SANASA's operations and ethos. Rather than just supplying start-up capital, these organizations have found that long-term support—technical, financial and moral—can produce a mutually beneficial partnership.

Over the last few years, SANASA has increasingly mobilized resources from external sources, especially at federation level. External subsidy for the federation has risen from 13 million rupees (US$300,000) in 1989 to 33 million rupees (US$660,000) in 1992. This contribution, about 2 percent of the total value of SANASA loans, could be seen as a strength in that SANASA is able to mobilize external resources, especially to increase its revolving funds. It could also be seen as a weakness, in that the federation is depending on partners' money. It should be remembered, however, that the primary societies are entirely self-funding and do not receive any subsidies. They could operate even if central organizations were cut back, although probably not as effectively.

PERSONNEL

Until 1978, the movement was run entirely by unpaid volunteers and this high level of voluntarism, which has kept costs low and increased the societies' efficiency, remains important. Leaders are often retired professionals with useful skills who wish to work for their community and usually work exceedingly hard. In fact, there have been some cases where leaders want to resign but have not been allowed to by their communities.

As workloads increase and the primary society activities become more complex, full-time managers are needed to run the societies. These managers, who are usually young and female, work closely with the society's committee. Cluster officers are also usually young and work full time with the support of the cluster committee. Voluntary workers are still vital to these levels, but full-time workers are increasingly important. They are able to work closely with the district union and manage technical financial matters while also covering a small enough area to motivate and educate at the grassroots. At higher levels, management becomes more technical. District unions employ specialist general managers, education officers and financial officers. Some district unions employ up to thirty people. Their boards of directors have overall control and the full-time staff's role is to carry out the wishes of the general body. However, the technical nature of the work requires that it is conducted by trained professionals.

Training staff is essential to increase the movement's professionalism. A major role of the national education campus in Kegalle is to provide training to SANASA's full-time workers. Courses are given in accountancy, management and training methods to staff at every organizational level. All of the 1,400 cluster officers receive four weeks of intensive training at the campus; higher-level staff receive further training both locally and abroad.

Because an understanding of cooperative principles and ideology is vital for all SANASA workers, the movement tries to retain its staff and promote from within the movement. This has built up a cadre of staff who are very committed to the ideals of cooperative development. As a people's organization, SANASA cannot hope to compete with international agencies on wages. The staff at SANASA, however, are sufficiently committed to the cooperative ideology to be willing to work for long hours at less than market wages.

DANGERS OF GROWTH

As organizations grow, they can lose the strengths of simplicity and member control. SANASA has so far avoided these two pitfalls. SANASA staff have had to become more professional as regional and national levels have been formed, and there is some danger that these developments could result in a top-heavy organization that removes money from the rural base. It is also possible that procedures could become complex and less easily understood by members.

These problems have been mitigated by two measures. First, the different levels of the organization are fully autonomous. Although the activities of the primary societies have become more sophisticated, the management of societies is still wholly within the community. Thus, although the organization has radically changed, the management has not moved away from the members. Second, the top of the organization has remained compact and efficient, with clear procedures for membership control. To be sure, by forming regional and national-level bodies and by using more full-time staff, SANASA has created the possibility of members losing control, which would be a disaster. A cooperative's strength is its members and their ability to guide the organization in a direction suited to their needs. Centralized power leads to weaker feelings of ownership, resulting in diminished membership pride, confidence and empowerment.

This problem does not arise in SANASA primary societies, because they have remained small and independent, with an average of 100 members, so individual members can still influence the society. District unions do not dictate the societies' policies; the societies are fully independent.

Another potential danger is that district unions and federation policies could become out of touch, since these levels have more full-time staff and less contact with members. This danger is countered in two ways. First, the movement's bylaws give clear and full power to the members and their elected leaders; second, the staff remain fully committed to cooperative principles. They understand the importance for the movement of membership participation and democracy, and elected leaders reinforce this. The staff and their orientation are crucial in such a process. Without their commitment to accountable management, the movement could not remain democratic. Committed staff are, paradoxically, the key to successfully maintaining member control. The success of SANASA and the satisfaction this gives both to staff and members have thus far kept democratic principles well respected.

NOTE

The author would like to thank Angus Poston from the University of Manchester, who has worked with SANASA, for his assistance in drafting this presentation.

5 Six-S: Building upon Traditional Social Organizations in Francophone West Africa

Bernard J. Lecomte and Anirudh Krishna[1]

The Sahel region of West Africa is home to the Six-S network, a remarkable multinational organization for rural development. Established in 1977, Six-S provides support for the self-help efforts of thousands of voluntary village groups organized into unions across West Africa. By the late 1980s, the organization was serving several hundred thousand people organized into 3,000 groups, located in 1,500 villages, which were federated into seventy-five unions spread over Burkina Faso, Mali and Senegal, with additional zones created to serve enthusiastic groups in Niger, Togo, The Gambia and Guinea-Bissau.

Six-S's name—*Se Servir de la Saison Séche en Savane et au Sahel*, "Making Use of the Dry Season in the Savannah and the Sahel"—indicates its intention to support village groups, efforts to capitalize on the potential for undertaking development work during the area's long dry season, which lasts six to nine months. The largely agricultural population of the region has little work to do during this period. Through Six-S, latent human resources are harnessed to combat the poverty and drought that force many of the able-bodied, rural residents to migrate to towns in search of meager earnings during this time. These resources are used, instead, to build dams, wells and dikes, to plant vegetable gardens and trees, to construct roads and schools, and to establish savings as well as grain banks. Literacy and health care are important components of the development package, which in each case is determined by every village group for itself.

In all its activities, Six-S emphasizes the primacy of local capabilities and needs. It has a minimum number of staff who work in facilitative rather than supervisory roles; the vast majority of staff are selected by village groups from among themselves. Six-S does not assist in the formation of groups; instead it cooperates with ones that exist or spring up in villages, based on traditional patterns of local cooperation. Six-S works through unions of such groups, in Burkina Faso traditionally known as *naams*. It does not design or manage development projects on their behalf, believing that stating its own priorities will contribute to continuing dependence. Instead, Six-S seeks to strengthen local capacities by filling the gaps—with complementary resources and skills—that local residents encounter as they take on village-level development by themselves. The long-term objective is for village groups to gain expertise and confidence and to establish themselves as viable, independent agencies for local development, with little residual support from Six-S.

Two convergent streams of thinking went into the evolution of Six-S. The first came from Lédéa Bernard Ouedraogo, who was born in Burkina Faso and had worked in the rural areas there seeking especially to combat illiteracy. His ideal of developing without harming the traditional bases of social cohesion in African society resulted in Six-S becoming an authentically African experiment aimed at creating a model of social organization that is neither a carbon copy of the West, nor a return to the past (Pradervand 1989, 22).

A second set of ideas stemmed from Bernard J. Lecomte, a French national who, together with Ouedraogo and some other colleagues, founded Six-S in 1977. Lecomte's considerable prior experience with development assistance, and his disgust with its generally poor outcomes, led him to ask what could the outside world, governments or aid agencies do to support, or at least not impede, the development of local organizations (Lecomte 1986, 90). His rejection of projects as the vehicle for assistance led Lecomte to infuse the idea of "flexible funding" into the Six-S strategy.

Under the approach devised to promote local-level development, a fixed amount of funds (between one and two million dollars per year) is given over by Six-S to federations of village groups. At the general meeting of a federation, village delegates present the proposals that their village group wishes to pursue during the coming year. Except for some general restrictions set by Six-S—the same group should not get money several years in a row; money should not go to private companies or government departments; disbursements should be matched by some contributions from the recipients, including contributed labor—the federations are free to select among themselves from the lists of action proposals submitted by different village groups.

Through its arrangements with the federation committees and the simple but important restrictions it places on disbursement, Six-S insures that the people closest to and most familiar with the end-users will be allocating the money equitably. Delegates have applied a number of criteria in selecting among the action proposals before them, for instance, the number of people involved, past borrowing record, level of risks in the scheme, the feasibility of launching it quickly, whether the funds are to be in the form of grants or interest-bearing loans (in the case of economic activities), and any rate of interest to be charged. At no time does Six-S or any of its personnel intervene in the selection of proposals or in passing funds from federations to village groups; mutual trust is a basic denominator in the relationship. Vincent (1984) refers to this process as the "pedagogy of responsibilisation."

The risk—of failure, of misappropriation—inherent in advancing funds to village groups without prior approval of activities is balanced by the care taken in admitting groups to the organization. Not all groups can join Six-S, and none immediately upon request:

> The first stage . . . is to reinforce the farmers' ability to organize them-selves. [Six]-S helps the groups summon up their own resources, starting with savings, which in turn leads to the trust in their own capacities . . . [it] helps the group create a network, find grassroots communicators, master elementary concepts of management, and lay the groundwork for literacy training . . . All of these are fundamental steps without which one builds on sand. . . . Only at the second stage—once the federation has become better structured at the regional level, once the groups have demonstrated their ability to save, to manage, and to carry on a dialogue—is financial assistance offered (Pradervand 1989, 104).

Only mature groups that have proved to be responsible can avail them-selves of Six-S funding, through a process whereby funds are advanced not to individual village groups but to federations, which are composed of between ten and fifty such groups. Accountability to the federation puts pressure on village groups to use the funds wisely and to repay those that are due. This is reinforced by training in account keeping for the treasurers selected by groups and federations. The first two stages in the development of a federation can take between eight and ten years, with the first (pre-project) stage itself taking up to five years in most cases. Groups are slowly nurtured to become more capable and responsible.

Success, however, has sown some seeds of failure. An excess of enthusi-asm fueled by donors practically lining up to provide funding has stretched the organization out too fast. Many new groups have not taken the time they need to organize themselves and generate the collective self-discipline expected of them. Increasingly, groups have enlisted with an eye on the fund-ing alone, which has reintroduced the element of dependency that Six-S has been trying to avoid. With donor funds diminishing in recent years, disaffection has crept into the relationship between Six-S and many of the village groups. This presents a challenge to long-term program success.

I. THE EVOLUTION OF SIX-S

This is how Lecomte remembers the beginnings of Six-S in the early days. The drought, which besieged sub-Saharan Africa in 1973, was felt as a great shock in the villages, especially among the youth. Lecomte felt that he had to do something to help people deal with this situation, but his knowledge of the African farming system at that time was more on the administrative level rather than the social. His experience with Senegalese farmers, for instance, consisted of planning and foreign aid negotiations. To reverse this situation and become more socially involved, he decided to join the Center for Economic and Social Studies in West Africa (the French abbreviation is CESAO), located in Burkina Faso. In collaboration with several other experts in planning and with the support of UNICEF, Lecomte had the opportunity to analyze the emerging gap that existed between development projects and two important social groups, women and young men. To follow up on this analysis, in 1975 he organized a conference in Accra with the support of ENDA, an African nongovernmental organization, or NGO, and with the assistance of few friends, including Lédéa Bernard Ouedraogo.

Ouedraogo's contribution was particularly valuable because of his familiarity with rural youth. He had been working as a regional inspector of rural schools, which provided three years of schooling for a small percentage of young peasants. These school programs covered his own region in Burkina Faso (Yatenga) and several other countries, including Côte d'Ivoire. Ouedraogo was not satisfied with the results of his work because education was often followed by brain drain from the rural areas. Young, educated people, especially the men, often left the villages when they completed their schooling, hoping to gain more money and happiness in the urban areas.

The results of this process disgusted him as a school inspector. In order to remedy this situation, Ouedraogo sought to implement one section of the National Educational Act, which supported the formation of postgraduation associations, called les *groupeménts post-scolaires*. His intention was that young people, after their schooling, would negotiate with their fathers to get some land which, together with some ambition, would induce them to remain in their village. Both Ouedraogo and Lecomte had lost faith in the then-prevailing methods of government-sponsored development. In contrast to Lecomte's previous experience in planning, his work at CESAO consisted mostly of interacting with both the implementers and the recipients of development projects. He saw that rural men and women regarded themselves more like plantation workers than as persons responsible for their own development. This was producing a negative reaction, especially among young farmers, who were no longer willing to obey the project monitors. Often, the farmers' only concern was to take advantage of the animals and equipment provided by the rural extension workers (Pradervard 1989).

Then came the drought in 1973, and the farmers saw how little the government could do to help them cope with that disaster and that they would have to rely on their own efforts to overcome the drought. Consequently, by combining their efforts, they became more independent. "Before we were ashamed to talk about our problems with one another, but the drought has made us more united, since we recognize that we all share the same misfortune," a group of farmers told us in 1974–75. As they came to CESAO to discuss their problems, Lecomte could see the emerging conditions for the birth of autonomous grassroots organizations.

As the drought was spreading in Senegal, Mali and Upper Volta, it became necessary to combine efforts. The conference in Accra, with the theme of childhood and youth in tropical Africa, produced a report (Lecomte and Ouedraogo 1975) that identified the following five issues.

The first concern of the farmer associations was a desire for *more knowledge*. However, farmers strongly believed that this knowledge could be acquired only by traveling abroad. As one illiterate village woman said, "It's only in Ghana that one gets the best training." She did not refer just to academic training; short-term immigration, it was thought, would also provide the opportunity for self-development. The second concern identified was the desire for *better technology*. Farmers desired to possess some of the production tools being used in the coffee and cocoa plantations in neighboring countries, located only 1,000 to 1,500 kilometers away. There they had seen how one could use machinery and implements, which were more than anything they had ever dreamed of having in their own villages. The third concern was more radical; they desired *more authority*. The young men and the women wanted to gain the respect of their elders who held power in the villages and to participate in the decisionmaking processes. Their previous efforts to achieve a greater role for themselves had been rejected. The young men and women resented their inferior status and lack of power, yet another reason for wanting to leave the village. The fourth concern was their thirst for *experience*. This was best expressed by the young farmers' enthusiastic participation in the multiple training programs organized by CESAO. Finally, the farmers who aspired to live differently also wanted to become *autonomous*. This desire was expressed at the village level by creating numerous associations, particularly in Burkina Faso and Senegal, where people could have their own place under the sun and to try new things. Where the basis for local action was already formed, the key was to negotiate with other elements in the rural community to get them to join in.

In our report of this conference, Ouedraogo and Lecomte asked, "How can we assist sub-Saharan youth and women in carrying on self-help activities to deal with the drought?" This was the first seed sown toward the creation of Six-S. Taking actions to deal with the consequences of severe drought helped them further develop their methodology for action. During trips across the Sahel in 1976, they became aware of the multiple consequences of the drought. The dry season, traditionally the period for numerous social activities—festivals, funerals, marriages—become a dead season. Barns and granaries were empty, and two-thirds of the adult men had left to look elsewhere for work. The only adults remaining in the villages were the elders and the women with their children. This situation was resulting in social conflicts, except in few irrigated areas where some type of farming was still possible.

The main task of the farmers' associations involved finding an alternative to this scourge. As they faced the question, "Isn't there anything else to do in a village during the dry season?" they realized that market gardening (already practiced by a few farmers in irrigated areas) was a likely alternative. However, three main conditions had to be fulfilled. First, they needed to acquire adequate means of production; at a bare minimum, water supply was essential. Second, farmers needed access to, as they said, "knowledgeable" people. Third, farmers needed modest monetary support, sufficient to pay for at least thirty days of work during the dry months of December through June. Given this assurance, they could stay in the village, even if there were not sufficient stores of grain to feed the whole family.

Realizing these conditions proved to be difficult both for CESAO and the farmers' associations. It was not just a matter of implementing a given project; it was necessary to incorporate it within the existing local structures. The diverse activities of the farmers' associations covered many different areas, such as home gardens and health, and it was critical to consider every aspect of these activities—how to encourage and support them—in order to make the program sustainable. The availability of funds became a serious issue at this time, particularly because such broad projects did not easily find support from any government or private agency.

The drought made people aware that development was a challenge, not a present to be given by beneficent outsiders. They said: "Everybody must roll up his or her sleeves and get to work." Above all, the groups did not want to feel ashamed among their peers or to be seen as failures by their elders. Thus, it would be necessary to bring them assistance that could be integrated with their own efforts, that fit into their priorities, and that gave them a chance to succeed in a sustainable manner. It would be out of the question to provide one-time support to a group and then abandon it to help another. There had to be continuity as well as purpose.

Ouedraogo and Lecomte were working 400 kilometers from each other, one living in the north and the other in the south. Given all the constraints, the realization of their vision was a real challenge. About this time, they were approached by an external agency. A friend in a foreign aid organization, Swiss Cooperation, made a reconnaissance trip to West Africa after the drought to, as he put it, "find good projects." But Lecomte had become totally allergic to "projects" by this time. At the friend's suggestion, however, Lecomte and Ouedraogo tried to imagine a way of providing aid that was different from projects, and would reinforce grassroots initiatives and not make donors their patron. Why not a fund that could make loans available to these groups? Or better yet, why not form committees or associations that brought together several village groups? Actually there were already a few unions and several village groups in Burkina Faso. But with few exceptions, these dispersed groups did not know one another. Lecomte and Ouedraogo imagined an instrumentality for aid that would bring them material assistance, a little money for work if they needed it and ample opportunity for the new groups to meet.

In 1975—unlike today when local democracy and people's organizations are praised—peasants were urged to participate in organizations established by a government organization and often financed by foreign aid agencies. Any organization that showed signs of autonomy or threatened to form a peasant movement was unacceptable to governments. Even though peasant groups were necessary for indigenous development, they must be called something else. Thus the idea of a fund, in order to sound legitimate, needed a technocratic name. So they called the new association "Making Use of the Dry Season in the Savannah and the Sahel."

Before proceeding further, it was necessary to decide how the fund would be used and then to negotiate with the aid agencies. The fact that Ouedraogo and Lecomte, citizens, respectively, of Upper Volta (now Burkina Faso) and France, were backing this venture helped to get the enterprise going within two years. Thanks to a foreign grant, Ouedraogo found the time to put his thoughts together, and his appointment to a committee set up by the national government—controlled at that time by the military— gave him the resources and the time to extend his network.

Lecomte and his wife during their three years with CESAO became acquainted with the men and women who had established groups in six West African countries and reviewed with them the least harmful methods of providing support. Then, returning to Europe in late 1976, Lecomte acquired from Swiss Cooperation a research monograph, "How to Plan External Assistance So That It Promotes Local Initiatives." Through participatory research, and with the help of officials in the foreign affairs department in Bern, he was able to lay the groundwork for financing Six-S as an international association under Swiss law, but with Sahelian peasants and cadres as a majority of its administrators.

The first funding, the equivalent of US$12,000, was provided in 1977 by a private German foundation, Misereor, whose representatives knew both Ouedraogo and Lecomte. This enabled them to begin operating in Senegal, Mali and Burkina Faso. The dry season permitted them to launch three closely related activities: exchange and training sessions; individual and, above all, collective rural works such as water, housing and roads; and land improvement, for example, controlling erosion. In the following dry seasons, a variety of production activities were made possible by the improvements achieved during the preceding years.

There were three hypotheses about the selection of groups. The first was that it was enough to observe which groups effectively used their first round of assistance and to use this experience as a basis for selecting groups that could receive larger grants and loans. The security for these loans—the second hypothesis—would not be personal property, since these young men and women had none, but their record of success with the works and improvements already achieved. The third hypothesis was that these groups which enjoyed success could be persuaded to allow new groups to come in and join their zonal committees.

Lecomte and Ouedraogo intended that resources would be available each year at the beginning of the dry season so that the groups might decide—with the funds clearly available—how to use them in the weeks and months ahead. In some cases there would be investments from which everybody would benefit because the whole working age population would remain in the village in the wake of a good harvest. In other cases, daily payments would be made for labor to those who had chosen to remain, despite the empty granaries. The plan was that this decision could be made between October 15 and November 15 of each year.

Six-S provided that the decision to take an action would be made by the groups themselves, after negotiating with fellow villagers. People's initiatives, whatever their content, were preferable to implementing courses of action with outsiders' predetermined goals. Why? Because Lecomte and Ouedraogo had observed so much pressure, narrowness and rigidity in existing foreign aid programs and the demobilizing effects of these constraints on the more vulnerable classes such as women and young people in the villages.

It was necessary to find locations where decisions could combine these two kinds of resources—the group members' own resources and the financial support from Six-S. Rejecting such decisionmaking at the level of a single village because it tends to be the center of parochialism and egoism, Six-S chose to work at the level of thirty or so villages, with 15–20,000 inhabitants spread out over distances that could be covered on foot in one day. This area was called a zone. The purpose was to facilitate contacts between a broader set of groups and to enable collective decisionmaking.

Ten or so delegates from the groups in the same zone would agree to share, at the beginning of each dry season, the external support provided by Six-S in the interest of their members. Certainly, this possibility, offering the zone committees the opportunity to decide for themselves, constituted a revolution. One local Malian civil servant exploded, "How could you trust one million CFA [equivalent to about US$5,000 at the time] to these peasants without my participation in the meeting?" The villagers replied, "How could we not appreciate the Six-S since they are the first donor that gave us confidence that we ourselves could administer their money?"

The decision not to prepare programs or projects in advance or to divide the funds arbitrarily among beneficiary groups allows Six-S to limit its number of salaried staff. In Senegal, where in 1989 there were forty-three assisted zones, there was never more than one permanent staff person, who was chosen from among the peasant *responsables*. The staff burden was a little heavier in Burkina Faso because, at the zonal level, educated peasants were rare indeed.

It was necessary to choose, from among people who had some minimum number of years of primary education, zone chiefs to guarantee the coordination of the groups' projects during the dry season. A secretariat was established in Ouahigouya, Burkina Faso, where Ouedraogo was born and lived. From 1978 to 1990 Ouedraogo and Lecomte operated in tandem. Ouedraogo assumed executive responsibility for the first three countries, then for six, while Lecomte assumed the presidency of the administrative council and handled relations with the foreign aid agencies.

Negotiations with the aid agencies proceeded step by step and turned out quite favorably. After the first grant of 5 million CFA from Misereor, we benefited from Swiss Cooperation, which provided the first three years of financing for the position of secretary-general. This permitted Ouedraogo to leave his government position and join Six-S. After 1980, a kind of consortium was formed among different donors, such as several large German and Dutch NGOs and the aid directorate of the Swiss department of foreign affairs. An even greater innovation for them was to finance a fund for which nobody knew, before each annual meeting, how much would go to each country and how it would be used. Thanks to these three-year agreements, the flow of these funds was without exception very regular, enabling activities to be undertaken at the beginning of each dry season in a number of zones—which had grown from 3 in 1978 to 110 in 1989.

Until 1990, the Six-S budget doubled almost every three years. The stability of a number of men and women—who remained in the same positions in the Six-S administrative council as well as in the aid agencies and the emergent peasant federations—has been an important factor in the management of the association. Every year the general assembly brings

together various participants, Sahelian and foreign, peasants and administrators, for several days where they could decide where and how to
cooperate. This has preserved a process that assures local involvement
and control. After these pioneering years, Lecomte resigned as president
of Six-S at the end of 1989.

II. METHODS OF ORGANIZATION

From 1977 to 1990, various working methods were developed as Six-S
expanded its operations to extend support to rural groups located in
nearly 1,500 villages. The basic unit of organization has remained the village group, although there may be more than one group in the village (the
average is two). Village groups are federated upward into zones (encompassing from ten to fifty village groups). Zones (sometimes called unions)
are then grouped together into areas (sometimes also called federations or
regions). Areas have between 1,000 and 40,000 individual members,
depending on their size and on the number of zones they contain, which
can vary from one to eight.

Each level of organization has its own elected office bearers. Each zone
has a management committee composed of delegates from the constituent
village groups, who elect from among themselves a chairman, secretary and
treasurer. None of these posts carries any salary. Each zone has a coordinator who receives compensation for his or her services, but not a regular
income. The coordinator carries out Six-S activities throughout the dry season. Once the rains come, coordinators tend to their own fields. These coordinators represent their zones at federation meetings and also, once a year, at
the Six-S general assembly. This meets separately in each of the countries
where Six-S operates. The organization is thus composed entirely of farmers
and their representatives. Technical specialists are hired on a temporary basis
as need arises for specific services or for training in special subjects.

Flexible Funding

Having decided not to interpose any intermediaries between itself and the
farming communities, Six-S had to devise suitable systems and processes
that would draw upon the strengths of this arrangement while minimizing
its weaknesses. The project form of assistance was rejected at the outset.
Instead, Six-S adopted the system of flexible funding, which required that
Six-S develop and maintain long-term relationships with the agencies that
provide it with funds. The standard agreement between the donors and
Six-S provides funding on a three-year, renewable basis; the money comes

as a grant to Six-S at the start of each dry season; Six-S can pass on the money to zones—to be given as grants or as loans—without any requirement that projects be submitted by village groups; neither is Six-S required to submit any project proposals to the donor agency.

This relationship of mutual trust—between aid agencies and Six-S, and between Six-S and the groups it assists—is maintained on the basis of two principles: prequalification of village groups, and a strong emphasis on proper account keeping. Before it receives any funds, a village group must have proven its determination to achieve local development by completing a project of its own. Internal capacity has to be enhanced before receiving outside assistance (a condition that appears to have weakened somewhat as a feast of funds came in later years).

Donor agencies are invited to send their representatives to the annual general assembly meeting where, along with hearing the plans and prospects presented by farmer representatives, they also get to appreciate the problems faced, the mistakes and the assignment of blame for these mistakes. These meetings, like those at the village or federation levels, are held in a democratic setting; peasants and donors sit together as equals and are free to dispute each other's views.

Selection of Activities

Six-S makes no effort to shortlist a menu of options or to suggest a list of eligible activities, unlike government-sponsored self-help programs. The activities undertaken by the different village groups thus reflect the development priorities shared by group members. Although these priorities vary among groups, a number of similar activities have been dictated by common socioeconomic conditions and concerns. To deal with the scarcity of water during the long dry season, they have dug wells and built dams. To conserve soil and moisture on their fields, they have constructed contour stone barriers, using a technique first borrowed from Oxfam–UK, then adapted to local conditions. The experience with droughts has made clear the advantages of introducing vegetable gardens and livestock raising. Such activities have been taken up jointly as well by individuals. Other groups have planted village woodlots, raised chickens and constructed schools, theaters and stores. Along with these income-generating activities, a number of social sector activities have been taken up. Groups have appointed village health agents and established rural pharmacies. School rooms have been built, and adult literacy has been taken up by most groups.

Many groups operate grain mills and have organized cereal banks. These banks buy excess grain from farmers at harvest time, store it, and resell it at cost to farmers when they run low shortly before the next harvest. Before these banks existed, farmers borrowed at usurious interest rates to buy cereal at the end of the dry season in order to feed their families, then had to sell their grain immediately after the next harvest to pay off these debts.

As one observer of Six-S explains,

> Because the peasant is poor and has no access to imported equipment, activities are wherever possible low-cost, relying on local tools and materials. . . . Respecting the peasant's knowledge and experience means building on traditional concepts and technologies, rather than trying to supplant them at one blow by alien and unfamiliar Western approaches. . . . Techniques are spread by the channel the African peasants trust best, the proof of their own eyes. Visits are arranged to take people to villages where new methods are in successful use. And much practical training is undertaken in "workplace schools" where people learn by doing. (Harrison 1987, 280–81)

Training

This is a central component of the support provided by Six-S to the village groups. Six-S hires "farmer technicians" each dry season and organizes work schools in which they can master specific skills for agriculture, health, well construction, maintenance of equipment or handicrafts. These people then form mobile training teams and travel to villages that request training in such skills. For example, Six-S instructional teams train women to build three-stone cooking stoves that are 35 to 70 percent more fuel-efficient than existing stoves.

In a typical training session, an instructor will demonstrate to several dozen women how to build the stove. Each woman then makes a stove herself under the instructor's supervision, breaks it up and repeats the process several times. These women return to their villages and teach their neighbors to build the stoves. Use of these stoves can save a woman up to twenty days of labor each year, which she would otherwise spend gathering wood, and it slows deforestation. Apprenticeships for gaining specialized knowledge or skills are also arranged with more experienced village groups or at a specialized institution.

In addition to gaining experience in planning and implementing specific development initiatives, generating their own funds and being assisted to learn new techniques, village groups—or some selected members—are also trained in techniques of management, especially in accountancy and record keeping. The objective is twofold: to promote transparency in all money matters ("accounts in the sunlight") and to instill within groups the management skills and accounting procedures that will later enable them to have a financial record good enough to establish creditworthiness with commercial banks and other modern financial institutions.

Each group has a person who is trained by Six-S in modern accounting, and the accounts of each union are audited annually by a professional auditor. Groups and unions whose accounts are in arrears cannot avail themselves of further funding. A Swiss-chartered accountant regularly reviews the books of Six-S, and copies of this report are freely available.

Use of Funds

Six-S recognizes that the need to repay loans helps guide a group's operations toward productive activities. The requirement of repayment also promotes social equity as it prevents a few powerful groups and individuals from appropriating a disproportionate share of funds; it also fosters solidarity within groups. Members realize that, by working together to repay loans, they will be able to avail themselves of fresh loans in the future. However, Six-S also admits that it is too much to expect that the groups can repay all of the funds they receive; they will need some grant-based assistance to meet the costs of training, community works and at least part of their operating expenditure. A mixture of grants and loans is therefore commonly found in the pattern of funds advanced to any group.

The condition that part of the funds—at least those that have been advanced for productive activities—will need to be returned, along with interest due, permits recycling of resources among groups. It is a powerful factor in knitting together the village groups in a network of mutual responsibility and assistance. An example is "son and daughter mills," a social innovation that was developed spontaneously and has now become part of the common lexicon of village groups everywhere.

There is a large demand for diesel-powered mills that can grind grain into flour. Without them, women are forced to spend long hours pounding grain by hand, often at the end of a long, tiring day. When one such mill was offered by a Western church group to a women's group in Yatenga, they were reluctant to accept it purely as a gift. They decided that each woman who used the mill would be charged a small sum. When enough money had been collected, they would buy a new mill and give it to the neighboring village. It would be a "daughter mill," since daughters marry outside the village. Later, when still more user charges had been collected, a "son mill" would be purchased to retire the original mill, which would by then have become old and worn out. Social pressure from the villages waiting for their mills keeps the process going. This innovation was further developed by other groups who decided to divide their contributions into four parts—one each for the son and daughter mills, one for the upkeep of the original mill and also an amount for assisting the helpless and the handicapped. Similar analogies are to be found for financing livestock, where the offspring are given to other groups or individuals.

Innovations have been constant in Six-S's use of funds. Ouedraogo recalls how, in one village, a particularly conscientious peasant was in charge of a village granary.

> We had told people in such positions not to make gifts, and he followed our recommendation. During the 1984 famine, old people, widows and others in need begged for gifts of grain, but he refused. One day he appeared at our headquarters and offered his resignation. "How can you expect me to perform my task so heartlessly?" . . . We convinced him to return to his village and find a solution with the management committee of the granary. They came up with an idea: each person who purchased grain from the granary would be asked to pay a modest supplement, which would go into a Social Solidarity Fund [for free distribution to the needy]. . . . Once more, as with the son and daughter mills, here is an example of a system created by the grassroots, applied by the grassroots and taught by the grassroots. That's our method. (Pradervand 1989)

This unique relationship between a support agency and the grassroots, what Ouedraogo calls being "mastered by the grassroots," has rested so far on definite understandings of the obligations and responsibilities that each party has to the other. Thus, while Six-S provides flexible funding and arranges for specialized equipment and training, the groups themselves must constantly prove themselves worthy of qualifying for this support. This arrangement requires a delicate balance. Unfortunately, there are some recent indications of creeping imbalance that may erode the system of incentives, checks and balances that has been evolved as the scale of operations and their speed of expansion pick up.

III. REFLECTIONS

The clearest result of the Six-S experience is the existence today of a very large number of unions and autonomous peasant federations in Burkina Faso and Senegal, although Six-S was only one of a number of causes contributing to this result. These grassroots organizations have their strengths and their weaknesses, but they carry on.

If Lecomte had it to do over, he would:

1. Establish a totally flexible fund, not committed in advance.

2. Organize by zones, which act as foundations for the creation of unions of groups.

3. Not hesitate to trust the decentralized management of the fund to committees of responsible peasants, while checking to see that decisions are taken properly at their level, with minimum interference by the directors of the federations.

4. Develop better methods for self-diffusion of experience through workshops, training, visits and meetings—minimizing the role of nonpeasant outsiders.

5. Be more hesitant about emphasizing loans over grants.

During periods of drought, loans pose dangers, especially if full payment is demanded from fledgling groups. It would be best, when beginning to work with peasant organizations, to operate more with grants. However, one has to ensure that such a flexible and undemanding method should not last more than a few years. In Six-S, some zones were supported by this method for as long as twelve years. In retrospect, this was probably twice too long. To provide such unconditional support to young organizations and their fledgling unions for five to six years is long enough. This should be followed by a period of increasing loans and diminishing grants.

To be certain that this flexibility is fully beneficial, one must establish—better than we did in Six-S—the critical function of continuous monitoring and evaluation. This function should be performed by the people themselves—by self-evaluation—but also by external evaluators. Training by reviewing successful experiences and mistakes is effective if it includes an element of reflection–information–correction. This function is not easy to introduce from the outside when a union of groups already exists. Thus, it would be better if this function were incorporated from the very beginning in the activation of flexible funds and in their management and control. The systematic examination of work already done is the precondition for planning better work to be done in the future.

After several years of a regime of flexible financing with continuous monitoring and evaluation, the unions of groups and the groups themselves can be inspired to program their own activities; indeed, they will desire to do so. At this moment, it is appropriate that they develop their own programs and negotiate them with funding agencies without the need for tutelage from a supportive NGO. Otherwise, there is the risk of persisting with this tutelage, and then its growth, like a cancer, in a number of NGOs is inevitable. NGOs are not there to become a new administration but for another purpose—the awakening and the development of the inherent capabilities of people.

NOTE

1. The editors made several attempts to contact Lédéa Bernard Ouedraogo in West Africa to invite him as cofounder of Six-S and its president since 1989 to contribute a chapter to this book. When we could not reach him, Krishna drafted a case study of this program to be able to include it in this volume. Subsequently, we were able to get in touch with Bernard J. Lecomte, Six-S's other cofounder, who is retired and living in France. Since he found this draft satisfactory, he declined to write a case study himself, preferring to contribute his perspectives on Six-S to our account; these are incorporated in Sections I and III.

6 DESEC: Thirty Years of Community Organization in Bolivia

Juan Demeure and Edgar Guardia

The *Centro para el Desarrollo Social y Económico*, widely known as DESEC, is a Bolivian nongovernmental organization (NGO) set up over thirty years ago to support peasant cultivators, initially those located in the rural regions of the Cochabamba valley. Bolivia's agrarian reform of the early 1950s had created an institutional vacuum in the rural areas that state extension agencies and state-sponsored rural trade unions could not adequately deal with. The agrarian reform annulled the old feudal land-holding patterns, abolished forced labor, and transferred land ownership to peasants. However, little was done by the state or its agencies to follow up on the reform. Apart from attempts to organize the new owner-cultivators in state-sponsored trade unions, virtually nothing was done to provide them with credit or technical advice, modern agricultural inputs or marketing support. The rural trade unions quickly became vehicles for local leaders to project their political power, supported in some cases by armed militia.

Despite the much awaited reform in land rights, most peasants ended up owning as little as one to three hectares of cultivable land per family and were, by and large, not supported in their quest for a better life. Not only were agriculture extension services extremely thin on the ground; social services, health and education were also scantily provided by government. Infant mortality rates were as high as 180 per 1,000 children born, and illiteracy levels in the rural areas ranged from 30 to 70 percent.

In 1963, against this background, DESEC was formed by a group of young Bolivian professionals, under the leadership of Juan Demeure. They set themselves the task of assisting in the organization of the peasant sector and of promoting the participation of peasants in the country's social and economic development. With these objectives, DESEC took action on two broad fronts: promoting and consolidating peasant organizations at the local and regional levels, and providing support services to assist these organizations.

Over the years, DESEC has worked in several areas of the country, mainly in the altiplano, highlands and valleys located in the departments of Cochabamba, La Paz, Oruro, Potosí and Santa Cruz. In recent years, DESEC's annual budget has been around US$300,000, employing close to eighty full-time staff, all Bolivian, with foreign consultants engaged only for short periods to provide assistance in specific spheres of work.

DESEC's work has reached more than 1,000 rural communities that have a combined population of some 50,000 families. We currently work with more than 250 peasant organizations in diverse programs related to agriculture, livestock, forestry, artisan production and community infrastructure. Although several of these programs are in relatively new areas of work, some have been carried out over a long period of time, making a considerable impact on rural production and incomes. Most notable has been the work done with potato cultivation and the programs in support of rural handicrafts. Potatoes are the main crop of the country's hilly Andean regions. In the Carrasco and Tiraque provinces, located in the department of Cochabamba, potato production for some 800 farmers has increased almost fourfold since the program began, from 1,440 tons to 6,400 tons. Amerindia is an artisan branch created by DESEC in the early 1960s. In its early years, it received some external support for promoting the technical and commercial viability of local artisan groups. It is now a mature, self-supporting organization. In spite of frequent crises due to the economic chaos in Bolivia since the 1980s, Amerindia has survived and grown, working now with nearly 400 artisans, the majority of whom are women.

Other areas of work, recently taken up, are progressing well and promise to raise rural incomes in a sustainable fashion. Work with agroforestry, with cooperative consumer stores and with livestock production are some examples. All activities are undertaken with a view to make them eventually self-supporting and fully managed locally. To this end, each activity is associated with an appropriate local organization that gradually takes over an increasing share of program management. It is our intention to start activities that will be taken over and managed by people's organizations. The transfer of responsibility from the support agency to a local organization is, however, a matter that requires extreme care. Done prematurely, it can destroy the program that has been built up and severely set back the local organizations. Only when there is good management, good information and good understanding among local leaders and members will they be in a position to assume full local control.

We better understand this process of local self-management (and its counterpart, the withdrawal of the support agency) after making a number of mistakes. The most costly mistake was trying to hand over the successful potato program too early and too much to a local organization. Although the potato program has been restored to its former growth path, after some years of stagnation, we realize that a critical mass of conditions needs to be generated before the support agency can withdraw itself. We will later describe our experience in this regard. Suffice it to say here that program sustainability more often than not requires that the support agency continue over the longer term to play a role, which, though residual and much reduced, can rarely be dispensed with entirely.

The support functions we have provided are usually financed from the project assistance received from various international, mainly European, donors, usually private organizations assisted in some cases by their governments. Until recent years, this project assistance was given to us in the form of one- or two-year grants. The short time frame of most project financing posed a major hurdle. We could rarely plan for the medium or long term, even though most of the activities that were started required sustained action for at least five to seven years. Some activities had to be aborted prematurely as donor funds were not renewed, and some were continued but only on a smaller scale. Rarely could efforts be carried on long enough for a critical mass to be generated.

Since the end of the 1980s, however, we have been getting longer-term commitments from our donors. This has allowed us to stabilize our programs and to give firmer commitments to our staff and to the people we serve. A more stable cadre of staff is now in place. We have also started to network with international agencies and domestic institutions—banks, technical institutes and government agencies—in a new "triangular relationship" that has given a wider scope to our activities. This will enable us to draw more effectively upon our experience to cope with the institutional vacuum that arises as state extension agencies are shrinking ever more in the face of structural adjustment policies.

PHILOSOPHY AND APPROACH: ORGANIZING RURAL COMMUNITIES

Since DESEC was formed, a number of other voluntary action groups have been set up, not always with a development objective, by political parties and church groups. Although DESEC has consciously and deliberately avoided affiliation with any political or religious group, our theoretical framework for social action drew initially upon the Catholic Church's teachings on social service and upon the marginality thesis that was put forth at the beginning of the 1960s by the Center for Economic and Social Development in Latin America (DESAL), a private social science research institute based in Santiago, Chile. Changes in attitudes and social structures were thought to be essential aspects for forming a social organization that facilitated the responsible participation of each person.

This frame of reference has continued to influence DESEC in the thirty years of its history.

In theory, changes in attitudes and structures are to be achieved through organizing the peasants into groups that could then be encouraged and supported to take up activities for social and economic advancement. There were, however, in the early 1960s no Bolivian and few Latin American precedents that could show us the way forward. We had to start slowly and learn for ourselves.

DESEC's initial staff was composed of young Bolivian professionals who were self-motivated and idealistic without being politically bound. Almost all of them were then less than thirty years old. These staff came together in seminars and workshops to analyze the rural situation and to evolve a methodology for the new organization. They realized that local people had to be organized, building from the village level up to higher levels of organization. The higher-level organizations would provide essential support services and would serve as a channel for the technical and managerial advice that would be provided by the DESEC professionals.

Juan Demeure had been active in evaluating rural development projects on behalf of external financing agencies. His contacts with local action groups and his connections among international agencies brought together the first set of Bolivian and international collaborators. Several local groups, mostly formed by local workers of the Catholic Church, invited us to work in their areas.

Peasant leaders from these groups participated in our early deliberations and became the first set of local outreach workers for DESEC. They went about getting rural residents to organize themselves into groups that could take collective action to address commonly felt problems. The first steps were financed internally. Many among DESEC's founders contributed their own resources to underwrite the early activities and programs. Donors were approached after our experience with these early programs and observation of the first results helped us formulate a coherent set of schemes and funding proposals. The first set of donors were European nongovernmental organizations, such as Misereor (Germany), Vastenaktie (Netherlands), Fastenopfer (Switzerland) and Entraide et Fraternité (Belgium), which contributed about US$1 million during DESEC's first five years.

Soon after the initial peasant organizations began work in the Cochabamba valley, people from other nearby villages began to approach DESEC for assistance. The lure of program funding may have been the attraction for a large number of local groups, but they all had to fulfill certain conditions before they became eligible for DESEC support. The groups had to hold periodic meetings and keep a meeting register; they had to select their leaders through regularly held elections; they had to build up a common fund from members' contributions; and they had to have some prior experience of, or at least be well prepared for, undertaking activities for mutual benefit. We found that groups that underwent such a formative period were more likely to remain stable.

We adopted no fixed formula for community organization. Depending on the situation, we supported existing peasants' organizations in some areas, especially those where traditional organizations were strong, or set up new organizations where people felt these were required. In villages where the trade unions had a strong socioeconomic character and were weakly, if at all, linked to political parties, we opted to work directly with these organizations. In some cases, entire villages joined together in an organization, while in others a subset of inhabitants got together to form a group.

The size of the group depended in most cases upon the nature of activity that the group wanted to take up. Groups that favored activities such as forestry, irrigation and cattle health generally extended to entire villages; on the other hand, groups that took up crop or cattle improvement, credit or marketing support, did not always include full villages. In each case, the choice regarding activity and membership size remained exclusively with group members.

DESEC has taken special care that our promoters maintain a subsidiary role in relation to the communities' elected leaders, strengthening their roles and never substituting for them. We do not designate group leaders nor do we help in their selection. Any external influence in the process tends to inhibit the emergence of leadership that is freely elected by, and, hence accountable to, local residents.

We support the formation of people's organizations first at the community level. To arrange for coordination among the village groups, establishing associations of village-level organizations is encouraged at zonal and regional levels. Such second-level structures are indispensable for consolidating the efforts of community-level organizations. It is here that many services can best be made available.

In 1963, the first regional association, ARADO (*Acción Rural Agricola de Desarrollo Organizado*) was set up by grassroots groups of the Cochabamba valley. As DESEC activities expanded to other areas, peasant groups from these areas joined in ARADO. Village groups in some other departments formed zonal chapters affiliated loosely with ARADO. In other cases, depending upon the programs that they decided to undertake, peasant groups of different regions opted to form separate cooperatives and producer associations. They contributed cash and labor to the activities that their associations promoted. DESEC has supported these efforts by arranging for complementary funds and, more important, by providing training and technical and managerial advice. To help it perform these functions adequately, DESEC has created specialized support agencies.

As zonal and regional organizations become stronger and more capable, more and more functions of the support agency are transferred to them. Factors that helped make some higher-level organizations stronger than others include a clear definition of the social and economic basis for affiliation, a well-articulated internal structure at each level of organization, and, above all, success in developing and managing an economic program that brings significant benefits to a wide range of members. However, the capability of leaders and managers has to be balanced by mechanisms that make for internal accountability. At all times, leaders and managers must be accountable to the organization's members and submit to members' control. Otherwise, there is a great danger that leaders and managers will fall prey to the lure of private gain.

We know of this danger because we have seen it happen. Our very successful program for potato cultivation was almost destroyed as a result of an ill-conceived operation in the early 1980s that aimed to transfer control from a DESEC support agency entirely to ARADO. ARADO has had difficulties finding good managers, and it failed to require them to report regularly and truthfully to its membership. The transfer of responsibility was total, with no provision for the support agency to give up its functions gradually, in step with the growth in capacity of ARADO's membership.

We have since realized that such transfers are best effected when the higher-level organization has capable management that is balanced by member oversight. This mix of skills, experience, self-confidence, mutual responsibility and economic volume of operations—a critical mass— needs to be attained by the people and then incorporated by them into organizational procedures. Until that time, the support agency has to continue to discharge several functions, albeit at a reduced level over time. Without such support, the services managed by peasant organizations run the risk of failure and frustration.

ESTABLISHING SUPPORT AGENCIES

A number of support agencies have been set up, each performing a particular function. The earliest of these, ASAR, the *Asociación de Servicios Artesanales y Rurales*, was established in 1964. ASAR was set up to extend assistance in the agriculture and livestock sectors. Its functions include providing technical assistance, extending credit, supplying inputs, producing and providing improved seeds and making arrangements for marketing the produce.

ASAR's greatest success is in the area of potato production, the most important crop of the Andes. ASAR support functions have taken a number of forms, including introduction of new and improved varieties; developing a seed multiplication program; training peasant paratechnicians; setting up an input distribution system, credit program and storage infrastructure; and promoting local trade fairs. This has resulted, in the provinces of Carrasco and Tiraque, in yield increases, from six tons per hectare, which we had achieved after the first set of early interventions, to ten tons per hectare. Combined with an increase in the area planted for potatoes—from, on average, 0.3 hectare to 0.8 hectare per family—this has meant a fourfold increase in production.

Though ASAR works directly with local groups comprising about a thousand families, the program's impacts are felt over a much wider area as farmers have rushed, either as individuals or in groups, to take advantage of the new technology. They have formed local organizations that have enlisted in ARADO, or that have taken up similar arrangements by themselves. The resulting increase in the region's marketable surplus is observed in the impressive growth and development of the main agrarian trade fair that is held each week in El Puente.

The *Instituto Campesino de Educación* (ICE) has been working since 1967 to provide training in organization and administration. ICE's staff visit the communities and participate in their meetings, helping communities organize themselves and take up initiatives for joint action. As grassroots organizations and their higher-level associations start functioning, ICE's promotion role changes to providing support and advice. Specialized training is provided in agriculture, animal husbandry, forestry and other production techniques. Since its origin, ICE has organized more than 600 courses that have been attended by more than 16,000 of the area's farmers. Training has been supported by disseminating audiovisual material and by publishing a rural newspaper, *Ayni*.

To support our activities in house construction and health, we have created the *Asociación de Vivienda Popular* (VIPO) and the *Servicio Popular de Salud* (SEPSA). Yet other institutions have been created in recent years as funds become assured for longer periods by our donor agencies.

In an effort to strengthen the potato improvement program, we established a new tripartite program for producing seed potatoes. ASAR contributes its experience and production capacity and participates as a shareholder in a new enterprise, the *Unidad de Produccion de Semilla de Papa* (SEPA). This is a joint public–private undertaking, with the Bolivian government's *Instituto Boliviano de Tecnologia Agropecuaria* and the

Swiss Technical Cooperation Agency as the other partners. This arrangement allows us to work closely with the public sector and expand our activities within the larger scope of a bilateral technical assistance program. Other such arrangements give us a means of scaling up our activities in a mutually beneficial partnership with public agencies and foreign donors.

Scaling Up Through Triangular Operations

A similar tripartite program has been taken up for livestock and sheep rearing. In this program, DESEC works alongside the government agency in charge of the livestock sector, with the support of the Food and Agriculture Organization (FAO) and the office of the Spanish Cooperation Agency in Bolivia. The program has strengthened DESEC's and ASAR's capacity for livestock improvement and allowed us to have some influence in national policymaking insofar as the livestock sector is concerned. A similar arrangement has been made for our rural credit operations. We have obtained refinancing, through local branches of commercial banks, from the Bolivian central bank's development department. The process of refinancing continued well from 1974 to the early 1980s, when galloping inflation was let loose in the country. Currently, some credits are still being obtained from private banks.

Our programs in the forestry sector expanded rapidly until they reached a level where we could coordinate our forestry support agency with a regional public institution. Within this framework, our program has been supported with bilateral financial and technical assistance. Due to its connections with the public sector, it has been able to negotiate successfully with the government on behalf of communities that take part in the program. This joint program has been able to resolve satisfactorily matters related to communities' rights to common lands, planting contracts and arrangements for protecting and utilizing forests.

Achievements in these areas have brought us offers of technical and financial assistance that are more stable and spread over a longer period. This makes it possible to concentrate our efforts, to work long enough with communities for them to attain the critical mass needed to take over these functions by themselves. Our involvement in these triangular operations is facilitated by our professional and nonpolitical character, which allows us to negotiate with the public sector from a position of independence and strength, giving us enough space to nurture our autonomy while simultaneously learning from others.

Obviously, we can participate best in those public sector activities that are undertaken with the least political motivation, as well as those least encumbered by large amounts of paperwork. These considerations make it difficult for us to draw funds from the government's *Fondo de Desarrollo Campesino* (Peasant Development Fund) and *Fondo de Inversión Social* (Social Investment Fund).

Where we feel that our identity and independence may be compromised, we prefer to go it alone. We have maintained several agricultural and livestock services without any external assistance, financing them through the margins we earn in the distribution of inputs and sale of produce. Thus, these activities have paid for themselves. We have a large number of cooperative consumer stores set up by many village and second-level organizations. The peasant organizations we work with charge membership dues which, although often very modest, contribute to financial independence. The support agency that has sustained itself financially for the longest period is Amerindia, which helps support the activities of rural crafts associations.

MONITORING AND EVALUATION

The activities of local organizations and DESEC support agencies are regularly monitored and evaluated. The oversight and self-correction activities have improved over the years, assisted in many instances through the evaluations conducted jointly by the staff of DESEC and donor agencies.

In our early years, monitoring was mostly carried on through informal means. Only at the end of the 1980s was a permanent system of monitoring and evaluation established. This system drew upon the guidelines suggested by the United Nations agencies' Administrative Committee on Coordination (ACC). We piloted the monitoring and evaluation system first in a small part of our operations and extended it progressively to include each of our different activities. The system was first applied in our forestry program. With some refinements, it was made part of a project that was taken up to extend DESEC operations to the western part of the Cochabamba department. This project includes several components assisting with agriculture and livestock production, forestry and community infrastructure, plus the organization and training of peasant communities.

Formal monitoring and evaluation force us to make detailed analyses of projects and to gain a clear definition of their objectives, expected outcomes, associated activities and indicators of success. The experience gained so far has allowed us to fine-tune our working methodology and provided valuable information as we expand our activities to neighboring zones. The formal system is complemented by periodic meetings with staff and people's organizations. Conceived as a tool for effective management, the system has yielded good results through assisting supervision and providing the feedback necessary to adjust planning and execution. A system of periodic joint evaluations has been established alongside some of our bilateral donors. This has proved to be an interesting learning exercise on both sides.

Although formal monitoring and evaluation were introduced relatively recently, participatory evaluations with area residents have been ongoing over all these years. In our livestock and agriculture programs, a system of participatory testing has been introduced in which the farmers and technicians come together to share knowledge and experiences. Each year, hundreds of local-level tests are planned and undertaken on farmers' fields with a variety of different crops. Since results are there for all to see, these tests have proven to be a very useful method for provoking discussion on matters of technology. The results are discussed and conclusions are drawn in groups organized at the village level. The spread of technical knowledge in this manner supplements the formal training given by ICE as well as the extension training provided by our technicians and village paratechnicians.

WHERE DO WE GO FROM HERE?

In the past, DESEC has often been forced to interrupt and abandon initiatives, due to the drying up of donor funds. This has often placed us in an unenviable position, even though it was an unavoidable and consciously chosen risk. If DESEC had waited to have full financing from the start, we never would have initiated several of the activities that we began and in the process we would have lost the opportunities for learning that presented themselves. This is a good example of Albert O. Hirschman's concept of the "hiding hand" (1995). It is also true, however, that in these early years we took too much upon ourselves, both in geographical expansion and areas of activity. Experience has taught us that excessive dispersion is far too hard to handle, especially where we seek to ground our work in the organizations of local people, most of whom are poorly educated and have little time to spare. One or a few specialized economic activities in each region are much easier to consolidate and manage locally as skills, confidence and the appropriate organizational arrangements are progressively acquired.

Extended support provided over a longer period of time is essential for local associations to develop their skills and to build up their organizations to a level where they can progressively take over the tasks of the support agency. The implication is that the support agency will itself have to stay in existence continuously over a number of years, although in a changing and evolving role. This, in turn, points clearly to the need for sustaining donor assistance over a fairly long time, much longer than has traditionally been envisioned, especially in the project mode of assistance. In the absence of such sustained assistance during its first three decades of existence, DESEC has not been able to consolidate all its initiatives, nor to find an anchor for them in experienced and proven local organizations.

The situation has improved somewhat since the early 1980s, with the commencement of triangular operations and the longer-term commitments that donors have started to provide. This provides a more stable environment for our staff and for the people among whom we work. Our long years of experience, of good results mixed with some inevitable mistakes, stand us in good stead, as will our reputation of being apolitical and independent.

AGRICULTURE-BASED DEVELOPMENT

7 The AMUL Dairy Cooperatives: Putting the Means of Development into the Hands of Small Producers in India

V. Kurien

In an age when it is assumed that structural adjustment and liberalization will solve the problems of underdevelopment, it may seem somewhat old-fashioned to make a claim on behalf of agricultural cooperatives as an instrument of rural change. Let it not be forgotten, however, that liberalization and all the other trappings of India's new economic policy (and those of other less developed countries) can at best engender change from above. We have experimented in the past with introducing change from above, but even when these policies were led by an enthusiastic state, they did little to improve the lot of the rural poor. How can it be imagined that the private sector, motivated as it is by profit, can make any deeper dent on rural poverty? Even if opening up the economy will lead, as claimed, to faster economic growth, there is little chance that the rural poor will derive much benefit from it. Urban jobs cannot be created fast enough to absorb more than a small share of the rural poor.

Unless the rural poor can profitably produce something for the urban market, and unless they have some control over the institutions that deal with this produce, economic growth will continue to pass them by this time, just as before. When we speak of India's rural population, we are talking of hundreds of millions of people, fully two-thirds of whom are landless or cultivate tracts of land too small or too poor to sustain themselves adequately.

For them to increase production and to derive profit from it, both reliably and consistently, a new set of institutions will have to be set up, not institutions that treat the rural poor as objects of charity, but institutions that they can hold accountable and that are responsive to their needs. This is only possible when the instruments and institutions of development are placed in the hands of the poor. They need to be assisted in setting up these institutions for themselves, so that they can harness the best of modern science and technology to their small production base and can bring sophisticated marketing skills to their service.

The private sector is not going to do this for the poor, nor, sad to say, does the public sector have much to contribute. Although they have tried for all these years, civil servants are, with some rare exceptions, ill-equipped and ill-trained for this task, and anyway they have little incentive to serve the poor, given the way their bureaucratic system works.

Cooperative institutions are a third sector that, to my mind, represents the way forward. They provide means whereby the poor can act together to obtain for themselves the benefits of modern science and technology and a fair share of the country's economic growth. In the process, they obtain the means to build for themselves, in every village, a society that is confident and at peace with itself, secure in the vision of a better future for its children. This also represents real growth in the nation's social and political capital, as a plurality of local institutions is created and strengthened that can underpin democracy at the grassroots.

When I speak of cooperatives, however, I am speaking of institutions controlled by the people themselves, and managed by hired professionals—managers and technicians who are accountable to them and not, as has most often been the case, to some remote political or bureaucratic authority. Not only has the cooperative spirit been so often subverted to serve the narrow need of political parties, our potential for cooperative-led growth has been stifled by excessive and totally unnecessary bureaucratic controls. I am convinced, however, that when cooperatives are placed firmly where they should belong—in the hands of their membership—they can serve as a powerful instrument of economic and social change.

Let me illustrate by recounting the story of the cooperative dairy industry in India, with which I have been associated—as an employee of farmers—for more than forty years. Starting from a narrow base in one of India's more than 500 districts, we have progressively expanded the cooperative dairy network to a point where it now provides assured incomes and services to more than nine million farm families, which include almost 50 million people.

The cooperative dairy network today operates in 170 districts. Its 70,000 village milk cooperatives are linked up in mutually supportive networks with district-level unions and state- and national-level cooperative federations. Together, the unions market more than ten million liters of milk every day, delivering clean, hygienic milk and milk products to the urban consumer and providing steady incomes and support services to the rural producer. Nearly US$700 million are paid out annually to these milk-producing families. Most of these families are poor. Fully 21 percent are landless, another 66 percent are small and marginal farmers who operate less than four hectares of land, and over 70 percent of them have only one or two cattle. An income supplement to each participating family of almost $90 each year means a lot in a country where gross domestic product per capita is still only $310, and most rural people make much less.

Yearly milk production in the country has increased from a stagnant level of 21 million tons during the 1950s and 1960s to over 60 million tons today, resulting in a rise in per capita milk availability from 107 grams per day in 1969–70 to 186 grams in 1993–94. India, which once imported milk and milk products, has reached a point where, with the second highest milk production in the world, it can now generate a surplus for export. Milk is second only to rice as a source of agricultural incomes.

Important as these income and consumption effects have been, there are spinoff social impacts of the vast dairy network. Imagine, if you will, nine million producers lining up twice every day—regardless of caste, religion or economic differences—in each of 70,000 village collection centers. Membership in village milk cooperatives is confined to milk producers, so the management committee and the executive in each village are selected by these farmers from among themselves. Over two-thirds of these farmer-members come from among the poorest groups in rural India—small and marginal landholders and those who own no land at all. These new dairy institutions—that have substantially enhanced rural incomes and whose impact is felt twice a day, every day through the year, and is visible over the entire village—are under the control of the very same groups.

Milk delivered by each producer is tested for its fat content, and a record is kept by collection staff hired by the village cooperative. A chain of trucks, chilling plants, refrigerated vans and railway wagons, and processing plants—all owned by the cooperative network—links the producer in the village with the city-based consumer. Twice a day, this milk is transported from the village to district-level processing plants from where it is shipped as liquid milk or processed and packaged milk products to urban centers. Twice a day, with a lag of only twelve hours, producers receive the payments due to them. They are also provided with enriched cattle feed and have support from qualified veterinary services with whom contact can be made, in many areas, through our own network of radio telephones. Routine cattle illnesses are dealt with by trained village paraprofessionals. To help improve the genetic strain of our cattle, the dairy network performs about 18 million artificial inseminations annually, with paraprofessionals performing the operations at the village level and highly trained professionals managing the semen banks and stud stations.

Dairy cooperatives have catalyzed road building, and occasionally they have themselves taken up the construction of village-approach roads. Some of the dairy cooperatives have set up rural health services for their members, and some are using their incomes to provide other social and economic services. None of these activities are part of the original charter;

they have been taken up incrementally as farmer-members gain the confidence to act for themselves through the institutions that work for them.

EXPANSION

Noting its achievements in the dairy sector, the cooperative network has been asked by the government to operate in other sectors. The organizing principles that we learned in our dairy operation have proved useful as we branched out, but the specific context of each commodity system has required a different operational strategy, which was devised after careful study. In the late 1980s, a major oilseeds operation was mounted to counter rising consumer prices and an annual outflow of scarce foreign exchange of more than $750 million. Our oilseeds operation was successful enough that today hardly any vegetable oil is imported. Nearly half a million oilseeds producers are members of a growing network. Lately, we have taken up organizing cooperative production and marketing in other sectors—cotton, fruit production and the manufacture of salt, to name a few. To deal with the growing rural shortages of fuel and fodder, cooperative tree growing has been begun as a separate project.

All this did not happen painlessly or all at once. It took us almost twenty-five years to acquire the learning required to establish well-managed, farmer-controlled cooperative dairying institutions in one district. The Anand model, named after the town in Khaira district of Gujarat state where we first started, was developed gradually and came to serve as a basis for expansion. The knowledge that we acquired in this living laboratory was then adapted to serve another district, Mehsana, 100 miles to our north. This, too, took a long time to develop, nearly ten years. The third district organization—in our neighboring Baroda district—took four years to set up. The fourth, fifth and sixth, also in Gujarat state, took close to two years each.

After that, the pace of expansion was much faster. Impressed with the possibilities represented by the Anand model, and assisted with commodity aid from the European Community (EC) and the World Food Program topped with a World Bank loan, the government of India has embarked since 1970 upon a series of ambitious programs designed to extend cooperative dairying throughout the the country. This became known as Operation Flood.

The pressure for rapid expansion stemmed from a desire to end growing milk shortages in our large cities and to increase farmer incomes in the process. State-owned dairy plants set up in these cities had proved largely unsuccessful. The bureaucrats knew neither how to operate the plants, nor how to organize milk collection. Identifying their primary constituency as the vocal city-based consumers, state-run dairies did not provide farmers with the incentives that could lead to consistent increases in milk production. Prices were kept low. Farmers were never confident that increased supplies would be absorbed by state dairies, especially during the winter flush.

The relationship with farmers was only one way: state dairies would buy only as much milk as the city could consume at the moment, and at a price that was kept artificially low for political reasons. Private traders continued to supply a large proportion of each city's milk consumption, typically inflating their margins through a host of unfair practices, such as diluting the milk with water and flour and hoarding milk products until prices rose in the lean season. Since farmers had little incentive to invest in dairying operations, total milk production stagnated and fell in per capita terms from 132 grams per day in the early 1950s to 107 grams by 1970.

It was perceived that merely adding to the already huge physical investments in the dairy sector would not reverse this trend. Future expansion would have to be based upon a different institutional approach. The Anand model had by then made a major difference in Khaira district, supplying milk and milk products not only to Bombay, but increasingly to other parts of the country. Our brand name, AMUL, was already well known all over India, and we had started installing parallel operations in other districts of Gujarat. When the prime minister of India visited Anand in 1965 to inaugurate our new cattle feed mixing plant, he spoke with our dairy farmers and emerged impressed with the spirit that had inspired these farmers. He was quick to perceive that farmers would respond best to an institution that they felt they owned and that was responsive to their everyday needs.

The prime minister asked us to create a network of Anands that would cover the entire country. The National Dairy Development Board (NDDB) and its sister organization, the Indian Dairy Corporation, were set up to carry out this task, and I was asked to be their first chairman. Since I wanted to continue to live and work among the Khaira farmers, the new organization was headquartered at Anand, and not in the national capital, New Delhi, as some would have preferred. This has been one of many factors that has kept our feet on the ground. NDDB has never become an ivory tower institution because we have stayed in touch with the field and continued to relate our plans to the needs of farmers.

In the national drive for expansion, however, we had to proceed very fast and work with the tools that were available. To begin with, eighteen district unions were to be organized on lines similar to the Anand pattern in the period between 1970 and 1978. In the twelve years after that, the drive has accelerated to encompass 170 districts. It is the largest agricultural development program undertaken anywhere in the world. But its urgency and vast spread have meant that it was not possible to have the luxury of following a slower learning curve and to gradually build cooperative institutions from the grassroots upward in many of the successor districts.

Given the overriding national objective, the stages of growth had to be telescoped and attenuated. District unions would be formed first by state governments. Then, using the funds and technical expertise made available by NDDB, the newly formed district unions would set up the necessary physical infrastructure—chilling plants, village collection centers and truck routes. Spearhead teams, consisting of personnel trained by NDDB, would go into the villages to organize milk producers into local milk cooperatives. State-level federations were created to administer policy and to assist the district unions. Since the large investments in existing state-run dairies could not be simply wished away, the state federations had to absorb within them the existing bureaucratic apparatus of state dairy boards.

In some instances, the management of state federations and district unions has passed over to cooperative structures that are regularly elected from the bottom up. But in other places, politicians and bureaucrats continue to cling to power, no matter how irrelevant or unproductive they might have become. Even these latter states have made substantial contributions to increased milk production and rural incomes, although their responsiveness to farmer needs and problems has been limited.

Since true development is the development of people, not of cows or milk routes or dairy plants, the process of management transfer to genuine cooperatives is a necessary further step. Thus, the achievements of our dairy cooperatives, although considerable and well remarked upon, are still in the making, rendered incomplete in some respects because of obstructions posed by bureaucrats and their political masters. Let me, however, go step by step and tell the story from its beginning.

THE BEGINNINGS: 1946—65

As even a child knows, India is the land of cattle and of milk. For millennia, we have revered cattle, and milk and milk products have a special place in our culture. But, unlike other large milk-producing countries, our cattle are not fenced off in huge ranches nor can they be fed high-quality fodder. Most of India's cattle—over 70 percent of those in our dairy network—are owned in small herds, often even one or two cows or buffaloes per family. India has 15 percent of the world's human population, but only 2.5 percent of its cultivated land area, and an even smaller share of global pastures.

As a growing human population places overwhelming pressure on land, nearly all our cattle live off crop residues and scrubby forage. Milk production is thus very small-scale and scattered. Cattle owners have had neither the resources nor, until recently, did they have the incentive to provide better feed and thus increase their milk supply.

Urban consumers of milk have obtained it from traders who transport the commodity in small quantities from nearby villages, or from city-based dairy operations. Neither of these options has afforded sufficient quantities of clean, healthful milk to city folk. None has provided an incentive to rural producers to increase milk production. Trader margins have been high, partly to compensate for the fact that milk is highly perishable, but mostly because the trader is a monopoly procurer. The situation is made worse in the flush season of the winter months when urban dairies can procure more milk from nearby producers and there is consequently little demand for the increased supply from rural areas.

The situation was no different in the villages of Khaira district in the 1940s. A private dairy had been given monopoly rights by the British colonial government to procure milk from the villages surrounding Anand— then a sleepy town of some 10,000 souls—in order to meet part of Bombay's growing demand. In 1946, local farmers revolted against the private dairy. Spurred as much by the unfair dealings of the dairy as by a desire to fashion a better deal for themselves, these farmers organized themselves into a cooperative, the Khaira District Cooperative Milk Producers' Union.

In 1949, this was a group of twenty village cooperatives, who had struggled to gain the right to send their milk to Bombay. Although each village cooperative had an elected management committee and employed a part-time secretary to manage its day-to-day affairs, the cooperatives were sorely limited by lack of technical capacity. Because it had no processing plant of its own, the union of dairy cooperatives had to depend upon a private dairy to process its milk before it could be shipped to Bombay. This cut into the margins that cooperative members earned and placed the fledgling district union at the mercy of an unreliable partner.

I had just returned after studying for a masters degree in the United States and was assigned to Anand by my employer, the government of India, to manage the government experimental creamery. It was with considerable dismay that I, a city-bred lad with metropolitan aspirations, arrived in this outlying town. The creamery was equipped with just one outdated pasteurizer; I had little to do with my time and soon began to take an interest in the activities of the budding milk cooperatives. I had gone abroad to study dairy technology and was thus in a good position to recommend, after studying their operations, that they invest in a modern processing plant.

My interest in and concern for the cooperative dairy continued to grow, and instead of running away from Anand as I had first imagined doing, I stayed on to help the cooperative dairy. After an initial period of assessment, I was hired by the district union to work as its general manager for operations, a position I have very happily retained in all these years. I have been responsible all this time to the board of the district union, which is composed of members elected by the chairpersons of village cooperative societies.

The Anand milk union grew rapidly during the 1950s and through the 1960s until it reached nearly every village in the district and collected close to a million liters of milk every day. As the dairy expanded, we included a range of services in our operations, which were introduced in response to farmer demands as they saw useful outlets for the growing cooperative incomes. We found resources for these services and additional new investments from out of the margin that accrued to the union from the sale and purchase of milk. What was left from the margin amount at the end of the year, after meeting the expenses of services and investments, was given back to members in the form of a tidy and steadily growing bonus.

Our first major investment, after a new pasteurizer, was a milk powder plant. At that time, there was no technology available in India or abroad that could convert buffalo milk into storable powder. Since most of Khaira's milk was produced by buffaloes, we were forced to take up the challenge and develop the technology by ourselves. Our new milk powder plant enabled us to accommodate seasonal fluctuations in demand and supply. In the flush season, we made and stored milk powder, converting it back into liquid during the lean season. With the consistent and reliable supplies made possible by this process, we were able to seize a major share of the Bombay market. We set up a cold chain to move chilled, pasteurized butter from Anand first to Bombay, and then to every large city in India. We also constructed a new facility to make infant food, the first time this had been done in India. Through each of these investments, better prices were made available to producers. Milk production in Khaira district continued to grow.

With the growth in incomes, confidence levels and market presence, our members began to place larger demands upon us. A veterinary service was installed. Regular visits to every village by a team of qualified vets was complemented by a program of training and equipping village paraprofessionals. A cattle feed plant was constructed to provide farmers with cheap and nutritious concentrates for their cattle. Over 350 tons of feed are now produced every day and sold to farmers—carried to villages in the same trucks that return with milk.

At the village level, this process has resulted in a steady flow of modernizing influences. First, the milk collection center itself, swabbed down by disinfectant twice a day, is usually the village's first introduction to modern sanitation. Then the veterinary doctor's visits stimulate curiosity in scientific health care, which is heightened when the effects of artificial insemination become visible. Many farmers have visited our plants at Anand, and we have helped this process along by sponsoring tours by village groups. The women among them have been especially impressed with improved cattle feed and with pasteurization. Their curiosity is whetted regarding improved nutrition and food safety when they see that measures for better health, whether for cattle or humans, are possible and can become available to them.

More important than our growing range of products—at Anand, we now produce butter, cheese, malted beverages and chocolates—has been the growth in confidence as village people identify their needs and take action to secure the changes they want. They are saying, "We can do this," rather than "They should do this for us." In large part, this change in farmer attitudes has been brought about by their learning that, as owners of the dairy cooperative, they have a right to create more and better services for themselves. With the profits they earn, farmers have employed the best professionals the country can offer. These professionals are accountable to farmers. Unlike government employees, they do not look upward to some remote authority; their services are evaluated by the farmers themselves.

Cooperative employees are forced to function with high standards of responsiveness and professionalism. Only those who are alive to the needs and constraints of farmers will stay. Farmers expect the veterinarian to arrive on time; they expect him or her to cure their animals. They will not take the advice of the fodder extensionist at face value; they expect him or her to convince them that the advised investment is profitable. Through their elected representatives on the board, they direct and discipline all employees. All members and elected representatives have to be milk producers and deliver milk to the society that elects them. Thus, self-serving politicians cannot cynically treat the dairy, as they have other cooperatives, as a vehicle for personal advancement.

Clear evidence of the farmers' sense of ownership was visible when, a few years ago, there was a flash strike called by employees of the Anand dairy in support of higher pay. Milk that was collected began to spoil and no fresh milk could be collected, resulting in a loss to farmers of half a million rupees a day (about US$17,000). Farmers were naturally quite angry. They had no objection to paying good wages to employees—in fact these are among the best in the country—but they could not stomach being blackmailed. About 900 chairpersons of village cooperatives came together to discuss the matter. They instructed me to clear the dairy plant of employees and to make arrangements to receive 30,000 young farmers, men and women, whom they would send from the next day on to help run the dairy. The farmers ran the plant long enough and well enough for employees to see that they would do well to seek an early settlement.

GROWTH: 1970–95

In this period, the roots of the dairy cooperative structure were penetrating deeper, at the same time spreading wider to other parts of the country. As we began to expand by organizing parallel operations in neighboring districts, the basic principles of an organizational strategy became clearer.

These principles stood us in good stead as we took up the task of Operation Flood I, the program that was designed to extend dairy cooperatives to the first set of eighteen district milksheds covered by NDDB. To assist the government of India in this program, 125,000 tons of skim milk powder and about 40,000 tons of butter oil—worth a total of forty-two million dollars on the world market—were donated by the EEC under the World Food Program. NDDB began by organizing operations in each milkshed on the following principles:

Link the Producer with the Market

Only a good market will enable a district union to provide remunerative prices to the producers. We started our national operations by concentrating on the eighteen districts that would supply milk to the four metro cities— New Delhi, Bombay, Calcutta and Madras—which account for 3 percent of India's population but 6 percent of its milk consumption. Once we could service these large markets, we would go on to the state capitals and other large towns in the second phase of Operation Flood. To establish a reliable presence in these markets, we needed to supply a substantial proportion of the day's milk in the flush season as well as the lean season. Unless we could procure and supply milk consistently throughout the year, neither producers nor consumers would find satisfaction in associating themselves with us.

Initially, the donated skim milk powder was recombined to tide over shortages during the dry season. Liquid milk produced this way was sold not at a subsidized price, but at a price that we felt would cover farmer costs and give them a fair profit. We used the revenues that came in from the sale of this milk—almost $125 million during Operation Flood I—to build the infrastructure for all our operations. Thus, commodity aid became for us not simply a means to overcome the shortage of milk, it was our only source of program funds. There was no demand placed on the public exchequer. The program funds generated in this manner were used for two main purposes, first, to upgrade the facilities of the state dairies in the four metropolitan cities, and second, to create the cooperative dairy infrastructure in the eighteen milksheds.

At one stroke, the strategy helped us overcome milk shortages in these four cities, generate program funds and provide a price incentive for the domestic producer. Since 70 percent of the program funds were advanced to state governments as interest-bearing loans, these became a source of revolving funds for future expansion.

Further, our manner of distributing the food aid did not result, as it so often does, in depressing the prices available to domestic producers. Over the years, we have been careful to maintain reliable milk supplies and fair prices for consumers while assuring producers of remunerative returns. A survey conducted in 1985 revealed that while the prices of all food commodities had gone up by 260 percent since 1970, those of milk and milk products had increased by only 175 percent. To maintain the incentive to producers, we have had to increase the efficiency of our dairy operations, passing over an increasing share of the consumer rupee—over 70 percent now—to the producer. As they have maintained and even increased their level of services, cooperative structures at the village, district, state and national levels have had to work on smaller margins.

Invest in Modern Facilities and Trained People

When dealing with a perishable commodity like milk, you must be able to conserve seasonal surpluses, transform them into products that have a longer shelf life, and then reconvert them when supplies fall short. You also need to send a message to the consumer in the city so that he or she will respect the product, even though it is produced by an organization of poor villagers, and not by a glossy multinational firm. Hygiene and quality have to be maintained, underwritten by modern technology, so that a brand image can be successfully built up.

To do all this, you need to invest in plant and equipment—not second-rate throwaways, but the best that is available. In the case of milk, the cold chain has to be reliable, and the product has to be delivered to consumers at the times and in the manner they prefer. Most of the plant and equipment were designed, constructed and installed under the supervision of NDDB technicians. Since Indian consumers prefer to purchase liquid milk in bulk, rather than in a packet, bulk vending machines needed to be installed at points scattered throughout the four megacities. Even though we would have preferred to import these machines, we could not do so in the face of government intransigence, and therefore had to design and manufacture them ourselves. This resulted in a delay of two years for the program. This is but one example of the obstructions put up by the civil servants with whom we were forced to cohabit in the national program, although they have played a reduced role over the years.

A cadre of professionals—scientists, technicians and managers— needed to be trained and deployed to run these facilities honestly and efficiently. Along with their professional qualifications, their attitudes and personal traits are also important. As we saw earlier, these persons must be accountable to farmers and responsive to their needs. Training therefore needs, at least at the initial stage, to avoid the sorts of superficial academism that is far from the practical need. In our case, training was mostly on-the-job and action training, complemented by short courses at Anand and sometimes abroad. In the early 1980s, we set up the Institute of Rural Management at Anand (IRMA) to provide specialized managerial training for rural producers' organizations. The institute aims to build a national cadre of professional managers with a strong field orientation.

Follow a Logical Sequence of Program Activities

Unless farmers are assured of higher incomes, they will not invest in improved cattle feed, and until they improve the feed, there is no point investing in better breeds of cattle. Thus, it is futile to introduce a component of artificial insemination (AI) until the first two stages have been achieved and there is both an opportunity and a felt need for genetic improvement. Project activities have to be designed to follow this natural sequence.

Crossbreeding and AI have grown over the years, but we have been careful to plan these activities to suit the typical conditions faced by Indian farmers. It will not do to indiscriminately promote full-bred herds of Jersey and Holstein cows that need special and expensive care in the altogether different Indian conditions. We have relied upon propagating exotic breeds selectively, choosing instead to rely more extensively upon better suited indigenous breeds. Though India has a variety of excellent breeds, lack of incentive had hitherto prevented our farmers from investing in breed improvement. One consequence of this is that cattle have been bred more for their draft power than for their milk-producing qualities.

We have started programs to reverse this trend. The mix that we can sustain over the long haul is about 40 to 50 million sturdy work animals, and about 15 to 17 million high-yielding milch cows, with about 7 to 10 million improved buffaloes. During the second phase of the program, Operation Flood II (1981–88), we began to set up such a national milch herd, to be distributed nationwide. The animals in the herd will serve both as core production centers as well as a source of further genetic improvement. Already the cooperative dairy program has had a considerable impact on breed improvement through the improvement in incentives backed by the AI program, and also through obviating the need to maintain large numbers of milch cattle in urban centers.

This last practice had resulted over the years in a significant annual depletion in India's stock of prime milk-producing animals. Traders in Bombay and New Delhi would scour the countryside for the best animals, bringing them when lactating to the cities, along with the newborn calves. There, the calf would be starved to death and the mother buffalo, after a year or two of producing returns for the milk trader, would be driven off to the slaughter house. Since it was generally unprofitable to send the animals back to the village for fresh impregnation, the finest animals would be prematurely led to their deaths. Thankfully, this is now a thing of the past. Milk is produced where it should be—in the villages. There the animals are better cared for, seen not only as profit-producing assets, but as a valued part of the farm household.

A national milk grid is being set up to store and conserve milk and to transport it from surplus to deficit areas. A vital backup to the grid will be a pooled buffer stock of conserved milk solids that are being stored at strategic points, to be drawn upon flexibly whenever local shortages arise in any part of the country. Both commodities donated from abroad as well as indigenous supplies are being used to build up the stocks.

Operation Flood II extended the cooperative dairy network to all states in the country, serving, in addition to the four metropolitan areas, another 150 or so large cities and some small towns that fall within the 170 milkshed districts presently covered. As the network has been expanded to serve other parts of the country, the relative importance of its initial base, the state of Gujarat, has fallen. Between 1974 and 1986, Gujarat's share in countrywide membership of village dairy cooperative fell from a massive 95 percent, reflecting the preeminence arising from its early start, to 26 percent. Gujarat's share in national milk procurement fell from 87 percent to 27 percent during the same period. A third phase of Operation Flood is currently in operation to carry cooperative dairy operations to other parts of the country and to strengthen them where they currently exist. A fourth phase is under consideration that will reinforce and consolidate this process.

In 1979, the national government asked us to intervene in the edible oils and oilseeds sector. We went in gladly enough and now have a substantial marketing presence, but the intervening years were filled with nightmares. Oil was a totally different sector. Whereas the vested interests in the dairy sector—traders and urban dairies—were small and ill-organized to resist changes in the system, the *telia rajas* (oil kings) were large parties who were unscrupulous and ruthless. They attacked us both politically as well as personally with violence. Our officials have been brutally assaulted, our offices ransacked and our processing plants sabotaged and burned.

Before domestic oilseed cultivation could be supported by other means, it was necessary to gain some control over domestic prices. A market intervention operation to arrest market price fluctuations would simultaneously serve two ends: it would result in a larger share of the consumer rupee passing back to the farmer, and thus it would break the monopoly hold of trader groups (and their capacity for overt and covert organized violence). By the time such an operation was conceived and set up in the late 1980s, the situation had become precarious. Edible oil imports had grown, amounting to a third of domestic production, until they accounted for $750 million in the year 1987–88. This was a large out-flow of scarce foreign currency, second only to that for petroleum. How-ever, even as international prices fell in the 1980s, Indian consumer prices continued to rise. There was little increase, however, in the prices received by farmers.

The NDDB strategy was to proceed simultaneously on a number of fronts. First, the market intervention aimed at controlling 15 percent of marketed edible oil. With a market share of only 5 percent, it helped estab-lish a price band within the narrow limits of which prices could fluctuate. Second, we went about organizing and federating village oilseeds producer cooperatives initially in seven states that would engage in producing and procuring oilseeds. Third, we set up modern processing plants, integrating oilseed crushing with solvent extraction techniques. Finally, we launched new products under own brand name, *Dhara*, that have since become very popular among Indian consumers. To help reinforce the incentives that these measures would provide to farmers, we asked the government to rationalize its public distribution of oil and reduce its subsidies to cover only the poorest among urban consumers.

Farmers have responded splendidly to the new system. Already, even as our operations in this sector are being expanded, over 500,000 farmers cultivating oilseeds on close to a million hectares of land have enrolled themselves as members of village oilseeds cooperatives. India's imports of oilseeds are insignificant today compared to previously. NDDB staff to service the new edible oil operations has never exceeded a complement of 200 persons. The experience with this sector, initially quite frighten-ing, has enabled us to learn an important lesson that will serve us well as we extend ourselves into other commodity sectors. The organization to serve each commodity needs to be geared to the specifics of its produc-tion and trade.

LOOKING AHEAD

Lately, we have been criticized, mainly by economists affiliated to the International Monetary Fund or other Western institutions, for using subsidies to set up our dairy and oilseeds operations. These academics claim that India has no international comparative advantage to specialize in dairy or oilseeds production, and thus that subsidies ought not to be used to buttress what is not economically justifiable. I have no disagreement with the argument for removing subsidies. In fact, they should have gone long ago, but, among the dairying nations of the world, only New Zealand has abolished state subsidies. The other large producers—the United States, Australia and the European Community (EC)—all persist with subsidies. In 1991, the EC paid its dairy farmers ECU 23.1 billion as subsidies, which works out to ECU 204 per ton of milk, or 69 percent of the price. No wonder the EC's milk is cheaper than ours! For oilseeds, the EC has been paying producers a subsidy amounting to 67 percent of the price. This makes a mockery of the advantages of competition that economists like to talk about.

Comparative advantage is a dynamic phenomenon that is influenced by a range of considerations. As Indian dairy farmers have gained larger control over the conditions that govern the production and market price of milk, they have delivered many times more milk than before. So have the farmers who produce oilseeds. So too will many other farmers in other parts of the country when they are given control over the instruments of development.

The potential that genuine cooperatives have for sustained and sustainable rural development is nothing new for India. But we have forgotten the words of our country's founder, Mahatma Gandhi, who told us that cooperation that is rooted in the soil always succeeds. His vision of cooperation has been tarnished as politicians, acting through bureaucrats, have cynically exploited cooperatives as a vehicle for distributing state largesse and garnering political support. The cooperative model has not been proven wrong; rather our homegrown version of state-manipulated cooperatives—which has rightly been vilified—has detracted from the ideal. The experiences of Indian dairy cooperatives and of their successors working under the NDDB banner show that the ideal can be made to work, provided that the institutions of cooperative development are controlled firmly and finally by the farmers themselves.

8 Plan Puebla: An Agricultural Development Program for Low-income Farmers in Mexico

Heliodoro Díaz Cisneros, Leobardo Jiménez Sánchez,
Reggie J. Laird and Antonio Turrent Fernández

In the mid-1960s, when the seeds of Plan Puebla were beginning to germinate, maize was being grown on over 6 million hectares, mostly under rain-fed conditions. Yields varied greatly from year to year and from one part of the country to another, but they averaged around 900 kilograms per hectare. More than 80 percent of rain-fed maize was being produced by small farmers and consumed mainly on their farms. Most of the land was prepared using animal traction. Local varieties were planted, and little use was made of agricultural chemicals.

To improve crop production, research was conducted by the National Agricultural Research Institute (INIA is the Spanish abbreviation), with experiment stations located in the major agroclimatic regions of Mexico and through trials on farmers' fields; agricultural scientists at the undergraduate level were trained at the National School of Agriculture and at the graduate level at the Postgraduate College (CP). All three institutions, plus the National Extension Service, were located at Chapingo, 40 kilometers east of Mexico City. Research activities were initially concentrated in areas with irrigation or favorable rainfall, although some research, especially with maize, was conducted in less favorable areas.

By the mid-1960s, we were part of a small group of researchers who had become concerned that most research results, however useful they might be for larger-scale commercial agriculture, were having little or no impact on maize production by small-scale, subsistence farmers. Based primarily at INIA and the Postgraduate College, we had been working on plant breeding to develop improved varieties, on soil fertility to arrive at optimum fertilizer recommendations and on communication to promote the transfer of maize production technology for small, subsistence farmers under rain-fed conditions. Experience and various studies showed that the large majority were receiving little benefit from the prevailing research and development strategy.

In early 1966, a pilot study was planned to develop and validate maize production technology in a rain-fed area populated mainly by small farmers and to transfer this technology to local producers. A meeting was held with representatives of all the agricultural institutions at Chapingo to discuss details of this proposed study. All present expressed interest in the project. However, the proposed strategy required not only working closely with small producers to develop technology and get it adopted, it needed participation by various agencies to provide credit, inputs and crop insurance. As it was not clear how such an effort could be implemented, no immediate support for the idea was forthcoming.

When the International Maize and Wheat Improvement Center (CIMMYT) was established in the fall of 1966, its director decided that CIMMYT would be interested in supporting this pilot project. We submitted a proposal for funding to the Rockefeller Foundation by the end of the year and received a three-year grant of $100,000 in May 1967. CIMMYT and the Postgraduate College agreed to work together to implement Plan Puebla both to develop, field-test and refine a strategy for rapidly increasing yields of maize for smallholders, and to train technicians from other regions in the elements and spread of the strategy. We expected that increased yields of maize would raise net farm incomes and be a first step in improving rural family well-being.

The Puebla Valley in the state of Puebla was chosen for the pilot because the physical environment was favorable for achieving substantial yield increases, and there was political support for efforts to increase maize production. As the plan evolved, the basic approach would be applicable in most regions of the world, if adequate attention were given to the constraints posed by specific environmental, social and economic circumstances in the target area.

From 1967 to 1973, Plan Puebla was administered by CIMMYT, with management by staff from the Postgraduate College. In early 1974, responsibility for the plan passed to the college, with support from the Mexican ministry of agriculture. The Rockefeller Foundation gave further financial support of $560,000 between 1967 and 1973, while CIMMYT contributed $333,000 to the operation of the Plan; $32,500 was provided by the college and other institutions in Puebla, so the total operating cost of Plan Puebla for its first seven years was a little over $900,000.

STRATEGY

The Plan Puebla strategy developed initially was an integrated attack on those problems that limit farmer use of productive technologies. Available information indicated that farmers needed access to:

• high-yielding maize varieties,

- advice on appropriate production practices,

- reliable sources of agronomic information to farmers,

- adequate supplies of agronomic inputs at accessible points when needed,

- credit at a reasonable interest rate,

- favorable relationships between input costs and crop values,

- crop insurance,

- accessible markets with a stable price for maize.

When the plan began, several institutions were providing agricultural inputs, credit, crop insurance and markets for maize producers in the Puebla area; also, the relationships between the costs of inputs and the price of maize were thought to be satisfactory. So these factors did not appear to present problems. But only limited results were available at the time from scientific research in the area, and only one extension agent was working in the area. Plan Puebla was conceived as a joint undertaking involving the participation of local farm families, the institutions providing agricultural services and a technical team. This team would be responsible for: agronomic research including varietal improvement of maize and on-farm research to develop appropriate production practices; assistance to farmers on the proper use of new recommendations; and coordination of activities among the service agencies, the technical team and the farmers. A fourth component, socioeconomic evaluation, was added during the first year.

The production and dissemination of information were seen as a continual process, with constant interaction among staff members and feedback of information, from the planning of research through the delivery of findings to farmers to the evaluation of results. The technical team consisted of a small group of capable, well-trained, highly motivated agronomists with an adequate budget and favorable professional opportunities. The members of the team lived and worked in the project area, cooperating closely in conducting the field trials and demonstrations and attending farmer meetings.

EVOLUTION OF THE CONCEPTUAL FRAMEWORK

From an initial focus on increasing maize production, the program was extended in 1970 to include research and extension work on beans, since these were also an important part of farming systems. Attention was given also to other crops for later planting, and Plan efforts were later expanded to cover all priority farming activities, including the production of animals, fruit trees and irrigated crops. A survey of household incomes in 1967 showed that only 30 percent came from the sale of crops, indeed, only 21 percent from selling maize. Almost as much, 28 percent, came from animal production, with 40 percent of income from off-farm employment. This reflected the limited access these households had to land and also the extent of their poverty. Beginning in 1975, assistance was provided to farm women for improving their homes and for the general well-being of their families. As the number and variety of activities covered by Plan Puebla expanded, the composition and expertise of the technical team were adjusted accordingly.

Efforts to reach large numbers of small, scattered producers with an improved technological package for maize production demonstrated clearly the advantages of working with groups of farmers rather than with individuals. Supporting farmer organizations became a main component of Plan Puebla strategy, first to facilitate the technical assistance process, and later to deal with a broad spectrum of production problems. As the Plan proceeded, still other farmer priorities became apparent, such as irrigation facilities, warehouses and access roads. Plan Puebla accepted that improvement of rural infrastructure was an essential element of rural development strategy and arranged for funding, equipment and materials to assist organized farmers.

THE PUEBLA AREA

The project area, which initially covered thirty-two counties in the state of Puebla, comprised about 117,000 hectares of cultivated land, with 80,000 hectares used for maize production, mainly under rain-fed conditions (CIMMYT 1969). The center of the area is a two-hour drive from Mexico City, from CIMMYT and from the Postgraduate College. Most of the farmers in the project area are descendants of the Indian populations present at the time of the Spanish conquest, and they live together in villages, most of which are connected by a network of all-weather roads. In 1967, there were an estimated 47,000 farm operators in the project area, with an average farm size of 2.5 hectares of cultivated land per family. Around 38 percent of the farm operators were *ejiditarios* (land reform beneficiaries), 28 percent were private holders, and 33 percent farmed both *ejido* and private land. Farm operators had attended school for an average of only 2.4 years, but 77 percent were able to read and write. The average annual cash income per family amounted to US$667 at the time, not much over $100 per capita.

The two official credit banks operating in Puebla in 1967 provided credit to only 7 percent of project farmers, while another 5 percent obtained credit from other sources, mainly private lenders. Fertilizers, improved seeds, insecticides and herbicides were available through merchants in the four principal cities, while eighty storekeepers in forty-two villages made fertilizer available at the local level. Only 39 percent of the households marketed maize in 1967. This was sold throughout the year mainly to cover the costs of medical care, another indication of the level of economic hardship. As noted, in 1967, there was only one extension agent working in the whole project area.

Plan Operations

Once CIMMYT decided to support Plan Puebla, we moved ahead to arrange for transportation, equipment and supplies, as well as to engage project staff. By March 1967, a soil scientist and plant breeder had been recruited, and in April, even before project funding was approved by the Rockefeller Foundation, agronomic research was initiated in the Puebla Valley, with maize breeding and fertilizer trials at several locations on farmers' fields. The first coordinator joined the project in August 1967; an evaluation specialist was added in late 1967; and the first technical assistance agent joined Plan Puebla in early 1968.

Plan Puebla sought to provide working conditions that would enable its staff to work harmoniously and effectively. These included attractive salaries and perquisites, supporting facilities to get the job done, encouragement of innovation and opportunities for advancement. During the first seven years, the number of person-years of professional time invested annually varied from two to twelve. Beginning in 1967, young farmers were hired as assistants to help with field activities, and over the next seven years, Plan Puebla involved about twenty-five such paraprofessionals in its program.

Specialists in agronomic research, maize breeding and communication from CIMMYT and the college served as advisors to Plan Puebla. Having drafted the original Plan Puebla proposal and arranged for funding, they also selected the area, made the necessary arrangements with local institutions, prepared the first operational plan, and set up the technical team. These advisors assisted the team in evaluating and modifying operational strategies, preparing detailed plans at the beginning of each year, selecting appropriate methods, resolving problems obstructing progress and interpreting research findings. The total time provided by these advisors averaged 172 days per year for the 1967–73 period. The four Plan Puebla components—agronomic research, technical assistance to small-scale producers, evaluation and coordination—each had clearly defined objectives and responsibilities, with its own operating procedures (CIMMYT 1974).

Agronomic Research

Crop production depends on many factors, including soil and climatic conditions, the variety planted and production practices. The physical environment cannot be readily changed, and this determines yield potential. Varietal characteristics and management practices, on the other hand, are more easily manipulated. Plan Puebla sought to produce information on management practices and varieties that would yield higher returns for the local producers. As a first step, information was gathered on possible factors limiting production. Then experiments were carried out on farmers' fields to assess these constraints and find ways to surmount them.

At first, field trials were distributed fairly evenly over the whole area, but, as more knowledge was gained about ecological diversity, different environmental situations were identified in the Puebla area where climate and soil factors were reasonably constant. Experiments were located so as to sample these typical systems, assessing factors influencing production at each site. Also, a maize varietal improvement program was carried out with farmers, taking into account their preferences regarding grain type, earliness of harvest and other characteristics. Outstanding native varieties in the area were collected, and promising local and exotic varieties tested at representative sites throughout the area. Cryptic double-cross hybrids were developed, as were open-pollinated varieties through mass selection.

Technical Assistance to Small-Scale Producers

Extension agents promoted adoption of new recommendations by informing farmers about Plan Puebla and its recommendations, assisting farmers to obtain credit and other inputs, and instructing farmers on the most efficient ways to use the recommendations. Agents also collected information about obstacles limiting use of agricultural services, transmitted this information to the technical team, and helped find ways to overcome the difficulties. This component is discussed more below.

Evaluation

Plan Puebla was conceived as an experimental approach to develop and test strategies for rapidly increasing yields for subsistence farmers on small landholdings. Thus, the evaluation unit had two main objectives, to measure

progress made by Plan Puebla over time, and to identify obstacles and collect the information needed for modifying activities.

At first we considered contracting an independent agency to make the
evaluation to achieve greater objectivity, since the more objective findings
would probably carry more weight with policymakers. There were, however,
important reasons for making evaluation an integral part of the plan: it
would assure continual feedback of information to other members of the
technical team, and obstacles limiting farmer participation could be identified and studied more effectively. After considering the alternatives, evaluation was included as an integral part of Plan Puebla; having objective criteria
and following accepted methodologies would assure sufficient objectivity.

Following the first experiments in 1967, it was evidently necessary to
establish benchmarks on yield, farmers' technology and living conditions,
for future comparisons. Personal interviews of a random sample of 251
farm operators were conducted in early 1968, using a two-stage sampling
technique, covering twenty-five 100-hectare segments randomly distributed
over the project area. The survey obtained information on crop yields,
farming costs, family income, use of modern inputs, marketing of produce
and living conditions of the farm family. Follow-up surveys were conducted in 1971, 1982, 1983 and 1985 to monitor and measure progress.

Coordination

The coordinator handled all staffing, budget and planning matters. Weekly
meetings were held throughout the year to discuss progress and problems
of the staff. Adjustments in operational plans as a result of new information were made at these meetings. A large part of the coordinator's time
was dedicated to working with the agricultural institutions in the state. Initially he was involved in informing them of the philosophy, objectives and
activities of Plan Puebla, and in becoming acquainted with their operating
procedures. Then, as information flowed in from the field work, he communicated new findings to the institutions. After each harvest, the coordinator was in frequent contact with representatives of these institutions,
explaining the plan of operation for the following year and working to
obtain their approval and support. When a problem arose due to the operating procedures of an institution, information on this was prepared by
staff and communicated by the coordinator to the responsible people.

Field Activities, 1967–77

With the installation of maize breeding and fertilizer trials on farmers'
fields in April 1967 field activities got underway. The coordinator started

work in August with a general reconnaissance of the area, followed by a formal survey to gather more detailed information on the characteristics of farm families. A baseline survey with personal interviews of farmers was conducted in early 1968, as noted above. Recommendations made based on 1967 research results included higher investment in fertilizers; using fertilizer combinations appropriate to specific fields instead of a standard formula; applying only part of the fertilizer at planting time and the remainder later, rather than all at the first cultivation; planting more densely; and controlling weeds in a more timely manner. These required considerable change in the management practices of Puebla farmers.

During 1968, the program assisted 103 farmers, who used the new recommendations on 141 "high-yield" plots varying from one-quarter to one hectare. Demonstrations on these plots showed cooperating farmers and their neighbors how to mix the fertilizers and apply them evenly, and how to plant the right number of seeds. Field days were held just prior to harvest so farmers could see the effects of these practices on maize yields. Pamphlets describing the recommendations were distributed to farmers, and a 16-millimeter color movie was made, describing the new technology for maize production.

The next year, 1969, the program sought to extend the improved technology to 10,000 hectares operated by about 5,000 farmers. The area was divided into four zones, with a technical assistance agent given responsibility for each zone. Meetings were held throughout each zone to inform farmers about the new technology and to assist them in organizing into groups. But the target was too ambitious. The goal was only about 60 percent achieved, as a total of 2,561 farmers, organized in 128 groups, were assisted in using the new recommendations on 5,838 hectares. In all villages with one or more groups, demonstrations held at planting time instructed farmers in the new techniques. An indication of farmer interest in the new technology was that, during the summer, eleven groups invited farmers from other parts of the area to visit their high-yield plots. Six regional demonstrations, attended by 1,200 farmers, were held just prior to harvest of the high-yield plots. During subsequent years, technical assistance agents continued to organize groups and work with them on using Plan Puebla recommendations.

The number of farmers and the area served in 1970 were roughly doubled, with 4,833 farmers applying the new recommendations on 12,601 hectares. The agronomic research program was expanded at this time to include studies on the production of beans and alternative crops for later planting. This broadening continued in 1971, when technical agents' activities included the management of orchards, the use of small trench silos, and helping arrange for loans to finance well drilling for irrigation and purchasing farm implements. By this year, 5,240 farmers were being assisted in employing the improved technology on 14,438 hectares.

In 1972 agronomic research was broadened to include developing recommendations for the maize–pole bean association, as farmers commonly grew these crops together. The project helped 6,202 farmers use the improved recommendations on 17,533 hectares. Early that year, CIMMYT announced that it would terminate its participation in Plan Puebla at the end of 1973, because it felt its research mandate was not broad enough to encompass the scope of activities that the plan needed to undertake.

The technical assistance program during 1973 included promoting improved technology for the maize–pole bean association. It also introduced the use of agua ammonia as a source of nitrogen for maize. By then, 7,194 farmers were using the improved technology on 20,604 hectares. Near the end of 1973, the Mexican ministry of agriculture announced that Plan Puebla would continue and assigned the responsibility for its implementation to the Graduate College.

From 1974, Plan Puebla was operated by the college with resources provided by the ministry of agriculture. PRONDAAT, the National Agricultural Development Program in Rain-fed Areas, was set up by the ministry to extend the experiences of Plan Puebla to other rain-fed areas of the country. This ambitious program was operated jointly by INIA, the extension service and the college. Research was broadened to include studies of animal production by farm families as well as fruit production. During the first year of this new management system, 8,130 maize farmers used the improved production practices on 27,485 hectares.

Technical teams for ten PRONDAAT projects in seven states received five months of training with Plan Puebla in late 1974 and early 1975, and field activities elsewhere were initiated in April 1975. Technical assistance staff began organizing and working with women's groups, promoting improvements in fruit production in four communities while they assisted 8,589 farmers improve their maize production on 27,769 hectares. The momentum for expansion was being lost, however.

Technical teams trained in Puebla initiated five additional PRONDAAT programs in 1976. The Teaching, Research and Training Center for Regional Agricultural Development was inaugurated in the city of Puebla the same year. Technical assistance extended the promotion of fruit production to other communities, helped farmers produce beans on trellises using improved technology and helped 8,352 maize farmers use the recommended practices on 26,342 hectares. The maize component of the program also contracted somewhat during this year.

The ministry of agriculture was reorganized in 1977, and a new program was initiated that divided the rain-fed areas of the country into approximately 200 districts, seeking to coordinate better the public sector's agricultural services at the district level. Technical assistance coverage for maize production diminished somewhat more in 1977, reaching 8,350 farmers cultivating 20,273 hectares of land.

Activities Since 1977

The Rain-fed Districts Program became operational in 1978 and underwent frequent structural changes in the following years. Efforts were made to accommodate Plan Puebla to the new program with as little loss of autonomy as possible. However, many important changes occurred. The project area was enlarged, and the coordinator became responsible to the government's district head. Instead of gradually evolving Plan Puebla activities based on farmer priorities, new activities that were of interest primarily to the central office were introduced. Technical personnel from several departments of the ministry of agriculture, with different backgrounds and work habits, were assigned to Plan Puebla (within about three years, the number of Plan Puebla technicians increased more than threefold). Finally, many decisions previously made by Plan Puebla personnel were now made at a higher level. In spite of these changes, the four components of Plan Puebla continued to function. Experienced observers of Plan Puebla, however, reported that the enlarged technical team operated less efficiently than before. There was less evidence of creative thinking in planning and implementation, and the team gave less emphasis to documenting field experiences.

Nevertheless, important initiatives have continued to be taken in the area of Plan Puebla.

- In 1980, when a National Plan to Support Agriculture (PLANAT) began to provide funding for improving agricultural infrastructure in several parts of Mexico, Plan Puebla technicians assisted farmer groups in using PLANAT funds, together with their own resources plus other sources of public funding, to bore irrigation wells, repair roads, build bridges and construct warehouses.

- In 1983, farmer groups with years of experience in Plan Puebla joined together to form the Cholollan Regional Cooperative, with about 12,000 members. The cooperative has served as a forum for expressing farmer opinions and has been active in improving agricultural infrastructure in the area.

- In 1981, research scientists with years of experience in Plan Puebla initiated a research program in two area communities to develop a prototype of what the modern family farm should be. Using a farming systems approach, studies were carried out to improve the production of maize, beans, irrigated alfalfa, vegetable crops, fruit trees and milk cows, and to take full advantage of interaction among these components. By 1985, improved technologies were available for most of these activities. Widespread adoption of the improved practices was slowed, however, because the services required to apply the new technologies were not always readily available. Local farmers were assisted in developing small enterprises that offered the required services. Presently, twenty-three small farm enterprises operating in ten communities are facilitating the use of the new technologies by local farmers.

• The most recent innovation resulting from Plan Puebla was the organization in 1993 by former Plan Puebla staff of a credit union to provide loans for farming and nonfarm activities. Membership assessments and matching government resources furnish the funds for loans. This credit union will facilitate the financing of agricultural production for many farmers in the Puebla area.

ACCOMPLISHMENTS

Plan Puebla contributed to many changes in the local farming population, in the research and development strategies employed in Mexico and in other countries, and in the agricultural service agencies operating in Puebla. Some of these changes can be quantified, and data below indicate the degree of change. Other changes are more subtle, and the statements made about these reflect the understanding of long-term participants in Plan Puebla. As in other enterprises, changes in farming activities come about as the result of many influences. No attempt is made to assign credit only to Plan Puebla or to allocate it between Plan Puebla and other sources of change mentioned here.

Farmer Adoption of Improved Maize Production Technology. Information collected in 1982 estimated the degree of farmer adoption of Plan Puebla recommendations, comparing the practices used by the farmers surveyed in each production system with the practices recommended for that system. The percentage of farmers with low or zero adoption of the five key recommendations was only 21 percent. Nearly 97 percent of farmers had adopted the key practices in some degree, although only 18 percent reported a high level of adoption (Díaz et al. 1995).

Increase in Maize Yields. The initial objective of Plan Puebla was to develop a strategy for rapidly increasing maize yields. Average yields for a random sample of all farmers in the Puebla area for 1968–90 are given in Table 8.1. These yields, measured in kilograms per hectare, vary from 980 in 1983 to 3,356 in 1976. Drought, which reduces yields in varying degrees in about 80 percent of the years, was extremely severe in 1982 and 1983, accounting for the very low yields observed in those years. Maize yields are also reduced occasionally by frost damage, and this was a major cause of the low average reported in 1974.

In spite of the great variation in maize yields attributable to climate, the impact of farmer's use of Plan Puebla recommendations can be seen by comparing the multiyear averages at the end of the table. The 1968–71 average (1,888 kg/ha) probably overstates slightly the average yields using traditional technology. The 1972–75 average suggests a 17 percent increase in yield, likely due to the improved technology, while the 1976–81 average indicates a 62 percent increase over pre-Plan Puebla levels. This is probably a reasonable estimate of average maize yields in the Puebla area under average weather conditions with most farmers having adopted—as noted, in varying degrees—the improved technology. The reasons for the reduction in the average yield after 1984 are unclear. This coincided with a period of economic crisis in Mexico when the relationship between the costs of growing maize and its price in the marketplace was not so favorable for Puebla farmers.

Increase in Farm Income. Although the immediate objective of Plan Puebla was to increase maize yields, its long-term objective was to improve the general welfare of rural families. Increasing farm income was seen as a necessary first step toward this goal. Surveys indicate that average net family incomes of Puebla area farmers rose from $667 in 1967 to $1,985 in 1984, adjusted for inflation. The percentage of family income derived from crop production grew from 30 to 36 percent, with crop production income increasing 252 percent, from $203 to $714. This was due mostly to an increase in the average area cultivated (from 2.47 hectares in 1967 to 5.05 in 1984), which accounts for 104 percent of the increase in income; and to greater use of improved technologies, which accounts for most of the remaining 148 percent.

Family income derived from off-farm employment increased by 181 percent, from US$271 in 1967 to US$763 in 1984. There were significant welfare implications from a shift in income sources. Before Plan Puebla, most nonfarm income was generated by heads of families, many of whom found temporary employment elsewhere when there was little work on the farm. By 1984, a large proportion of nonfarm income came from young family members with more formal education who had found permanent

Table 8.1   Average Maize Yields for Random Sample of All Farmers
in the Puebla Area, 1968–90

Year	Yield (kg/ha)	Year	Yield (kg/ha)
1967	1,310	1981	3,095
1968	2,090	1982	1,300
1969	1,662	1983	980
1970	1,917	1984	2,281
1971	1,883	1985	2,664
1972	2,442	1986	2,008
1973	2,552	1987	2,172
1974	1,714	1988	1,523
1975	2,099	1989	2,414
1976	3,356	1990	3,159
1977	2,953	1968–71 (avg.)	1,888
1978	3,011	1972–75 (avg.)	2,202
1979	2,803	1976–81 (avg.)	3,052
1980	3,096	1984–90 (avg.)	2,317

jobs in the service sector in the city of Puebla and in several new industries in the Puebla area. So family disruption due to poverty conditions was somewhat alleviated by the improved technology.

Improvements in General Welfare. It was expected that higher family incomes would lead to improvements in the general welfare in Puebla. Information from surveys conducted in 1967 and 1982 showed changes in food consumption, child education and the facilities available in the homes. Since changes in family welfare are influenced by many factors, especially the availability of public services, we cannot say exactly how the measured changes were brought about.

Almost 70 percent of the farmers interviewed in 1982 reported substantial improvement since 1967 in the variety of foods consumed by their families. About 68 percent of these farmers mentioned that in using the additional income, priority was given to improving their children's education. The average number of years of schooling of the age group sixteen to twenty years old increased from 5.4 in 1967 to 7.1 in 1982; for the twenty-one to twenty-five year age group, the average years of schooling increased from 3.6 to 7.8 during the same period. Substantial improvements in the quality of rural homes was also reported by Puebla farmers.

Improved Development Strategies. The experiences in Plan Puebla, together with findings from similar programs in other parts of Mexico and in other countries, support the importance of the following elements in initiating and operating a development program in areas of traditional agriculture.

1. A program to promote the development of traditional agriculture should be initiated in a defined area. Presently there are very few successful experiences that provide guidelines for accelerating the development of traditional agriculture. There is no way to decide a priori which activities should receive priority, or which operational strategies can assure success. For this reason, the best course is to initiate activities in a defined area where there is an opportunity to test strategies, learn from the local farmers and train technical personnel. Once a degree of success has been demonstrated, it should be feasible to extend the program to other areas.

2. At the beginning, the pilot area should not represent the most difficult agro-socioeconomic conditions in the country. On the contrary, the circumstances in the selected area should be reasonably favorable for change. It is necessary to achieve fairly quickly a degree of success in increasing crop yields and family incomes that guarantees sufficient continuity of the program to permit a fair test of the operational strategies.

3. The most critical factor for success or failure in a development program is the ability and dedication of the technical team members. They should be people motivated to work closely with farmers and to assist them in improving their production and general welfare. Besides having academic preparation that enables them to comprehend well their specific responsibilities, they must be able to win the confidence of farmers and work harmoniously with their colleagues.

4. Priority activities should be defined, and the program of operations should be planned with a thorough understanding of the circumstances of local farm families.

5. Local farmers are valuable sources of information and ideas about how to improve crop production and family income. They should participate fully in planning and implementing program activities and in interpreting findings.

6. Technical assistance agents should dedicate all their time to helping rural families improve agricultural production and their general welfare. Farmers should be informed about the advantages of group action and assisted at local and regional levels in forming effective organizations. Although mass communications media are useful, the most effective way agents can influence farmers is by interacting directly with them in village meetings, as well as through demonstrations, crop inspections and interchanges among groups in farmers' fields.

7. Frequently, the agricultural production technology available to traditional farmers in a given area has not been validated under local conditions. It is very important that crop production research be carried out on farmers' fields to generate adoptable recommendations.

8. Close integration of research and technical assistance activities (weekly meetings, a shared training program and collaboration in all areas) leads to greater effectiveness at the operational level. Likewise, an essential component of development programs is coordination among the farmers, the technical team and agricultural service agencies, especially those that provide the information, inputs and credit needed for improving crop production.

9. Agricultural development programs should have an evaluation component, with responsibility for identifying the problems that limit progress and for helping find solutions. Evaluating the program's progress may be the responsibility of this same evaluation component or of an external element. If reliable methodologies are used, having evaluation integrated into operations need not compromise objectivity.

INSTITUTIONAL CHANGES

The agricultural service agencies operating in Plan Puebla in 1967 were accustomed to working mostly with large farmers or credit societies. Banks viewed small farmers as poor credit risks and reported that small loans were not profitable because of the paperwork. Farmers, on the other hand, had little interest in seeking bank credit because of their negative past experiences, such as the credit not being made available on time.

Although service agencies were reluctant to modify their operating procedures, over time most of them made significant changes. The Agricultural Bank, for example, made several changes in its lending procedures:

- credit, which had earlier been available only to larger producers, was extended to farmers with five hectares or less,

- credit was provided to solidarity groups with three to nine members, without requiring an individual guarantee,

- temporary personnel were hired to facilitate the preparation of loan documents,

- solidarity group contracts were made for five years instead of one,

- farmers were permitted to pay off their loans early, thus reducing interest costs, and

- the president of a solidarity group was able to make transactions with the bank on behalf of all members of the group.

By adjusting their operating procedures, the service agencies played a vital role in increasing crop production and farm income in the Puebla area.

The Graduate College itself has changed in the course of participating in Plan Puebla. In Puebla, an outreach center was established that trains technical teams and administers Plan Puebla and similar programs in many parts of Mexico. The center in Puebla initiated a master's degree program in regional agricultural development strategies in 1989 and a doctoral program in 1994. The college's Communications Center is now the Center of Rural Development Studies. Its Genetics Center gives greater importance to developing improved maize varieties for rain-fed agriculture. The Soil Science Center has improved its methods for conducting research on farmers' fields. Many students in soil science, rural development studies, genetics, and economics have carried out their thesis research in the Puebla area.

EXTENSION TO OTHER AREAS

From its beginning in 1967, Plan Puebla sought to communicate its progress and experience to agricultural and political leaders in Mexico and other countries. By 1969, as field activities were progressing very satisfactorily, plans were made to publicize these findings in other parts of Mexico and in other countries. Plan Puebla's coordinator began meeting with representatives of Mexican institutions to report on the experiences in Puebla and to offer assistance to other programs. In 1970, the director of CIMMYT, together with Plan Puebla staff visited Colombia, Peru, Ecuador and Bolivia; similar visits were made to Argentina, Venezuela and Honduras in 1971. As a result of such activities, several agricultural develoment projects—the East Antioquia Project in Columbia, the Cajamarca-La Libertad Project in Peru, a basic grains program in Honduras, a maize program in the state of Mexico, and the Tlaxcala Project, also in Mexico— operating along similar lines began operation in 1970 and 1971. Plan Puebla staff assisted these projects by training technicians in Puebla and providing technical assistance. These regional production projects in Mexico and elsewhere in Latin America had considerable impact on the agricultural programs in their countries.

In the early 1980s, Plan Puebla staff began to work with a nongovernmental organization, the International Liaison Committee for Food Crops Programs. Its goal was to reduce hunger and poverty of the rural poor by promoting villager participation in programs to increase food production and income. Pilot programs were initiated in Mali, Tanzania, Zimbabwe and Peru between 1982 and 1985. Again, Plan Puebla assisted these programs by training technical teams in Puebla and providing technical advice in the project areas.

RETROSPECTION

Looking back over the evolution of Plan Puebla, it seems likely that overall progress could have been greater had certain things been done differently. During the early years, from 1967 to 1971, Plan Puebla operated with almost complete autonomy. Staff and advisors were encouraged to think innovatively and were given the opportunity to test new options in the field. There was an abundance of new ideas and great optimism. Five years, however, is a short period when faced with the complexities involved in achieving rapid change in the production and net income of small-scale traditional farmers under rain-fed conditions. Had the period of generous funding and operational autonomy extended another five or ten years, much greater progress could have been made in understanding and documenting the process of development of traditional agriculture. By 1972, however, Plan Puebla activities were constrained by the imminent loss of CIMMYT funding and support.

Another area in which Plan Puebla activities might have been implemented more effectively was in selecting and training field staff. During Plan Puebla's evolution, it became clear that progress in a difficult undertaking such as rural development depends more on the capability, enthusiasm and motivation of project staff than on any other element. In Plan Puebla's early years, top priority was given to selecting the most highly qualified professionals available, and Plan Puebla advisors participated actively in the in-service training of new technicians. Over time, however, hiring new staff became more institutionalized, with advisors and senior staff playing a minor role in selection and training; the process and criteria became more subject to bureaucratic and political considerations. This undoubtedly had some adverse impact on overall progress.

In the early days of Plan Puebla, the evaluation component was understood to have two main objectives: identify problems limiting progress and take an active role in finding appropriate solutions; and document quantifiable changes brought about by plan activities. In the early years, some attention was given to the first objective. With time, however, almost all the effort of the evaluation unit was directed to the measurement of progress. It is likely that many adjustments in Plan Puebla strategies would have been made and would have been better focused had greater attention been given by evaluation professionals to diagnosing conditions limiting progress and to prompting corrective action, rather than simply trying to document and report performance. The loss of a diagnostic capability with some administrative authority behind it constrained Plan Puebla from remaining as engaged with learning and adapting as it was in the beginning—and as is required for effective and sustainable rural development.

9 Farmer-to-Farmer Experimentation and Extension: Integrated Rural Development for Smallholders in Guatemala

Anirudh Krishna with Roland Bunch

The San Martin program functioned between 1972 and 1979. It was located in the *municipio* (subdistrict) of San Martin Jilotepeque within the department (district) of Chimaltenango in the central highlands of Guatemala, approximately 30 miles west of Guatemala City. The program covered about half the municipio, an area of 550 square kilometers and a population of approximately 33,000, most of them Cakchiquel Indians of Mayan descent.

The economy of the department is overwhelmingly agrarian, with one-third of area farmers owning less than two acres of land, and another one-third owning between two and four acres. The steep terrain is easily eroded, and soil fertility was quite low when the program started. Most of the best lands belonged to descendants of the Spanish conquerors, while the Indian people's remaining hillside plots had been divided up again and again. With only a few acres remaining with each family, they had been forced to abandon the agricultural practices, such as long-term fallowing, that previously made their land use sustainable. They watched helplessly as their soil's fertility was depleted by continuous cropping and as the topsoil washed away because of continuous exposure to seasonal rains. As a consequence of low and decreasing yields, thousands of farmers (49 percent of those surveyed in San Martin) were periodically forced to work for subsistence wages on large-scale commercial farms near the Pacific coast.

During a seven-year period (1972–79), the San Martin program was successful in addressing these problems, not only by substantially raising agricultural yields and arresting soil erosion, but also, and far more important, through being able to develop local capacities that have resulted in local farmers' continuing to develop their own agriculture, without further external assistance. When we conducted a survey in March 1994, we found that impressive yield increases have continued to occur in program villages, as shown in Table 9.1, while neighboring villages in which the program did not operate have not shown similar improvements. Maize yields in control villages went from 400 kilograms

Table 9.1   Average Maize Yields for Four San Martin Jilotepeque Villages

Village	1972	1979	1994
	in kg/ha, rounded to the nearest 100 kgs		
San Antonio Cornejo	400	2,800	4,800
Las Venturas	400	2,400	5,200
Xesuj	300	2,000	3,200
Pacoj	500	3,200	4,800
Control villages (outside program area)	400	600	1,200

per hectare in 1972 to 600 in 1979, reaching only 1,200 by 1994, when the resurvey was done. These large and continuing yield increases, and the consequent improvements in income levels, were achieved with total program expenditures of less than US$50 per family benefitted (Bunch and Lopez 1994).[1]

The important change here is not just that a large number of people adopted a list of program-promoted technologies, but that they developed a new attitude of increased innovativeness, trying out new ideas and new technologies continually. Without any major provision of outside information, they have continued to raise their yields and incomes, even after the program ended in 1979.

In San Antonio Cornejo and Xesuj, many farmers planted sustainable hillside coffee groves during the 1980s, after any formal extension activities had ceased. Similarly, people of Las Venturas have, on their own initiative, developed a sustainable system for wood and timber harvesting and planting. They have also adopted a system of intensive cattle raising. During the 1980s, many villagers moved into production of vegetables for export. Local farmers, recognizing the potential returns of these crops, quickly learned how to grow and market broccoli, cauliflower, brussels sprouts and snow peas. When that market dried up, they worked to develop other alternatives.

Although the people suffered severe setbacks from the protracted civil disturbances, which lasted from 1978 to 1985, the program's results—continuous individual and institutional innovation—continue to this day. Furthermore, the principles of agricultural extension developed in the San Martin program have been adopted by a number of grassroots development efforts in over twenty nations of the developing world.

INITIATION THROUGH THE CHIMALTENANGO PROGRAM, 1962–75

The work that led to the San Martin program began in 1962 when Carroll Behrhorst, a young Kansas physician sponsored by the Lutheran Church, opened a clinic in Chimaltenango, a major town fifteen kilometers from San Martin. Major health problems in the area included respiratory infections, malnutrition and intestinal disorders. An informal house-to-house survey near Chimaltenango reported that 105 out of 450 people had active cases of tuberculosis.

Within weeks, the doctor was seeing fifty patients a day. One man's leg had swollen to twice its size because of a small bruise, complicated by a severe protein deficiency. A little four-year-old girl arrived so underfed that the doctor had trouble locating a vein in her body that was large enough to take an intravenous solution. And a young mother tearfully admitted that her son had just died because "her milk was not strong enough." "What can I do," she said, "when we do not have enough to eat?"

Behrhorst quickly realized that this mother's question was crucial. The great majority of the diseases he was treating were either caused or complicated by inadequate diets which, in turn, were due to low levels of agricultural production. In a rural, agriculturally based community, the results of poor agricultural production are all-pervasive. Poor harvests mean low incomes, which in turn cause malnutrition, poor health, poor schooling and, perhaps most destructive, lack of control over one's own destiny.

Consequently, in 1963, he asked World Neighbors (WN), a small Oklahoma-based nongovernmental organization, for help in establishing an educational program. With a $25,000 grant from WN, a combined health and agricultural program was begun. A small hospital was built, and Behrhorst began training health promoters through practical hands-on learning. Once a week, a group of volunteers spent a day at the hospital and made rounds with Behrhorst or Carlos Xoquic, a promoter who later became a supervisor. In time, the volunteers learned to take the patient's history, examine the patient, describe the symptoms and prescribe treatment. When faced with a problem that they could not treat adequately, they referred the patient to the hospital. Promoters who passed a periodic practical examination were authorized to give injections and to sell medications in their home community, at a price significantly below that charged by local pharmacies.

Behrhorst quickly demonstrated through this approach that local Cakchiquels could treat most common local ailments as competently as could university-trained physicians. They could reach people who, for various reasons, could not come to the hospital. Medicine sales, along with a small treatment fee, were the promoters' only source of remuneration. Selection of volunteers for the training was originally based on recommendations by local priests or Peace Corps volunteers, but, with time, Behrhorst encouraged communities to establish their own health committees, which selected a community member to receive the training and provided oversight once that member began working as a promoter.

Along with health, volunteers were also trained in improved agricultural practices. In 1968, the agriculture program picked up when Oxfam–US, recognizing the potential of the work already begun, offered to fund a more concerted development effort. A $82,000 grant enabled three expatriate WN personnel—Paul and Mary McKay and Roland Bunch—to begin working directly out of Chimaltenango rather than simply making periodic supervisory visits. Paul was trained in agriculture and sociology, Mary was a teacher and a nurse, and Roland had a teaching degree. Three local agricultural promoters trained by WN filled out the team.

The new project concentrated on forty-six communities, mostly in the department of Chimaltenango, that were already participating in the health promoter program. Health, nutrition, veterinary medicine, fruit production and vegetable production were the major subject areas addressed. Fertilizer use combined with a soil analysis service was also promoted, along with soil conservation ditches and terracing.

However, we were trying to do too much, spreading ourselves too thinly over too many interventions and too many farmers. As a result, errors were made. An internal evaluation showed that the agricultural program had been almost totally ineffective. Major changes in the program strategy were required. These were carried out to some extent in the Chimaltenango program, but they were articulated more fully in the San Martin program. The San Martin program began in 1972 and, while it drew upon the lessons and the personnel of the Chimaltenango program, it was developed separately.

THE PROGRAM IN SAN MARTIN, 1972–79

The event that most clearly marked the beginning of the San Martin program was a short, two-paragraph memo from Oxfam–US to John Peters, WN's president, proposing the establishment of several integrated development programs as a new and logical way to attack rural poverty. Three main considerations underlay Oxfam's suggestion of a new approach. First, it thought that since most of the problems of developing areas were interrelated, progress could be stimulated most efficiently through an *integrated* approach in which any major bottleneck in the development process could be worked on when necessary. Second, although the Chimaltenango program was having a major influence in the area, there was no systematic process for measuring its accomplishments. Third, Oxfam was convinced that, in the long run, development must be carried out by the local people themselves. Expatriates could provide important ideas about new program approaches and new institutional mechanisms, but program leadership had to be handed over to local Guatemalans within two years of founding.

WN chose the area around San Martin Jilotepeque both because of its need and its potential for progress. In 1972, San Martin was known for being the most conservative municipio in the Chimaltenango department. People were still using centuries-old techniques of cultivation on worn-out, badly eroded fields. Our survey of 600 families in the area indicated that practices in the corn fields were a good barometer of what was happening in the rest of the region's agriculture: people had not improved their other crops and did little to keep their animals healthy and well fed. One agronomist told WN that it would be a mistake to work in San Martin because people there would never change.

"Potential for progress" was reflected in a complex set of closely related preconditions for development. In the San Martin area, these preconditions included the area's familiarity with the earlier project centered in Chimaltenango and the presence of a strong leadership base in the local church. Some work done in the area by the earlier Chimaltenango program had won a great deal of faith and goodwill among the people of the area. Hundreds of people had benefited from the program, and hundreds more had heard about it. Ideas for specific design and program interventions had emerged out of both the successes and the failures of the earlier program.

The new program was to work for five years in an area roughly 15 by 20 kilometers, with a total funding of $104,000 from Oxfam. Its general aim was to cause a permanent improvement in the standard of living of the area's people. The approach embodied the following long-term goals: agricultural development, human development, health and family welfare and road construction. Program goals were expressed in terms of actual benefits that would accrue to the people. Among the more important goals was a doubling of the area's agricultural production and a significant decrease in child mortality. The initial three-year goals were to help at least 20 percent of the population to produce corn yields of 3000 kilograms per hectare; 15 percent were to have built contour erosion control ditches, and 10 percent to have planted fruit trees.

The program was to involve absolutely no handouts; it would encourage only such interventions for which people would themselves be willing to pay. Program funds received from Oxfam were to finance salaries of full-time and part-time staff, equipment and operating expenditures. All expatriate involvement ended when the program was turned over to Guatemalan leadership in mid-1973.

Anacleto Sajbochol, an Indian extensionist from the Chimaltenango program, and Roland led an initial staff of six part-time extensionists, all of whom had been involved as farmers in that program. They started by conducting a baseline survey of 600 area families. Since one of the most important resources available lay in the example of the work done in the earlier program, they took groups of farmers from all over the new area to see what the other farmers had done. Experience had shown that one of the biggest problems when beginning work in an area is convincing people that, if they work a little harder and risk a little bit of their harvest on the new practices being promoted, the program had both the technologies and the determination to make sure their efforts were rewarded. There was no better way of doing this than to show them what had already been done in nearby villages and to let them talk freely to villagers who had made the proposed changes themselves.

The Agriculture Program

From earlier work the program learned that spreading the organization's effort over a large number of interventions is of little use. Teaching a few ideas to hundreds of people is more effective than teaching hundreds of ideas to one person. People will understand the innovation better and will continue to use it and improve upon it. This will also contribute more to community solidarity and to overall social justice as a "critical mass" of people become involved with the new technique.

Another program emphasis was to concentrate on those techniques that had the potential to produce *early visible success*. The entire dynamic of people's involvement with the program depends upon their level of enthusiasm, and only recognizable success can generate this enthusiasm, particularly when failure and stagnation have been their main experience. Experience had further taught WN that it should try to teach people only such techniques as they can implement with the equipment that they already own or can easily afford. It was therefore decided to concentrate during the first year on improving the yields of corn and beans, which together account for over 80 percent of the area's agricultural production. Therefore, Anacleto's first job was to select agricultural practices that combined simplicity and low risk, and that would provide the largest initial yield increases with the least expense to the people and the program. Thus, he set about trying to pin down the one or two limiting factors that were responsible for the area's low productivity.

Experimentation around San Martin had shown that, because of erosion and nutrient depletion, soil nutrients and, particularly, phosphorus
were the area's limiting factors. Preventing erosion and adding nitrogen and
phosphorus to the soil would be the priority areas of action. The specific
activities to achieve these ends would, however, have to be adapted to local
soil types, climate and economic conditions, the prevailing state of technical knowledge and also the cultural preferences and skills of the local people. For the San Martin area, with steeply sloping fields and an average
annual rainfall of less than 900 millimeters, Anacleto and the village leaders chose a system of contour ditches that would prevent erosion with a
minimum of labor and lost planting space. These ditches were dug on a
contour every ten to twenty meters, and high-protein, drought-resistant
forage grasses were planted along their upper edges. These grasses trapped
eroding soil, leading over time to the build-up of natural terraces.

The decision on how to add nutrients to the soil was more complex.
The only sources of organic matter were either totally inadequate in quantity or very expensive and of unreliable quality. San Martin's Indian leaders
decided in favor of chemical fertilizers. Although this represented embracing dependence on external, and largely uncontrollable, sources of supply
along with potential for environmental pollution, these problems were
insignificant to local leaders when compared to the malnutrition their families were suffering without the chemical fertilizers. In hindsight, it would
probably have been better if program personnel had worked harder to promote green manuring instead (although knowledge about such technologies was almost nonexistent at that time). In any case, contour ditches and
the application of chemical manure based on soil analysis were selected as
the program's main agricultural priorities during the first year.

The determination of an appropriate technology was only the first step.
Even the best technology is useless unless there is a way of spreading the
word to literally thousands of farmers. WN had learned that efforts
should be concentrated on those people in each village who are most eager
and willing to make changes. Their example, by itself and with little extra
work, will convince others that they could and should do the same.
Thus the plan was to train local leaders as agricultural teachers, who in
turn gave weekly classes in their own or in nearby villages. These classes
were combined with field trials and field demonstrations done by farmers
so that people realized that they themselves, and not just trained agricul-
turists with special budgets for experimentation, could produce good
harvests.

In essence, we devised a three-step training process for multiplying our
efforts. During the initial year, Anacleto and his staff trained forty local volunteer promoters, respected village leaders who had previously shown a

willingness to work for their communities' welfare. The volunteers received practical and theoretical training one day a week for nine months. We organized field trips to farms that had benefited from their association with the Chimaltenango program and prepared training manuals for small farmers.

The second, concurrent, step involved small-scale experimentation with the new techniques conducted on the promoters' farms. The farmer-experimenters were regularly visited by program staff, who provided them with encouragement and further suggestions. These experiments, when successful, served as demonstrations of the new technology. Since they were carried out on-farm by area farmers themselves, they had tremendous value in generating conviction and enthusiasm among neighboring farmers.

Actual extension work was the third step of the strategy. Twenty-seven of these individuals continued with the project as volunteer promoters, learning to be extensionists by doing this kind of work. Due to their outreach, 450 farmers had built contour ditches on their land by the end of the first year. In addition, 500 farmers had their soils analyzed and fertilized them accordingly; eighty tons of fertilizer had been sold, and several hundred farmers were experimenting with program-introduced varieties of maize and beans. For 146 of these farmers from fifteen villages, the average harvest on their improved fields was 77 percent better than the best harvest they had ever before achieved.

The first year's success made it easier for the promoters to introduce more new ideas. Hundreds of farmers learned to turn over their compacted soils with a fork or an ox-drawn plow, and how to control the spread of insects. They built compost heaps, had their soils tested, planted narrower rows, vaccinated their animals and experimented with new crops. Most important, they learned the practice of crop rotation.

Yield increases continued throughout the project period. An evaluation study conducted on behalf of the U.S. Agency for International Development (USAID) in 1978 concluded, "After using the technological package for five years, projected-assisted farmers have shown average yield increases of 600 percent for beans and 1,100 percent for corn; individual farmers report far higher increases" (Gow et al. 1979). These increases were achieved at an estimated cost of $4.28 per farmer per year.

The Credit Cooperative

Although we sought to keep the cost of each new practice as low as possible, many farmers needed loans with which to purchase chemical fertilizer. To assist them, a credit cooperative was established in 1972 with an initial thirty-two members and $177 in share capital. It was called *Kato-ki*—meaning "self-help" in Cakchiquel, the local language. Requirements for membership and for receiving loans included attending lessons on financial management. This organization maintained its credibility during the program years by doing what it was supposed to do, namely, providing timely loans to its members.

By 1978, membership had grown to 732 with share capital of $38,000. The cooperative expanded its operations to provide a wider range of services for its members. Loans were given for livestock, commercial purposes, small industry, housing and consumption. An input supply store sold many kinds of agricultural inputs, such as fertilizer and seeds, either on cash or through a loan from the cooperative. Besides providing credit and inputs, it also undertook the marketing of wheat, thus furthering the objective of integration for which the project was first started.

The cooperative encouraged member savings to build up capital. Savings equal to 5 percent of the loan amount were compulsorily added to the total value of each loan and deposited in the member's savings account. Savings deposits amounted to $23,000 in 1977. The evaluation performed for USAID found a default rate on outstanding loans of only 8.5 percent, and this rate had been considerably lower before the 1976 earthquake. By the end of the program in the late 1970s, the cooperative had nearly 1,000 members, including most of the leaders and many farmers involved in the program. As the program was phasing out, the leaders drafted a plan through which they would carry on many of the functions of the program and circulated a proposal for support among a number of aid agencies. Thus, members planned to continue the work that the program had started now that it was formally coming to an end. However, at this same time, the civil war in Guatemala was reaching its zenith. Massacres were already occurring in San Martin and elsewhere. In one three-day period in 1982, thirteen villages in the municipio of San Martin were temporarily wiped off the map. Between 3,000 to 4,000 people fled to the mountains, surviving on herbs and tree bark for nearly three years before they felt safe enough to return. Amid this kind of upheaval, the cooperative was naturally unable to collect loans or conduct any other business and became largely dormant. Efforts made after the end of the civil disturbances have not succeeded so far in restoring the same dynamic as before.

Helping the Landless

The one major group that remained largely unaffected by agricultural improvements in the area was the landless. Increased yields on rented lands all too often resulted in the rental fees being raised, or even in the eviction of the tenant by a landlord who had become keen to farm the land himself. Thus, WN also set up, through the *Kato-ki* cooperative, a land buying scheme. For this purpose, the cooperative obtained a loan of US$33,000 from Church World Services. This money was advanced for individual and communal land purchases and was made available to members at 12 percent interest over a three- to five-year payback period. Through the years, this scheme enabled more than 250 families to become landowners.

Other farmer groups bought land on their own. This has been facilitated by the impact that the program had made on agricultural yields, as villagers could make more net income off their lands than could absentee landlords. The superior productivity of smallholders is due in part to their greater farming knowledge and heavy labor inputs, but it is also the result of the new technologies, which have reduced the scale advantages of large-size farms. Small farmers to this day continue to buy land from rich farmers. Virtually no land transactions in the area are going in the opposite direction.

HEALTH AND NUTRITION

The program's work in health and nutrition began slowly. As agricultural production increased, people's interest in this part of the program grew. By the end of the third year, over 300 women from eighteen villages had been organized into twenty groups and were regularly attending classes on nutrition, responsible parenthood, hygiene, latrine construction and vegetable gardening. Women became influential in motivating a large literacy program and several community drinking water projects. Men taking agriculture classes were, from time to time, introduced to the women's classes, and vice versa.

DEALING WITH AN EARTHQUAKE

In 1976, a major earthquake rocked Guatemala and, just in the township of San Martin, killed 2,900 people (8 percent of the population). Over 90 percent of homes in the program area were destroyed. The need for relief and reconstruction was obvious. Although international relief agencies quickly mobilized to rebuild the hardest hit areas, the residents of San Martin decided to take more direct action. The agricultural extension work in San Martin was suspended during this year, and paid as well as volunteer staff used their skills instead to promote education on earthquake-proof construction techniques.

Oxfam provided the program with an additional $1 million for relief, and the Guatemalan government provided a loan of about $30,000 to the cooperative to on-lend to its members for home reconstruction. The cooperative helped by buying and transporting food in bulk for distribution in the area. Outstanding loans of members who were killed in the earthquake were written off. Due to the extensive damage and disruption caused by the earthquake, the development program was extended for an additional three years and the total amount of Oxfam funding was increased to $150,000 from the initial $104,000.

COMMUNITY PARTICIPATION AND PROGRAM MANAGEMENT

From the very beginning, local people played an important part in the program's planning, organization and management. Through their participation, they kept the program working on their most important needs in ways consistent with their cultural values. The local leadership became the personnel of the program. Except for the original two directors and an accountant, all staff were recruited from among local villager leaders. Prospective extensionists were chosen based on their observed willingness to help others. They had to spend up to two years attending training courses, conducting small-scale experiments on their fields and teaching agricultural classes in other villages before being hired by the program. By 1978, the staff had increased to eleven salaried individuals and twenty-seven volunteers. All of them were from the Chimaltenango department (all but two were from San Martin), spoke the local dialect, and were subsistence farmers themselves, thus they could easily relate to other farmers.

Training and supervision were continuous and heavy until these promoters had gained a good deal of experience. WN saw supervision as having two aspects: information/skills and motivational. Supervision to provide information and skills was thorough; however, supervision to keep people at their work, to make sure that they were doing what they were supposed to do, was practically unnecessary. The entire training process used—based on experimentation and early, visible success—was built around positive reinforcement, which was constant and repeated often. The promoters were supported in their extension work, so that they could have a high rate of success and positive feedback from that work.

The whole process was permeated with an appreciation that motivation is of utmost importance. People are constantly rewarded for their efforts by evident success, which is a powerful motivating force for people who have been taught all their lives that they are useless. WN feels that this is the only way extension programs can work. Extensionists have to be self-motivated. There is no feasible mechanism other than self-motivation for supervising a dozen extensionists spread over several villages on any given day. Even if you could make sure they showed up in their respective villages, no amount of outside pressure would ever force or push them to do their very best at providing good, well-planned, motivating and enthusiastically presented classes.

WN motivated staff and local leadership by every means it knew. They were selected according to proven motivation, and if, in the end, someone's work suffered from lack of motivation, the program was prepared to let him or her go. This happened to only one health extensionist and to no agricultural extensionist during the eight years of the program. Team spirit among staff was maintained through continual supervision, a high level of success in the work, a participatory style of management in which the vast majority of decisions were made by consensus and frequent participatory discussions of what we were doing and why. Also, once every couple of years, we had a one- to two-week session with experts in group dynamics who helped the team get out the inevitable complaints and resentments that built up. This was a very important activity that helped to maintain a spirit of camaraderie and close personal and working relationships between the members of the team.

Planning was done with the participation of the whole team through consensus, usually on an annual basis, with each extensionist establishing his or her own objectives after consulting with the villagers with whom he or she worked. If the director felt the objectives were too low, or another should be added or subtracted, he would question the extensionist, but the final decision would be made based on consensus.

All of this served to build cohesion between the program and the people whom it sought to serve. Relying primarily on local personnel and locally-valid technologies, and encouraging people to adopt program-introduced innovations with no subsidies being provided, promoted a spirit of confidence in their own abilities.

An illustration of the degree of independence achieved in the area came in 1978 when USAID and the Guatemalan government proposed to include the San Martin area in a regional soil conservation program. Suddenly, farmers were to be paid to undertake the same kinds of soil conservation techniques that they had been practicing voluntarily for years. Local leaders, recognizing the potential threat to the sense of independence and self-help that had developed over the previous decade, petitioned the government and succeeded in convincing it to drop their area from the project.

EXTERNAL LINKAGES

At the village level, these connections were managed by the extensionist concerned, and at the municipio and national levels by the program director.

Any problems in this respect were discussed by the staff as a whole. Relationships with officials were often fairly rocky, as local officials were all Latin, while the vast majority of the poor, and those with whom the program worked, were Indian. Discrimination and mutual suspicion between these groups made it difficult for Latin groups to cooperate with an institution that so openly trained Indians in leadership skills. The election of an Indian mayor of San Martin in 1974 changed this situation as far as the municipal government was concerned, but the relationship with traditional sources of power became, if anything, progressively worse as they increasingly realized that the program was achieving considerable success.

SUSTAINABILITY

The San Martin program operated during a period of rapidly increasing political polarization that eventually resulted in one of the most repressive and violent periods in the history of Latin America. San Martin was directly between the major area of conflict, El Quiche, and the capital city, and in the early 1980s it became one of the most heavily hit municipios in the nation. People became afraid to travel outside their villages, and saving their lives became a higher priority than continuing with the development process. Managing an agricultural program was a low priority for people who were preoccupied with basic survival. In spite of the efforts that area farmers made to continue program activities, little could be done until the situation normalized.

It is sad that we could not see what might have happened in San Martin had the violence not erupted. Although the farmers of San Martin were quick to return to their fields after the carnage ended and to continue with the unfinished work of innovation, the major institutional development, the *Kato-ki* cooperative, never fully recovered. However, as Table 9.1 showed, agricultural yields have continued to rise, and newer and more remunerative activities have been added by the farmers themselves. The downside is that the agricultural technologies have spread from village to village only to a limited degree—much less, we suspect, than they would have, had the cooperative continued to function.

DISSEMINATION

At first WN was uncertain about the value of the new methodology and about its usefulness in other areas. However, as its results became more apparent, WN decided to try out the new methodology in at least one program in each area around the world where it was working. This decision resulted in serious attempts being made to recreate the methodology in Mexico (Oaxaca and Tlaxcala), Honduras (Guinope and El Rosario), Peru (the highlands around Ayacucho), Bolivia (North Potosí), Togo (Bassar), Kenya (Machakos), Indonesia (Sumba) and the Philippines (Cebu, in a program now carried on by the Mag-Uugmad Foundation, a Philippine NGO). All of these, with the possible exception of the Kenyan program, grew eventually into respected programs recognized nationally, and in many cases emulated by other institutions as examples of desirable agricultural development.

In the late 1970's and early 1980's, another source of dissemination of the San Martin experience resulted from the international recruitment and deployment of the program's farmer-extensionists, many of whom continued to serve as project directors for WN or other nongovernmental organizations throughout Central America. Beginning as peasant farmers who first attended agricultural classes, they developed their leadership skills as volunteer promoters and later as paid extensionists. Many of them, with relatively little formal education, now oversee projects with a dozen or more employees and annual budgets of $40,000 to $50,000. These accomplishments are even more exceptional when one notes that most of the projects to which these highland Indians were assigned have been staffed by Latinos who, in many cases, previously had strong anti-Indian prejudices.

A further channel for disseminating the learning and philosophy of the San Martin program was created with the publication of *Two Ears of Corn: A Guide to People-Centered Agricultural Development* (Bunch 1982). It gained a wide readership and has been translated into nine languages, encouraging people in a variety of programs and projects to engage farmers as partners in agricultural research and extension.

LESSONS LEARNED

Successful replication of the San Martin approach convinced us that the methodology was not one that would work only among Guatemalan Indian people, or in Latin cultures, but that it is applicable and needed throughout much of the developing world. Specific agricultural techniques will vary, of course, from program to program, depending on climate, land tenure, culture and access to market, but the basic principles of agricultural extension are valid across a range of cultural and ecological settings.

The methodology of organization for mobilizing farmer participation has been independently discovered, promoted and widely adopted by many different organizations, under various names, for example, the "farmer-to-farmer" extension approach spreading over Asia and Latin America, the "farmer first" approach, the "participatory technology development" approach and the "campesino as protagonist" philosophy of the Food and Agriculture Organization in Latin America. What is common to each of these is one or more of the basic principles for rural development that were first, as far as we know, integrated in the San Martin program:

- Start where the people are—Begin with the things in which they are already interested and in which they are already involved.

- Discover the limiting factors—What factors, when corrected, will make the greatest difference in solving key problems?

- Choose simple, limited technologies—The best tool is the simplest one that will do the job.

- Test ideas on a small scale—Introduce small trials run by farmers in their own fields to learn if a new idea is applicable to a given situation, without exposing the people and the project to the risk of major failures.

- Work to attain early visible success—This maintains the momentum of enthusiasm.

- Evaluate results—The principal evaluators must be the beneficiaries themselves.

- Train trainers—The most effective way to multiply efforts is by preparing villagers who can train others.

These principles have become widely adopted and implemented worldwide. Nevertheless, a very useful and worthwhile learning process with further adaptations has been going on in terms of the details of the process. Different organizations continue to try out a series of related processes, maintaining the basic principles but experimenting with what could be called variations on a theme. We in WN, and, more recently, COSECHA, a Honduran NGO, are constantly trying out new ways of approaching a community, new teaching techniques, different methodologies for phasing out and so forth. Any program or organization can learn from each of the others, and an urgent need exists for establishing networks among organizations and concerned individuals.

What might we have done differently if starting the program at San Martin with the advantage of hindsight? WN should probably have devoted more effort to building bridges and mechanisms for conflict resolution between the majority (Indians) and the minority (Latin). We are not sure that the program could have had much lasting impact, given the ethnic tensions at the national level, but perhaps some local amelioration would have been possible.

Considerable effort was put into promoting home vegetable gardens with no sustainable impact. These required too much labor and care compared to the perennial crops that people were growing already. WN should have been quicker to recognize that this innovation was not likely to gain favor and be accepted.

Finally, it is clear in retrospect that WN should have devoted more time and effort to involving women in our programs to improve agriculture. In rural Guatemala, the role of women in agriculture is probably not as great as in, say, most African countries. But there are widows and other women who are necessarily or by choice more economically active. In the past twenty years, it has become evident to most everyone working in international development that we need to give more support to women's education and expanded opportunities. If WN were initiating the San Martin program over again, it would do more to involve and support women in their various agricultural and household roles.

NOTE

1. To estimate this figure, the total program expenditure on agricultural activity between 1972 and 1979 was divided by the number of families considered to have benefited from this effort (about 5,000 households out of the 6,500 in the municipio). Only those families which at least tripled their maize productivity were counted as having benefited from the program. Discussed in Bunch and Lopez (1994).

10 The National Irrigation Administration's Participatory Irrigation Management Program in the Philippines

Benjamin U. Bagadion

After the National Irrigation Administration (NIA) was organized in 1964 as a semiautonomous government agency and absorbed the staff, functions and responsibilities of the irrigation division of the Bureau of Public Works, it had to find ways of addressing problems in the operation and maintenance (O&M) of national and communal irrigation systems. In national systems, those built and managed by the government, water distribution was usually inequitable, and farmers often complained about unsatisfactory service. Production was much below potential. Irrigation fee collection amounted to much less than the cost of O&M. This presented a big problem because NIA had to fund O&M from the fees it collected once it no longer received a subsidy from the government.

In communal systems, built and/or managed by farmers, funding for construction was increasingly provided through "pork barrel" funds, which were obtained by legislators to fulfill election promises. Although NIA policy required irrigation associations (IAs) to undertake the O&M in communal systems after they were constructed, IAs were generally weak and unable to operate and maintain the irrigation systems properly. Moreover, since construction was free, farmers felt that they did not have to worry about their systems' deterioration, as they could always ask politicians for funding to rehabilitate these systems.

In 1968, NIA started a water management pilot project in the Angat River irrigation system that organized farmers into groups, using agricultural extension methods, after irrigation facilities were constructed. This procedure was subsequently spread by NIA to other national systems. The groups were to serve as channels for credit and agricultural inputs, and it was hoped they would encourage farmers to take over responsibilities for O&M at the farm level, improve water management, increase production and increase the collection of irrigation fees. The process was essentially top down, as farmers were instructed on what to do and how; all decisionmaking remained with NIA. In communal systems, to reduce the dependency effects of the "pork barrel" system, NIA required farmers to contribute 10 percent of the cost of construction in the form of labor and local materials.

However, all these measures failed to meet their objectives. Although irrigation associations were organized in both national and communal systems, they were generally paper organizations. Studies, however, of indigenous irrigation associations such as the *zanjeras* in the northern part of the Philippines showed that these associations have been able to construct, maintain and operate their irrigation systems through many decades without assistance from the government (Siy 1982). This suggested that if a sense of ownership could be developed in the IAs being organized by NIA, they would undertake O&M, as farmers in traditional systems showed they were capable of.

In 1974 NIA's charter was amended to authorize it to recover funds for the construction or rehabilitation of communal irrigation systems. This was in addition to the right to collect irrigation fees in national systems under its original charter. Subsequently NIA initiated, and the president of the Philippines approved, a general policy mandating that water users pay for the operation and maintenance of irrigation systems. Moreover, the costs of construction, except for roads and flood control, were to be recovered as well. These costs could be repaid on generous terms, without interest and over a period not exceeding fifty years, provided also that the charges were within the paying capacity of the farmers. The new requirements were intended to develop a sense of ownership among water users in both national and communal systems.

To implement the new policy, NIA had to find an effective way to get farmers organized. First, it hired the Farm Systems Development Corporation (FSDC), a government agency that was already organizing farmers, to undertake the organizing of IAs in communal irrigation systems. The arrangement with FSDC did not solve the problem though. While its organizing methods seemed better than those NIA had used, many IAs still did not assume O&M responsibilities after construction was finished. Also, FSDC did not address the needs of the national systems, in which it declined to work.

At the time this experiment began, I was project manager of the Upper Pampanga River project, at that time the largest irrigation project in the Philippines. I had contacts with Jeff Romm, a program officer of the Ford Foundation in Manila, who was interested in communal irrigation systems, especially the organization of effective irrigation associations. Many years before, while still with the irrigation division of the Bureau of Public Works, I had gone on observation tours in Taiwan and the United States. There I had seen large irrigation systems being successfully managed by farmer associations. This convinced me that establishing strong and viable irrigation associations must be a major goal of Philippine irrigation administration.

Before I became project manager, I had done a lot of work with communal systems as part of my responsibilities as head of the engineering department of NIA, so Romm and I shared an interest in upgrading performance through participatory management. I also had a leading role in formulating the NIA charter amendments and the new irrigation policy mentioned above, so I wanted to try to develop ways of organizing effective irrigation associations. Romm facilitated a grant of US$30,000 from the Ford Foundation to support a pilot project in two communal irrigation systems in Nueva Ecija, an area under my control as project manager.

A new approach to organizing had to be introduced. From discussions with my son, Benjy, who had been helping organize urban associations in the slum areas in Manila, a new concept emerged of using "community organizers" and a field coordinator to do the organizing work. Thus was born NIA's participatory irrigation development program. What happened later in the pilots has been written about extensively (for example, Korten 1982), so there is no need to repeat it here. Several months later I became NIA's assistant administrator for finance and administration, but I retained control and supervision over the pilots as no one else was interested in them. In 1980, as assistant administrator for operations, I phased out the arrangement with FSDC, establishing another pair of pilot communal projects in Camarines Sur. Subsequently I oversaw the expansion of work in the communals to cover the whole country and the extension of participatory irrigation development to national irrigation systems, until my retirement from NIA at the end of April 1985.

INDICATORS OF SUCCESS

Since the program started in 1976, its indicators have evolved. At first the objective was to organize IAs that could undertake O&M responsibility in both communal and national systems. This meant having IAs with the following capacities and characteristics:

- an organizational structure with a strong membership base and a decisionmaking process that ensures participation of that base,

- strong, committed leadership at all levels, and at least one leader for every ten members,

- rules and regulations accepted by the general membership and properly implemented,

- recording systems for meetings, decision and other transactions,

- financial budgeting, recording, control and reporting,

- equity of water distribution as planned in water delivery schedules, with rotation of water in times of shortage,

- maintenance programs and procedures,

- collection of irrigation service fees and payment of amortized construction costs in the case of communal systems, and

- management of O&M conflicts.

To prepare IAs for taking on O&M responsibilities, they went through three training programs that covered basic leadership development, irrigation system management for IAs, and simplified financial management.

In recent years, the indicators for success have evolved to include sustainability of the systems. This implies achieving increases in production and in the income of farmers and their IA. The latter is needed to enable the association to undertake emergency repair. The government makes available some funds to repair irrigation systems that are damaged by typhoons almost every year. Such funds need not be repaid; however, they are often delayed and seldom sufficient. Thus, IAs need to raise more resources from their members to keep systems operating season to season.

The turnover of O&M responsibility to IAs in the communal systems has succeeded substantially—all the IAs that were organized and trained along the participatory development processes have taken over the O&M of their irrigation systems and are amortizing the construction costs. A study by the Institute of Philippine Culture in 1985 comparing participatory communal systems with nonparticipatory ones showed that the former were functioning better and were more responsive to farmers' needs; they also had higher incremental yields per hectare, more improvements in IA performance, higher contributions to construction cost, and better repayment of construction loans (de los Reyes and Jopillo 1986).

Assessing the sustainability of an irrigation system is more complex, as many factors affecting this are beyond the control of NIA. Nevertheless, some work has been started under the NIA/Ford Foundation program for building IAs' capacity to manage credit, agricultural inputs, postharvest facilities and marketing. We have seen that IAs that develop such capacities are able to increase average production of paddy in their irrigation systems from 3.5–4 tons per hectare to 5.5–6 tons per hectare, and irrigation fee collection has reached 100 percent of current collectibles. The program for introducing activities beyond irrigation management, however, is still in the pilot stage.

In the national systems, 1,260 IAs have entered into O&M contracts with NIA, covering over 370,000 hectares of service area, representing almost 60 percent of the total service area of national systems in the country. These contracts vary from maintenance of canals and collection of irrigation fees to full takeover by IAs of O&M responsibilities. Another 463 IAs, covering almost 150,000 hectares or about 25 percent of the total service area, have been organized but have not yet entered into any contract with NIA for undertaking either canal maintenance or collection of irrigation fees.

Turnover in national systems has been slowed by lack of funds to pay the costs of retirement and separation pay and other benefits due to NIA staff that would be made redundant by handing over system management to IAs. However, compared to the situation before, when IAs did not take any responsibility at all, the participatory irrigation development program in the national systems can be considered quite successful.

LEARNING PROCESS

Because the participatory approach to organizing IAs was new to NIA back in the mid-1970s, a process had to be developed for this. When the first two pilot efforts were started in Nueva Ecija, NIA did not have staff that could function as community organizers, so staff with some experience in community organizing were recruited. There was considerable debate about methodologies to be used. We were not sure that the confrontational approach, advocated by followers of Saul Alinsky and used in urban slums, would be effective in rural irrigation systems, and our experience bore this out. More cooperative methods had to be applied. The two pilot projects were considered "learning laboratories." Our assumptions were that farmer participation in the tasks and decisionmaking during planning and construction of an irrigation project would enable them to form IAs willing to assume responsibilities for O&M, and that this participation could be developed by trained community organizers.

The results of the Nueva Ecija pilots substantiated these assumptions, but the processes developed needed further improvement. So two more pilot projects were established in Camarines Sur province for improving the integration of technical and institutional activities, for programming funds to support timely technical and institutional activities, for developing procedures for farmers to map paddy field elevations, for testing procurement procedures with farmers' participation and contracting with farmers' groups, for identifying further training needs of community organizers and engineers and for producing manuals on financial management and water management suitable for irrigation associations.

Regular feedback, evaluation and self-criticism were encouraged during planning and review workshops held monthly for community organizers

(COs), engineers, the field coordinator and the program supervisor. More frequent were the reflection sessions among the COs and the field coordinator for improving organizing strategies. Field processes, problems and results were documented by trained process documenters. Monthly documentation reports were reviewed and discussed by a Communal Irrigation Committee established at NIA's central office and chaired by the assistant administrator for operations (myself). This committee was a multidisciplinary group composed of individuals interested in the program, coming from NIA, the Asian Institute of Management, the Institute of Philippine Culture at the Ateneo de Manila, the International Rice Research Institute, the University of the Philippines at Los Baños and the Ford Foundation (Korten 1988). It provided overall guidance for implementing the pilot projects and the capacity-building programs. Its members attended workshops in the field, often serving as advisers and resource persons.

The pilot projects were among several rural development initiatives cited by David C. Korten in his 1980 analysis of learning process approaches to rural development. The four pilot programs enabled NIA to learn, first, how to be effective and then how to be efficient; the gradual spread of the program that followed helped NIA learn how to expand. This is a good way of understanding the learning process as it took form in the NIA case. However, our experience indicates that during the expansion of the program, we had improvements to make in the program's effectiveness and efficiency.

POLITICS AND WORKING WITH COMMUNITIES

A cardinal principle emphasized by COs when working with leaders and members of IAs is to keep out of partisan politics, as this will create factions that damage the IA. We learned this lesson early in the program. In one of the pilot projects in Nueva Ecija, there was political intervention by the municipal mayor in the election of the IA president. Two factions emerged, one supporting the mayor's candidate and another supporting a candidate who was favored by more farmers. The COs mobilized the farmers for confrontational tactics against the mayor. The result was a deadlock that delayed organization of the IA for almost two years. Since then, COs have employed various ways of keeping the IAs out of politics, including courtesy visits with municipal and other local government officials. COs explain the program and let everyone know that decisionmaking in the IA starts from the base. As this base is quite wide and generally uninterested in partisan politics, this has served to discourage political interference.

Women have important roles in IAs. Many IAs have women treasurers, given a widely held belief that women are more trustworthy with money. IA meetings usually have many women in attendance, most of them on behalf of husbands unable to attend due to work on the farm or other business, and some on their own behalf as farm managers.

IAs hold general meetings of members at the beginning and the end of every cropping season, first to agree on plans and later to assess accomplishments. Various committees are responsible for presenting plans and reporting progress. Special attention is given to preparing the annual budget of the IA and to presenting an annual income and expense accounting that explains the overall financial situation of the IA. These measures emphasize the accountability of the leaders to members and maintain members' confidence in their leadership. Special general assembly meetings of the IA are called when emergencies arise and when decisions have to be made that require approval of the whole membership.

Most IA business is carried out by smaller Turnout Service Associations (TSAs), each managing a subdivision of a larger irrigation scheme, referred to as a turnout area. Each TSA holds a monthly meeting of its members presided over by the TSA chairman. During this meeting, the implementation of IA plans for water distribution, maintenance of canals and structures, conflict management and irrigation fee collection are discussed. Problems that need action by the IA are identified. At the IA's monthly board of directors meeting, the TSA chairpersons brief the board on the status of activities at the turnout level and inform them of any problems that need board action. The TSA chairpersons then discuss with their TSA members any decisions taken by the board.

PROJECT MANAGEMENT

Since the program required a combination of attitudes and skills not available in the NIA at the time, a cadre of community organizers had to be formed. The initial group of six COs worked on the initial pilot projects from 1976 to 1979. After roles were well defined and understood and after appropriate strategies and procedures had been developed, gradual expansion into other provinces was started. In 1980, twenty-four regional pilot projects were started to develop understanding and capabilities at the regional level. Thirty COs were recruited and trained. The first six COs in the pilots became supervisors of the new COs. The following year (1981), twenty-four out of the sixty-eight provinces covered by NIA were brought into the program, and an additional ninety-nine COs were recruited and trained. In the same year, a pilot project for applying the new processes in national systems was established in the 3,000 hectare Buhi-Lalo River Irrigation Project in Camarines Sur.

As noted previously, the organizing process employed initially by NIA was not effective in getting farmers to assume responsibilities. The process used extension concepts for organizing—telling farmers what to do and how to do it. It did not involve them in decisionmaking for planning and constructing the irrigation facilities they were going to use and for which they were responsible. When the participatory approach was applied in Buhi-Lalo in 1981, fifteen COs were recruited and trained to use the process developed in the communal systems, modified to suit the situation in the national systems.

Successful application of the participatory approach in this pilot national system led to expansion of the program to thirty-seven other national systems covering about 35,000 hectares. These were mostly small national systems, less than 1,000 hectares in service area, plus a few medium-sized systems, all of which were a part of the nationwide improvement program for national systems under the National Irrigation Systems Improvement Project.

At the height of the participatory irrigation development program in 1986, NIA had more than 400 community organizers in communal and national systems. COs were carefully recruited according to the following criteria: college graduate with bachelor's degree in the social or agricultural sciences; willingness to live in the project area with farmer communities; physically fit, preferably single, and between twenty-one and thirty years of age; experience in organizing the rural or urban poor; abiding interest in the welfare of farmers; proficiency communicating in the local dialect, and residence in the region for at least one year during the previous five years.

Before being fielded, COs receive predeployment training covering, among other topics, an orientation on NIA and the farmers' participation program, basic management principles, group dynamics, strategies and methods of organizing and mobilizing farmers, project preconstruction activities, coordination with technical staff during the planning stage, and field exposure in an operating irrigation system to learn its various areas and operating procedures. COs are fielded before the start of construction or improvement of the physical facilities. With new construction, the lead time for organizing is about nine months; in systems improvement it is less, but not less than six months.

Before the start of construction or improvement, COs are given training on what will be done during this stage. This covers construction schedules, methods of mobilizing farmers' participation to meet the required 10 percent equity contribution, formation of work groups that will undertake construction work to be arranged with NIA, monitoring performance of the IA and its leaders, and guidance to the IAs for strengthening the associations during the construction period.

Soon after the start of construction, COs are trained in simplified financial management for IAs. This includes single-entry bookkeeping, preparation of financial plans and budgets, preparation of financial statements, collection of irrigation fees, payment of amortization and auditing procedures. Before construction is finished, COs are trained to assist IAs in developing O&M plans, preparing a cropping calendar, a water distribution plan, a maintenance plan, conflict management procedures, resource mobilization and on developing rules and regulations.

Supervision of COs is undertaken jointly by an irrigation organization program supervisor and the senior provincial irrigation engineer. The supervisor is an experienced CO who has been in the program for at least two years. He or she supervises the activities of the COs and maintains an overview of strategies for organizing training and assisting IAs, assessing institutional work programs and accomplishments, providing guidance to COs, and coordinating with NIA personnel. Administrative support and supervision of COs is provided by the senior engineer. These officials see to it that the activities of COs and NIA staff are well integrated, that the COs get their salaries and other needs met on time and that the COs' employment contracts with NIA are duly complied with. COs are hired by NIA on contractual basis. As such, they are not entitled to payment of vacation or sick leave or to government insurance benefits. To compensate for this, they are given 25 percent higher pay than regular employees in the same position pay classification.

To facilitate monitoring of their work, COs submit an annual institutional work plan, a more detailed monthly institutional work plan, a monthly report on institutional activities and accomplishments and a monthly narrative report containing a brief description of every issue or problem identified, how it is being dealt with, the people involved, lessons learned, skills developed and any recommendations.

At the start of the program, central government agencies insisted that COs maintain daily time records in accordance with official office hours of 8:00–12:00 A.M. and 1:00–5:00 P.M., Monday to Friday. They could not get paid for all their work because much of it involved meetings with farmers in the evenings and on Saturdays and Sundays. I had to explain the program and the nature of COs' work to the top auditor in NIA. Thereafter COs were allowed to collect their pay on the basis of a certification of services rendered, issued jointly by the COs' supervisors. Various other aspects of the program—compensation rates, contractual appointments, civil service status—were not consistent with existing government policies and practices. Such matters required initiative on my part to deal with the initial obstructions presented by the central bureaucracy. But with patient and persistent effort, we found ways to get necessary approvals and accommodations.

FINANCES

External assistance for the pilot project came from the Ford Foundation, as noted already. Because of the program's pioneering nature and its potential impact on irrigation development, Ford continued making grants even after the pilot stage as more support was needed for expanding it throughout the country. Every Ford Foundation grant was matched by NIA from its project funds to support the activities of the participatory irrigation management program.

After the initial expansion of the program to twenty-four provincial offices, the World Bank and the International Fund for Agricultural Development (IFAD) considered a proposal to fund a nationwide program for improving communal irrigation systems. They were impressed with the results of the pilots and the initial expansion work. When the World Bank and IFAD adopted our approach in planning a nationwide Communal Irrigation Development Project, this accelerated widespread application. The program also caught the attention of the U.S. Agency for International Development (USAID), which agreed to adopt our participatory approach in the Buhi-Lalo River irrigation project that it was assisting. As the program became institutionalized in NIA, all irrigation improvement projects, including those with foreign funding, included institutional development components based on farmers' participation.

SCALING UP

A constraint to immediate nationwide application of the participatory processes was a lack of capacity, at the regional and provincial levels, for implementing them. Thus regional pilots were first established. In 1980 regional directors were convened for a two-day workshop on the program for farmers' participation. During the workshop the regional directors each resolved to set up two pilot projects for developing regional capacity and demonstrating the processes to provincial staffs. At the end of the workshop, the budgets needed for the regional pilots were agreed upon.

Workshops were then held in each of the twelve NIA regions to select two systems in each, to reach a total of twenty-four regional pilots throughout the country. With guidance from experienced COs, each regional office selected new COs for the pilot projects. These COs were trained by the program supervisor, the field coordinator and the six experienced COs, with backstopping from the members of the Communinal Irrigation Committee at the national level. The experienced COs became program supervisors, which ensured the proper establishment and effective supervision within the regional pilots. Similar expansion and institutionalization of the participatory approach for all communal projects throughout the country was going on concurrently. By 1983, all communal projects of NIA were being implemented with farmer participation.

The expansion effort designed for thirty-seven national systems, covering 35,000 hectares, planned to turn over full responsibility to IAs in systems under 1,000 hectares, to be operated in the same way as communal systems. Or it would bring IAs into joint management agreements with NIA, assuming responsibility for O&M within their own zones, the hydrological subdivisions within a large system. This expansion program was to be funded under a World Bank-assisted project, the National Irrigation System Improvement Project (NISIP I and II), which started in 1977. It did not originally use a participatory approach, but after I became assistant administrator for operations in 1981, with control over NISIP, a component for "Regional Strengthening" was added. This had not been spelled out in much detail, so the World Bank could be persuaded that expanding the farmer participation program constituted "Regional Strengthening."

With NISIP funding, NIA had enough resources for limited expansion of the program. By 1985, six IAs were operating small national systems totalling 2,560 hectares, and twenty-two IAs had joint management arrangements for 26,640 hectares of irrigated area. However, means had to be found to continue further expansion after termination of NISIP, when NIA resources would be much less. Thus we tested a modified approach that needed fewer financial resources. Instead of employing college graduates with degrees in the social sciences or agriculture, we identified potential farmer-irrigator organizers from local communities, and we trained those farmers to help organize IAs, under the guidance of experienced COs. The intensity of rehabilitation was also reduced so that per-hectare costs were lower than under NISIP. The essential component of farmers' participation in planning and construction was retained, and this modified approach was tested in two systems totalling almost 3,000 hectares, with good results.

When the irrigation components of the government's Accelerated Agricultural Production Program and the Irrigation Operation Support Program were implemented in 1987 to 1991, the farmer-irrigator organizer role was adopted as the means for organizing farmers. The arrangements with farmers were changed by NIA unilaterally (unfortunately) into two types of contracts. Under a Type I contract, the IA undertakes canal maintenance and assists in water distribution for a specified length of canal, and NIA pays the IA 1,400 pesos (about US$70) per kilometer of canal. With a Type II contract, the IA collects irrigation service fees for NIA and assists in water distribution. It gets to keep a certain percentage of the fees it collects from members, on a sliding scale that gives the IA a strong incentive to increase its collections. The IA retains 2 percent of fees it collects totalling between 50 and 60 percent of the total amount due; 5 percent of collections between 60 and 70 percent; 10 percent of collections between 70 and 90 percent, and 15 percent of all collections above 90 percent.

In terms of IA capacity building, these contracts are not as good as the joint management agreement previously in force. NIA has apparently had to resort to this alternative to be able to continue the farmers' participation program without having to terminate O&M staff who would otherwise be displaced. Staff reduction is very much resisted by many people, so pressing ahead with farmer participation is difficult if it results in laying off some NIA staff. Recent experience in NIA has shown the deficiencies in these newer arrangements, however, and the agency seems now to be moving back toward the previous agreements on joint management, where terms are negotiated between NIA and the IAs rather than laid down unilaterally.

By 1995, over 350,000 hectares were under participatory irrigation management. The breakdown is as follows: 472 IAs have Type I contracts covering 151,027 hectares; 348 IAs have Type II contracts covering 100,680 hectares; 385 IAs have both Type I and Type II contracts covering another 99,276 hectares; 22 IAs have joint management arrangements as discussed above, and 33 IAs have taken over all O&M on 11,617 hectares.

BENEFITS OF HINDSIGHT

Knowing what I know now, I do not think we could have done things much differently. I feel that the actions taken were probably the most feasible responses to the situation prevailing in the irrigation sector at the time and within NIA in particular. Although I was in top management in NIA for about eight years and held at the same time, for several months, the positions of assistant administrator for operations and assistant administrator for finance and management, and had full support from three successive NIA administrators, many influences on NIA top management were beyond our control.

Farmer participation in the irrigation sector is still not as robust and extensive as we envisioned when the program was started, but, then, few efforts can achieve all of their aspirations. This program has provided important contributions toward making the agricultural sector in the Philippines more productive, more self-sustaining and more democratic. Moreover, it has provided ideas and models for participatory irrigation development in other Asian countries—Sri Lanka, Indonesia, Thailand, Nepal, India and Bangladesh—to mention just those places where our NIA experience has been specifically drawn upon.

11 Farmer Organization in Gal Oya: Improving Irrigation Management in Sri Lanka

C. M. Wijayaratna and Norman Uphoff

In Sri Lanka, by the end of the 1970s it was recognized that the easiest and cheapest sources of irrigation in the country were already being utilized. If irrigation was to contribute to redressing rural poverty as well as meeting the increased demand for food arising from population and income growth, the efficiency of irrigation water use would need to be increased. Most irrigation systems were unable to serve adequately all the farmers within their respective command areas. Unequal and unreliable distribution of irrigation water was common. Unkept operation and maintenance schedules, lack of collaboration between water users and system managers, and faulty physical structures contributed to this state of affairs (Svendsen and Wijayaratna 1982; Murray-Rust and Moore 1984). Irrigation planners and managers needed to go beyond augmenting supply to make changes in institutional structures and procedures.

The government of Sri Lanka and the U.S. Agency for International Development (USAID) recognized this, and in 1979 they launched a major irrigation improvement project. This was to include both physical rehabilitation and the establishment of farmer organizations to improve water management. The work was to be started in Gal Oya, the largest and, reputedly, most disorganized and deteriorated system in Sri Lanka. The government's intention was to devise and validate approaches that could be used throughout all major irrigation schemes in the country to improve irrigation efficiency and productivity.

IRRIGATION DEVELOPMENT IN SRI LANKA

Sri Lanka has a tradition of irrigation more than two thousand years old. For more than a millennium, impressive civilizations flourished, based on food and financial resources drawn from a vast network of major and minor irrigation schemes (Brohier 1933). For reasons not yet agreed upon, the irrigation systems and the prosperous civilization they supported collapsed after the thirteenth century (Indrapala 1971). Only at the beginning of the twentieth century was large-scale irrigation revived, spearheaded by the British colonial government's Irrigation Department (ID).

Established in 1900, the ID restored many old irrigation schemes throughout the north and east of Sri Lanka. This area, known as the Dry Zone, receives monsoon rains only once a year and depends on irrigation for growing a second crop of rice that makes the difference between survival and starvation for peasant families. Given the colonial tradition and the professional orientation of engineers, the ID saw no need for farmer participation in the operation and maintenance of irrigation systems. Farmers were simply expected to follow the instructions given by system managers. Because the Dry Zone had become depopulated during the preceding centuries, the government in this century sought to restore Dry Zone agriculture and villages by supplying irrigation water from large reservoirs and by establishing settlement schemes that took in households from surrounding areas or from thousands of communities in the overpopulated Wet Zone.

The Gal Oya irrigation system, with its complex network of main canals, supplementary reservoirs, branch canals, distributary canals and field channels, was designed to irrigate about 50,000 hectares. However the area actually cultivated, expanded due to population pressure, was greater by some unknown extent. The Left Bank command area was planted mostly in rice and covered half of this area. This was where the farmer organization effort was started in 1981.

The most productive farming in Gal Oya was done in parts of the Right Bank and in the central portion of the system served directly by the Gal Oya river, because these areas had better water supply. The population in these areas was mostly Tamil and Muslim. In the Left Bank, in contrast, Sinhalese households were in the majority. Most of these were settled in the head and middle areas of the Left Bank, while Right Bank Tamil and Muslim households were located downstream. This ethnic distribution complicated the normal problems between head- and tail-end farmers.

Because of the serious deterioration of its physical system with silted-up channels, broken structures and maldistribution of water (and because it had some of the most severe poverty), the Left Bank area of Gal Oya was chosen in 1978 for a major rehabilitation effort by USAID and the government of Sri Lanka. Recognizing that simply restoring the physical system would not make lasting gains in productivity and welfare, the main objective of the project was to improve water management. Promoting farmer organizations and active involvement of farmers in water management was a belated, but integral, part of the project.

IRRIGATION MANAGEMENT PRIOR TO
FORMING FARMER ORGANIZATIONS

Reconnaissance surveys conducted by the Agrarian Research and Training Institute (ARTI) showed that the problems in Gal Oya, particularly the Left Bank, were far greater than acknowledged in the project's documentation (ARTI 1982; Svendsen and Wijayaratna 1982; and Wijayaratna 1986). The reservoir seldom filled up as planned because its water harvest was inadequate. Eighty percent of control structures were broken or missing. The amounts and timing of water delivered throughout the system seldom matched the schedules previously agreed on and announced. Some head-end areas got a continuous supply of water, while the middle reaches received only unreliable deliveries, and most areas in the tail-end never received water during the dry season. Even some head-end areas suffered water shortages because of haphazard delivery and wasteful use. The surveys also provided evidence of the lack of user participation in operation and maintenance activities and in decisionmaking generally.

The project commenced in late 1979 and was completed at the end of 1985. The ID as the implementing agency was assisted by a U.S. firm for the engineering work. Responsibility for socioeconomic research, monitoring and evaluation, and the formation of farmer organizations was assigned to ARTI. The Rural Development Committee of Cornell University, having at the time a cooperative agreement with USAID to promote participatory development, provided technical assistance to support ARTI's work.

ARTI and Cornell researchers worked as a team in this effort, developing and testing participatory strategies to organize farmer beneficiaries in irrigation management. The formation of irrigation organizations was based on hydrological boundaries, following the respective command areas served by the different field channels and distributary canals. About 19,000 households were thought to be cultivating about 22,000 hectares of irrigated land in the Left Bank command area. Both figures turned out to be underestimates, because they did not account for squatters or for area unofficially (or illegally) brought under cultivation.

THE EVOLUTION OF CONCEPTS AND
STRATEGIES OF LEARNING PROCESS

Analysis of the system's performance prior to beginning the project clearly showed the need for farmer participation in irrigation management. Organized self-management efforts by users at the field channel level could yield some benefits. However, in a large irrigation scheme such as Gal Oya, such localized efforts were unlikely to bring significant returns systemwide due to the interdependence of the hydrological units within the system. Farmers needed to become organized to make inputs, at least of ideas and suggestions, at all levels.

One reason that there was no farmer organization in Gal Oya was the differing social and cultural backgrounds found in this very heterogeneous settlement scheme (Govt. of Ceylon 1971, 40). In addition, with no bonds of kinship or village solidarity, cooperation was more the exception than rule. In much of the rest of Sri Lanka, there had traditionally been, at village level, an irrigation headman (*vel vidane*), a hereditary role passed from father to son. This local notable, in return for overseeing water distribution and channel maintenance, received a share of the harvest. Under British colonial rule, this role became more of a bureaucratic than a community institution. Because Gal Oya was a settlement scheme, such headmen, if they existed, had little influence or acceptance. Sri Lankans had a traditional practice of communal voluntary labor, known as *shramadana*, which could be mobilized for cleaning and repairing channels and dams. But such social organization was rare in Gal Oya. We were, however, able to capitalize on local knowledge and norms concerning how irrigation had traditionally been managed.

Although our mandate was to work with farmers, the ARTI-Cornell team examined the problems faced by the irrigation agency as well. Engineers could not carry out their tasks and get proper feedback and cooperation from farmers due to many reasons.

1. Problems arising from poor system design and inoperable control structures made equitable distribution of irrigation water an almost impossible task.

2. Disparity between planned and actual command area, due to encroachers increasing the cultivated area by 30 percent over the preceding thirty years, made the limited water supply all the more inadequate.

3. Insufficient allocations of funds for operation and maintenance compounded the problem of a lack of qualified staff willing to serve in the area.

4. There were few incentives and rewards for staff to do good work.

5. Local politicians altered agreed-upon schedules to benefit a few influential farmers.

6. No network of farmer organizations at various levels with a good information system capable of monitoring and following up agreed-upon schedules existed.

We anticipated that consultation with farmers when planning the physical rehabilitation and redesign of irrigation facilities would take care of the major drawbacks and would provide an opportunity to mobilize the local skills of the farmers for improving system performance.

Having analyzed the shortcomings of previous approaches to farmer organization in Sri Lanka (Uphoff and Wanigaratne 1982), and appreciating the heterogeneity of the agroenvironmental and social scene in Gal Oya, we concluded that rather than introduce a pre-formed organizational design, we should facilitate the evolution of organizations by the farmers themselves. Rather than promote a *model*, we sought to establish a *process* that would enable farmers to take responsibility for co-management of the irrigation system and to expand organized farmer efforts into other domains, once they had improved irrigation system operation.

This meant making a planned intervention that was strong enough to generate an internal dynamic of the community toward local organization but controlled enough not to dominate and direct such efforts of the community. The methodology required farmers to develop an understanding of their problems and needs, then to explore how these needs could be met through their cooperation and organized efforts.

To accomplish this, we recruited, trained and deployed young persons who were called institutional organizers, IOs for short. Their role was modeled after that of the community organizers already helping to improve irrigation in the Philippines (see Chapter 11). Their role was also similar to that of the social organizers described by Akhter Hameed Khan in Chapter 2 on the Orangi Pilot Project in Pakistan. To be successful, IOs should respect people and their ideas, values and beliefs. IOs should have faith and confidence in people and trust in farmers' ability to solve their local problems. They should be facilitators rather than instructors, promoting interaction among farmers to find solutions for their problems and encouraging the development of group consciousness. IOs should not do things for the farmers, such as obtaining fertilizer, because that would make them dependent on the IOs. The purpose of the role was to make farmers self-reliant. IOs engage in discussions with the farmers, with a view to getting them to analyze their own problems. When organizing farmer groups, IOs only promote the concept of organization, leaving decisions about membership, structure and rules to the members. In Gal Oya, farmers rejected the kind of complicated structure most government-instigated organizations had introduced, in favor of a simple structure based on farmer-representatives (FRs) selected by each field channel group throughout the system.

We explicitly adopted a "learning process" approach, rather than the "blueprint" approach that underpins most project planning and implementation. Because of their knowledge of the Philippine program described in Chapter 10, David C. Korten, author of the seminal article (1980) on learning process, and Benjamin U. Bagadion were brought to Sri Lanka by Cornell as consultants during the first year. Korten participated on the reconnaissance team that visited Gal Oya in January 1980, along with Wijayaratna, Uphoff and other ARTI and Cornell staff to begin planning the farmer organization effort.[1]

Project Implementation—Working with Communities

The institutional organizers were the key to the progress we made in Gal Oya. They were young men and women, university graduates in social sciences, agriculture or development studies, who had at least two of the following qualifications:

1. personal experience in rice farming,

2. experience in the Dry Zone, having worked or lived there,

3. past participation in village organizations, and

4. ability and willingness to live and work in rural communities in remote areas.[2]

ARTI managed to avoid interference by politicians to ensure a fair selection during recruitment, which is a story in itself. Since most of the applicants were from farm families, they did not feel socially distanced from rural people by their higher education. These qualifications contributed to getting IOs who could understand and win the confidence of farmers, quickly comprehend the tasks of organizing farmers and withstand the difficult conditions prevailing within farming communities. Thirty-two out of over 800 applicants were selected for the first batch of IOs. The number of applicants reflected the high unemployment level of educated youth in Sri Lanka, not the attractiveness of the job.

Training of IOs. During a six-week training program, IOs were exposed to the concepts and methods of a locality-specific approach and to techniques of organizing people, communicating with others and working with groups. To develop the requisite understanding and skills, there were lectures, discussions, role playing and group exercises. During four weeks of training in the field, IOs went in small groups into different communities with a particular topic or task each day. This acquainted them with farmers' situations. Each evening, the small groups' observations were discussed at length by the whole group. This practical field exposure, which included working with local people as part of the training, helped IOs learn how to enter communities, establish rapport and win farmer confidence. They learned how to familiarize themselves with the social and physical environment of villages, how to study farmer problems and needs as well as technical issues for irrigated agriculture, and how to establish a process of dialogue for problem identification and solution.

Once assigned to a specific area as a member of a team, IOs were expected to get acquainted quickly with the area's geography: location, climate and soils; sociocultural aspects: formal and informal organizations and leadership patterns within the community; economic factors: economic institutions, major occupations, income levels from agriculture, family budgeting, credit and marketing; political factors: political dynamics in community organization, political party identification and influence of party politics in water management; and administrative infrastructure: administrative organizations at different levels and efficiency of coordination between these levels and overlapping jurisdictions. Based on this information, each IO was expected to prepare profiles on the area concerning irrigation and water management, community organization, land use, land tenure and agriculture.

Deployment in Teams. In March 1981, six teams of IOs were deployed to different areas of the Left Bank. These areas covered 2,227 hectares with 1,686 farmers cultivating along seventy-one field channels. Subsequent teams were introduced to additional areas so that the total area covered by IO activity under the project was eventually 7,500 hectares. (This does not include about 4,500 hectares downstream where IOs worked with Tamil-speaking farmers for a year before threats from the separatist Tamil Tigers caused us to close down this work. The Tamil IOs were making good progress until they were withdrawn.)

The first year of the program, Gal Oya was gripped by a greater-than-usual water shortage, with the main reservoir only one-quarter full at the start of the dry season. We even considered postponing the start of the program because we feared that if there were a crop failure (a distinct possibility), farmers might blame our program for this and be more reluctant to participate the following year. (Most social scientists would predict greater likelihood of conflict when there is aggravated resource scarcity.) But the IOs, who were already living in the villages and being asked what they could do to help in this crisis, wanted to proceed. So we agreed, with the proviso that they never impose anything on farmers, always being sure that what would be done was of farmers' own choosing.

To everyone's surprise, within six weeks, channels in 90 percent of the pilot area had been cleaned by voluntary labor, water was being equitably rotated among farmers and about one-sixth of the water being issued was being saved and donated to downstream farmers. This demonstration of farmer cooperation and generosity in response to IOs' initiatives got the program off to a rapid and very positive start (Uphoff 1992, 54–107).

The IOs were appointed on yearly contracts, however, without permanent employment or career prospects, so their turnover rate was quite high. Of the 169 IOs we trained and fielded in six batches, only eight (5 percent) remained at the end of the project in December 1985. The average length of service was about nine months, and the effective IO presence in the field averaged about thirty. Nevertheless, they were immensely effective and successful because of their methodology and morale. Each time most of the cadre left for permanent jobs elsewhere, those few IOs who remained helped train new ones, and did so effectively.

Depending on hydrological boundaries and the number of farmers served by the given irrigation area, between four and seven IOs were fielded in each team. During the initial stages, each IO worked with between sixty and seventy farmers. With increased farmer cooperation, greater experience on the part of IOs, and, given the continuing loss of IOs, this number soon increased to between 100 and 200 farmers per IO, the exact number depending on hydrology. By the end of the project, once farmer organizations were in place, the number of farmers per IO reached almost 2,000.

While individual IOs were each responsible for a particular area within the assigned distributary canal command, overall responsibility for the entire area rested with the whole group. The IOs seemed to form, quite naturally, tight-knit teams that helped each other in identifying and solving problems with the farmers. Frequent team meetings helped them share their experiences and solve problems. If an IO was not available for some work, another member of the team would look after that task. Female IOs working late in the evenings (about 30 percent of IOs were women) could ask male IOs in their group to travel with them after dark.

Process Documentation. Mistakes are bound to happen in the process of learning about farmers' situation and in trying out promising approaches to obtain effective participation. It is important that these mistakes are quickly identified and appropriate adjustments made in the program based upon lessons learned. A monitoring program called process documentation (PD) was established.Some IOs were assigned to spend half of their time documenting the process of social dynamics generated as a result of the IOs' entry into the farming community. This had some advantages in that the PD was done by someone fully knowledgeable of the conditions and difficulties of farmer organizing. There was no mistrust from other IOs, and the team discussion of PD reports before they were sent to ARTI in Colombo introduced quick corrections and redirections in the program, based on what was being observed and learned in the field. What we lost in objectivity by this combining of roles we more than gained in better self-management.

The usual approach in development programs has been to conduct before and after evaluations to rectify defects. Our continuous monitoring and evaluation meant that the IOs themselves were identifying problems and possible solutions. About 10 percent of IOs' effort went into PD work initially. As IOs' work increased, this percentage declined, but by then we had developed through the PD some reasonably good ideas to work with.

Supervision. An experienced government officer was in charge of the overall supervision and administration of the program at field level. He was assisted by an IO project coordinator chosen from among the IOs. Each team had its own coordinator. A research officer at the ARTI head office in Colombo, appointed by the institute director, was personally responsible for the overall project. As it turned out, because of constraints on ARTI personnel and funding, plus the separatist violence that increased during the years of the project (Gal Oya crosses the boundary between Sinhalese and Tamil settlements in eastern Sri Lanka), head office supervision became much less than planned. But this may have been just as well, given that the IO program itself was set up to be self-reliant. The IO cadre proved to be self-managing and self-correcting in spite of—or, perhaps, because of—our limitations at ARTI.[3]

Facilitating the Formation of Farmer Groups. IOs met farmers initially one-on-one, then in small groups, and eventually got together for discussions all of the farmers (ten to twenty) cultivating along a field channel, all getting water from the same source. In this process, they encouraged active participation and facilitated unity and cooperation among farmers. IOs helped farmers take initiative and assume responsibility for solving common problems, motivated farmers toward more equitable distribution of water and encouraged better practices for water management.

Our strategy was to get farmers to work together informally before starting a formal organization, creating a demand for organization rather than just supplying farmers with it. Our motto was, "Work first, organize second." Eventually, explicit organizations were established at field channel level, with the broad objectives of improving operation and maintenance, reducing conflicts and having better interaction with ID staff.

In farmers' opinion, elections divide people. So each group, when ready to become formally organized, selected a farmer-representative by consensus. FRs functioned as facilitators for collective action and as spokespersons for the groups in meetings with officials. Being an FR was not a permanent or paid position, and the role generally rotated among members. A farmer-representative who was ineffective or failed to keep the confidence of the group was usually replaced, a sign that members took their organization seriously.

Federating Farmer Organizations. Field channel groups were federated, when members were ready, into a distributary canal organization (DCO) made up of their farmer-representatives. These same FRs also participated in a larger area council, which met periodically to consider issues affecting all the field channels and distributary canals served by a main or branch canal. Finally, a project management committee was created for the whole Left Bank, made up of FRs chosen by the area councils to represent them in decisionmaking with officials. In 1982, responding to a farmer's request, the district minister agreed to have farmer-chosen FRs participate in the district agriculture committee, a body that he chaired and that included members of parliament plus all the heads of relevant government departments (agriculture, irrigation, crop insurance). The DAC gave farmers another channel for expressing their needs and advancing their interests.

Even during the initial stages of forming organizations, farmers used them to achieve some benefits beyond irrigation. The end-of-project evaluation conducted by ARTI (1986) reports that the farmer committeess were dealing with input marketing, price of rice, crop insurance and savings and loans. Subsequently, Gal Oya farmer organizations have diversified their group activities to a still greater extent, as discussed below. By the end of 1985, over 60 DCOs were in place, representing over 500 field channel groups, and feeding farmer ideas into four area councils and an apex organization that could make overall improvements in system management.

INDICATORS OF SUCCESS

Lack of farmer participation in irrigation system management and a wide communication gap between the ID and farmers were highlighted in pre-rehabilitation studies. For example, the master plan of the Gal Oya Project stated:

> the farmers have absolutely no discipline in water management and are accustomed to take all they want when the water flows by their head gates (Part II, 37).

By contrast, the postproject evaluation for USAID done by the International Science and Technology Institute concluded:

one of the most important outcomes of this project is the change in attitude, communication and behavior among farmers and government personnel that has occurred in Gal Oya (ISTI 1985, 4).

As noted above, during the severe water shortage of the 1981 dry season, IOs mobilized farmer skills and cooperation for managing water
more carefully. Water-saving measures such as rotational distribution
within field channels and channel cleaning to reduce water losses from
seepage and percolation were undertaken by farmers even before physical
improvements were made in the system. These measures practically doubled water use efficiency. During the 1982 dry season, with even less water
in the reservoir than in 1981, farmers managed to get a successful crop
from 5,000 hectares when the ID had calculated there was only enough
water for 2,000 hectares. These voluntary measures by farmers won the
respect of engineers and other officials. By the end of the project, overall
water issues per hectare had been reduced by almost half, with greater
farmer satisfaction than before the project, when more water per hectare
had been issued from the reservoir. Evaluation studies done for the International Irrigation Management Institute confirmed this and found almost
a five-fold increase in the amount of rice produced per unit of water issued.
(See Figures 11.1 and 11.2.)

During project implementation, dialogue between farmers and ID staff
greatly improved with the development of farmer organizations. There
were joint meetings to redesign the channel network, monthly meetings
between FRs and field-level officers of the different departments, periodic
meetings with district officials, and formal representation of farmers on
the district agriculture committee. Radical improvements took place in the
mutual perceptions of officials and farmers as a result of cooperation promoted by organizers.

The average annual cost of the Gal Oya farmer organization program
during 1981–85 was less than two million rupees, about US$72,000 at the
prevailing exchange rate (ARTI 1986). Figured against an area of 10,100
hectares and 8,000 farm families (about 40,000 beneficiaries) served by the
program, the cost per hectare was US$7.10 (in 1985 prices) and US$9.00 per
farm family. It should be noted that this represents the cost to the Sri
Lankan government, which paid for the farmer organization program as
part of its local contribution—salaries and benefits of IOs, ARTI
researchers and staff, operating costs (travel, supplies, etc.) and costs of
training. This does not include the cost of consultants provided from Cornell, which was paid for by USAID.

The farmer organization component was only about 5 percent of total
project cost. A benefit:cost ratio of about 1.5:1—well above what most

Figure 11.1   Changes in Dry Season Water Duty[1] in Gal Oya

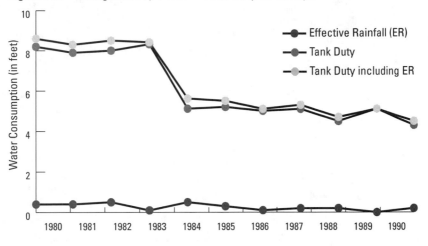

[1] Duty = water released from reservoir in acre-feet, divided by number of acres irrigated

Source: Study conducted by Engineering Consultants Ltd. and Associated Development Research Consultants, for International Irrigation Management Institute, 1992.

donor-assisted projects can show—has been calculated for the first two years of the program. This did not include many definite but difficult-to-quantify benefits and did not capitalize some of the expenditures that could reasonably have been spread out over more than two years (for example, training and capital costs). Moreover, this computation ignored some important benefits:

1. reduction in disputes (even murders) over water,

2. less breakage of irrigation structures by farmers,

3. farmer inputs to better designs for physical rehabilitation,

4. fewer crop failures due to more efficient water use,

5. economies of scale generated through group action,

6. more and better use of complementary inputs such as fertilizer, due to improved reliability and equity in water distribution, and

7. improved self-reliance within the farming community.

When the government introduced a water-user fee for operation and maintenance in 1984, Gal Oya farmers paid 700,000 rupees the first year (Uphoff 1992, 255). The fee collection program elsewhere was a failure. In

Figure 11.2   Production per Unit of Water in Gal Oya

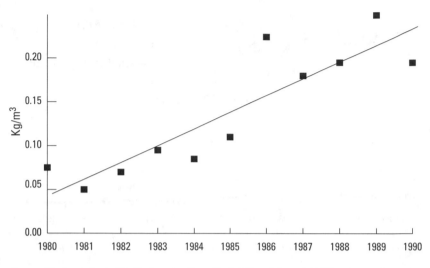

Source: Study conducted by Engineering Consultants Ltd. and Associated Development Research Consultants, for International Irrigation Management Institute, 1992.

recent years, the ID has reduced its expenditures on operation and mainte-nance considerably in real terms. However, this has been compensated for in Gal Oya by organized farmer inputs to carry out operation and mainte-nance activities.

The official end-of-project evaluation for USAID calculated an improb-able 47 percent internal rate of return for the Gal Oya project (ISTI 1985). ARTI and Cornell, in a more conservative internal evaluation, estimated this figure to be between 16 and 24 percent, depending on the assumptions made (ARTI 1986). In any case the rate was considerably higher than aver-age for donor-funded projects. A postproject evaluation commissioned by the International Irrigation Management Institute estimated the rate of return on investment to have been 24 percent (Aluwihare and Kikuchi 1991, 45). We are fairly sure that at least half of the project's benefits were attributable to the performance of the farmer organizations, which absorbed only a fraction of the project's cost.

The spreading effects and expanded benefits of the Gal Oya effort have been many. The demonstrated improvements in irrigation efficiency there led the government to promote and support farmer organizations in all the major irrigation schemes in Sri Lanka through its irrigation management division. At the end of 1988, a cabinet decision made "participatory irri-gation management" national policy for the whole country (Uphoff 1992, 261–2). All major schemes are now to be managed by a joint project committee made up of farmer-representatives and officials, with farmers in the majority and with a farmer serving as chairman. We had hoped for an outcome like this when we started in 1980, but we had no right to expect this would actually come to pass, given the resistance to farmer participation in ID and government circles.

Moreover, Gal Oya has contributed to international experience regarding participatory management. Many previous and present professional staff of the International Irrigation Management Institute have been involved with Gal Oya, and there have been contributions to the initiation of similar programs outside Sri Lanka. Uphoff and Ganewatte helped to establish a similar program using association organizers in Nepal, beginning with the Sirsia-Dudhaura system under a USAID-funded project there. Based on his Gal Oya experience, Wijayaratna initiated a program of restructuring base organizations and introduced a self-evaluation process for farmer organizations in the Bicol region of the Philippines. This effort was undertaken jointly by the International Irrigation Management Institute, the National Irrigation Administration, and Bicol University (Lauraya et al. 1990).

On the Left Bank, ten years after ARTI and Cornell left Gal Oya, there are over 500 field channel groups and 58 well-organized DCOs. These maintain a system-level farmer federation to handle business activities. As of September 1995, the DCOs had invested over $18,000 in shares in the system-level organization, and in addition had operating funds averaging about $1,000 plus assets like tractors. The system-level federation had engaged in business with a volume of about $100,000 during the first nine months of 1995, selling fertilizer, seed and other goods and services, so it was beginning to be a significant economic operator on behalf of farmer-members. The DCOs plan to pool all their resources, obtain a bank loan with that guarantee, establish four mills to convert their unhusked crop into polished rice, purchase two vehicles for transportation and establish contact with companies outside Gal Oya, to strengthen their bargaining capacity so that farmers get a better return from their production. Farmer-representatives said, "We learned a lot [from ARTI and Cornell] about water management in the 1980s. Let us show you what we have accomplished on our own since you left." This is the kind of self-reliant spirit we hoped for.

PROBLEMS, POLITICS AND BENEFITS OF HINDSIGHT

The farmer organization effort in Gal Oya faced many difficulties during its implementation from 1980 to 1985. Moreover, institutionalizing farmer responsibility for water management in that irrigation system and extending this experience to similar situations elsewhere in the country faced many constraints. We could have been much more successful with more time, resources and backing. Most of these constraints were associated with the external environment, bureaucratic procedures and resistance, land tenure problems and other issues. No in-depth discussion can be undertaken here, most of them having been treated in Uphoff (1992). Only a few main issues will be addressed.

At the peak of the organizational effort in 1984, it appeared to us that the sustainability of farmers' organizations was uncertain mainly due to the lack of formal support from the bureaucracy. Whatever support was being received from officials was initially quite personalized, coming from those few who perceived value in the concept of user participation. Others accepted participation as a kind of "special favor" to farmers. As farmers responded positively and productively to our bottom-up approach of institution building, the bureaucracy gradually took a more positive attitude toward farmer participation. ID staff became sympathetic to the aims of the program and agreed to share knowledge and authority with farmers. Personal experience suggests three main reasons for the change in attitudes of the ID staff.

- Farmers demonstrated their ability to handle operation and maintenance activities and conflict management at local levels.

- ID staff were pushed to accept farmer participation by their government's project agreement with USAID, by the efforts of the ARTI/Cornell group and by the support of a few officials within the parent ministry.

- A few senior ID officials, such as S. Senthinathan, the deputy director for Gal Oya, demonstrated commendable dedication, motivation and commitment to improving irrigation management with farmers.

There is no accepted formula for establishing user associations for irrigation management such that one can establish user associations once and for all and leave it them continue successfully by themselves. Both the form and machinery of participation have to be continuously adjusted in order to find solutions from day-to-day experience and from lessons learned through the process. The productivity and sustainability of participation will be promoted only through a progressive expansion of farmers' roles in development decisions.

Important characteristics of such institutional arrangements aimed at sustainability of farmer organizations include

- institutionalization of the learning process of institution building,

- increasing benefits to members, eventually through diversified profit-making ventures beyond irrigation,

- continuing adjustments in the organization to cope with new demands,

- agency reorientation and structural changes in the bureaucracy in favor of participatory management,

- legal support and protection for farmer organizations,

- adequate information systems and training,

- self-correcting mechanisms through participatory monitoring and evaluation,

- supportive financial policies and provisions, and

- political will to accept participatory management.

These need not all be tackled simultaneously and in advance. There was little political or bureaucratic support for our venture at the outset and no legal recognition of farmer organizations until after the project ended in 1985. Up to a certain point, the groups were able to function effectively based on social (consensual) authority rather than on political (formal) authority. Mostly, we depended on the fact that the government had agreed with USAID to undertake this experiment, and, thanks to farmer cooperation, impressive and visible results were achieved quickly in the first season. Over time, we were able to build various elements, however imperfectly and incompletely, into the program. Success depended on getting enough of these elements established well enough and soon enough, rather than creating all the ideal preconditions in advance, which is the way development projects are usually prescribed.

Another factor, difficult to write about, is the importance of the quality and commitment of the people involved. We were most fortunate to be able to bring together in this venture an unusually fine set of people in a great variety of roles. This was not necessarily predictable, but our experience was that the program, with its commitment to participatory means and equitable results, seemed to bring out the best in many persons—in farmers, IOs, engineers, top officials in government, and, to be frank, in ourselves. Once we got into the field, the first positive breakthroughs—especially during a dry season when the reservoir was only one-quarter full, and farmer and IO efforts got fields successfully cultivated that had not had dry-season crops for years—the program acquired a momentum that carried it along.

For improving irrigation water management, farmer participation is most effective when it begins with the initial stages of project development, including the stages of plan formulation and design. Such involvement is part of the ideal conditions for genuine participation, for a true partnership between farmers and government. However, in Sri Lanka this was not the case with most of the past rehabilitation efforts for major irrigation systems. The government had to be willing to bridge the gap between farmers and officials, if there was to be an atmosphere of cooperation to move forward with a participatory approach. It was fortuitous that the project was able to enlist the sustained efforts of ARTI, Cornell and a large, if transient, cadre of IOs who could catalyze a needed but unprecedented partnership with rural communities.

In promoting people's association and cooperation with each other, the ARTI-Cornell team supported methods and rules of farmers' own choosing, so they would regard the associations as their own. The catalysts used for this intervention—the institutional organizers—approached communities with trained but open minds, showing respect for what the communities had to offer. They promoted interaction among farmers, helping them find their own solutions to problems, with the goal of making farmers self-reliant.

We now see considerable potential in Gal Oya for the further intensification of irrigated agriculture. The foundations laid and the progress in participatory management there make it easier than in most other places to embark on new productive enterprises for better overall use of the area's land and water resources. Farmers support these efforts to gain control over the situation they face under the current policies of open economy in Sri Lanka.

We know that, just as it was important during the initial intervention to be always open to new ideas and directions coming from the farmers and the larger environment, the program and structure must continually evolve. If farmer organizations are to maintain their vitality, they must keep changing, growing and altering, according to the wishes and capabilities of the local communities. This is the most gratifying outcome of the Gal Oya experience: that farmers there are continuing to innovate with the organizational capacities they have created to meet the ever-changing circumstances under which rural people live in the contemporary world.

NOTES

1. Wijayaratna coordinated the program for its first three years, while Uphoff coordinated the Cornell involvement from 1980 to 1985. The program

involved a number of other faculty and students from Cornell in research, advising or evaluating.

2. Later, nongraduates with secondary school qualifications were recruited as IOs when the farmer organization program expanded under a follow-on USAID project in Polonnaruwa district. They also proved quite effective, but their way had been paved by the graduate IOs, who had won acceptance of the farmer-participatory approach from engineers and other officials.

3. We will not go into all of these problems, including the decline in ARTI's administrative support for the program. After Wijayaratna had served as program coordinator for three years and left to do his Ph.D. at Cornell, there were six different program heads in the next three years, indeed, one of them a research assistant for nine months. Several Sri Lankans hired by Cornell as local training consultants (particularly Sena Ganewatte and Nalini Kasynathan) provided excellent and much-needed continuity during this period.

12 Integrated Crop Pest Management with Farmer Participation in Indonesia

Ida Nyoman Oka

Rice is the major staple of the Indonesian diet, supplying nearly 60 percent of the total caloric intake of the average person, and even more for the poor of the country. But significant amounts of rice were imported regularly until the mid-1980s. Between 1960 and 1970, the yearly rice imports averaged about one million tons, increasing, in the face of growing population, to above two million tons by the end of the 1970s. While Indonesia's population growth rate has decreased from 2.4 percent in the 1970s to 1.4 percent now, its population will likely be over 200 million by the year 2000, up from 164 million in 1985. Food production must continue to increase in a sustainable fashion in order to feed this large and growing population, and to provide every person with a diet sufficient to meet at least their daily caloric needs.

A comprehensive food intensification program was initiated by the national government as early as 1969, with the following objectives:

- achieve and maintain self-sufficiency in food,

- increase farmers' income,

- provide job opportunities and alleviate poverty,

- increase foreign earnings through exports of agricultural products, and

- provide strong support for the rapidly expanding industrial, business and service sectors.

To achieve these objectives, four programs were promoted: intensification, diversification, rehabilitation and extensification (bringing new areas under cultivation). Of these, the intensification program has contributed most to increased food production. However, the drive to intensify yields has caused serious environmental problems, due in large part to the excessive use of agrochemicals. Most significant is pesticide use, which has contributed to ecological and other damage as farmers used pesticides far beyond the doses that are practically necessary.

Problems associated with pesticide use included increased health hazards to humans and animals, the emergence of pesticide-resistant strains of common pests, and large foreign exchange costs (pesticides were mostly imported or had a large import content). To deal with these problems, the government adopted a strategy of *integrated crop pest management*, known as IPM. This has resulted in dramatic, widespread and sustainable improvement in farming practices that have lowered production costs and reduced health and environmental hazards without compromising yields. Indeed, yields often increased as a result.

INTENSIFYING RICE PRODUCTION

The policy package for food intensification launched in the late 1960s included a number of measures, both technical and socioeconomic, including

- large-scale planting of modern high-yielding varieties,

- increased use of chemical fertilizers,

- expansion of the irrigation network,

- better price policies for rice,

- expansion of agricultural extension,

- extension of the rice producing area,

- supporting farmer cooperatives, and

- use of pesticides.

The prevailing belief at the time was that pesticides were a "mighty weapon" to guard and protect the rice plants from any and all pests. Pesticides, however, were wrongly regarded as highly effective "medicines" for plants afflicted by pests, and this belief led the government to subsidize the pesticides used in rice by as much as 80 percent of the total price. A special government agency was given the responsibility for making pesticides available to farmers in the field. Schedules for applying pesticides to the rice plants were fixed, usually four times during the growing season, regardless of the presence or absence of pests. In the event of pest attacks, pesticides were sprayed even more often. Aerial sprays were begun in 1968–69 to control the yellow rice stem borer in the northern plain of West Java province. To control the brown rice planthopper, aerial spraying was also conducted throughout the main rice centers of Java, north Sumatra and Bali, covering no less than one million hectares.

The package of measures was quite successful in achieving a large, continued increase in food production, as seen in Table 12.1. The average yield of rough rice per hectare in 1989 was 6.6 tons, the highest in the tropics. The average rate of increase was 4.5 percent per year, well above the annual population increase of 2.2 percent. Self-sufficiency in rice was achieved in the 1983–84 crop season for the first time in history, and it is still being maintained today. Rice, soybean and cassava production increased steadily between 1970 and 1989.

THE EMERGENCE OF PROBLEMS

During the early years of the rice intensification program, pest problems were regarded as separate from the health of the rice ecosystem. This view resulted in an ad hoc approach to pest control. The easiest thing was to apply pesticides at regular intervals. Even if no pests were observed in the fields, chemicals were sprayed prophylactically. In most, if not all, cases, this led to overuse of pesticides, particularly broad-spectrum chemicals. These kill not only harmful pests but also beneficial and nontargeted organisms, such as the natural predators of pests, parasitoids, bees and other pollinators, scavengers, earthworms, snakes, toads, fish, chickens and ducks. In addition, the chemicals used as pesticides polluted the irrigation water, the canals and rivers. Village people who used this water for bathing, cooking and other needs were exposed to health hazards.

Instances of acute toxicity in humans began to be reported. There were 450 cases in 1976, with 26 resulting in death; ten years later, 404 cases were reported, with the death toll up to 32 (Mustamin 1988). Undoubtedly there were many additional cases not reported because of poor communication with remote and isolated places.

Another detrimental effect was the development among certain pest species of resistance to pesticides, followed by resurgence of these species. This was clearly seen in the case of the brown planthopper and the green leafhopper. In 1976–77, the brown planthopper caused extensive damage to the rice crop, affecting more than 450,000 hectares. The estimated yield loss was 364,500 tons of milled rice, enough to feed three million people for an entire year. In the 1970s the rice tungro virus vectored by the green leafhopper caused damage to about 70,000 hectares of rice fields in South Sulawesi. In 1980, the same disease broke out in Bali, causing damage to at least 12,000 hectares of rice fields.

Based on our observations and backed up by research results, we know that a combination of factors contributed to the increasing pest problems in intensification areas.

Table 12.1 Increase in Food Crop Production Resulting from Intensification
Programs, 1970–89

Food Crop	1970	1980	1985	1989	Average Yield
	in millions of tons				metric tons/ha
Rice	23.4	29.7	39.0	42.2	6.6
Soybean	0.5	0.6	0.9	1.3	1.1
Corn	2.8	4.0	4.3	6.2	2.1
Cassava	10.2	13.8	14.0	17.1	12.2

- Planting just a few modern varieties over wide areas reduced varietal diversity, which made the plant population more vulnerable to pest attacks.

- Some new varieties, especially those with a narrow genetic base, did not possess resistance to all endemic pests.

- Increased and excessive application of chemical nitrogenous fertilizers made plants more susceptible to pests.

- Continual planting of rice in a staggered manner throughout the year provided continuous food and shelter for a growing pest population.

- Overuse of pesticides created pest resistance and led to pest resurgence, as noted above.

INTRODUCING IPM AS AN ALTERNATIVE STRATEGY

Integrated pest management as a potentially superior form of pest control had been mentioned in official documents already in the Third Five-Year Plan (1979–84). Although limited in application, IPM was seen as a feasible alternative, capable of delivering more permanent solutions to pest problems. In this initial stage, IPM was implemented by strengthening the existing plant protection directorate within the agriculture ministry. It supported cultural controls (synchronized planting, crop rotation and sanitary measures), extensive use of pest-resistant modern varieties, and intensive pest monitoring for more judicious use of pesticides.

The application of this strategy was, however, limited by various factors. Large pesticide subsidies remained in place, so it was easy for farmers to continue to use cheap pesticides, encouraged by the massive advertising campaigns mounted by pesticide companies. There was no systematic effort to educate farmers in implementing IPM for themselves, and extension workers, themselves not trained in the new methods, could do no more than mention IPM in a cursory way during their field visits. Finally, there were external factors such as pressures to promote and sell certain insecticides.

A systematic effort to promote IPM did not to emerge until a major crisis occurred. The massive outbreak of brown planthopper in parts of Central Java during 1986 generated the necessary concern. Covering as much as 75,000 hectares, the outbreak took on calamitous proportions, threatening the nation's self-sufficiency in rice that had been won at great cost. Shortages of rice could become a cause of large-scale public unrest, since rice is the staple food for most Indonesians. Resumption of large imports of rice would draw heavily on the country's limited foreign reserves, and presented the government with a reason for serious embarrassment.

When the National Agency for Planning and Development (BAPPENAS) became concerned about the threat of the brown planthopper, it sought advice from a few scientists from the department of agriculture and from universities on how to deal effectively with the pest problem. They suggested that the government implement an IPM strategy at the farm level, minimizing insecticide use and educating technical personnel and farmers about IPM. The department of agriculture, however, seemed convinced that the brown planthopper threat was not so serious and could still be handled by conventional means. The suggestions offered by the scientists to BAPPENAS were supported by evidence, however, and farmers' own experience showed that the pest outbreak was spreading in spite of (and quite possibly because of) the increased use of chemicals.

Once the matter was considered at the highest level of government, a political decision was taken to support and implement IPM. Presidential decree no. 3, promulgated in 1986, endorsed IPM as a strategy and stated three objectives.

1. Develop manpower at the grassroots level, both farmers and field staff, to expand education in and awareness of IPM;

2. Increase efficiency of input use, in particular of pesticides; and

3. Improve environmental quality and prevent adverse effects on human health.

To enforce a change in pest control practices, the decree banned fifty-seven broad-spectrum insecticides formerly approved for use on rice. It permitted only the use of a few insecticides with a relatively narrow spectrum that eliminated certain specific insects.

The most important step was the withdrawal of subsidies, which were reduced from 75–80 percent in early 1986 to 40–45 percent in 1987. In January 1989, these subsidies were totally withdrawn. The abolition of pesticide subsidies saved the government significant amounts of scarce foreign exchange, as much as US$100–150 million per year.

The decree brought about a major change in the task environment of the government officials responsible for plant protection. They were required to switch from a pesticide-oriented approach to a more comprehensive one, namely IPM. The pesticide companies were also challenged to adopt a new orientation; rather than concentrate just on making profits, they now needed to show more concern for the environment and for human health. The challenge we faced following the decree was how to implement this new strategy of accelerating IPM. To take this task in hand, a comprehensive rice-focused National Integrated Crop Pest Management Program was established in 1989. The main thrust of the program was human resource development at the farmers' level, as discussed below.

The new program, designed by BAPPENAS, was also charged with coordinating the implementation tasks. At the national level, an advisory board was established with high-ranking membership from BAPPENAS and the ministries of agriculture and of home affairs. This was the supreme policymaking body, and it had overall responsibility for the success of the program.[1] Below the advisory board, a steering committee was created with members from BAPPENAS, the ministry of agriculture, other ministries, universities, and the regional office of the Food and Agriculture Organization (FAO). This committee was assisted in its day-to-day operations by a working group consisting of IPM experts, administrators and FAO advisors, whose task it was to supervise the program and provide appropriate technical solutions. Members of the working group were also ex-officio members of the steering committee.

Given their common objective of hastening the pace of execution and to keep interest alive in the program, these three administrative levels were closely knit together. Policy issues identified by the working group during the execution of the program were brought up at steering committee meetings. In urgent cases, immediate solutions were sought from the chairperson of the board.

At the provincial and district levels, corresponding working groups were established, and field staff of the ministry of agriculture were directed to provide full support to these working groups. As the program began to make an impact, it attracted the support of provincial governors and district administrators. Local working groups began to establish their own

IPM programs, mobilizing additional financial support from local government bodies, a sign that this approach was understood and appreciated at lower levels.

IMPLEMENTING THE PROGRAM

The basic features of implementation were designed to reflect the following principles.

1. IPM is not simply a blending of various control tactics to manage pests. Instead, it treats pest problems as part and parcel of the dynamics of the particular ecosystem, due to various interrelated production, management and ecological factors. IPM therefore involves the totality of measures undertaken to achieve a healthy crop. To make such a system work and have it accepted by millions of farmers, it is essential to integrate existing, local sociocultural factors and traditional farming practices, making IPM a socio-agro-ecosystem approach.

2. Developing human capacity at the grassroots is the only way forward. It is not enough to increase farmers' technical capabilities (the how). More important is helping them understand the reasons for doing one thing and for not doing something else (the why). This makes them more independent when coping with other problems that they come across. Farmers themselves should become experts in IPM. Therefore, farmers were given a thorough education in IPM, using the methodology most suited to them.

Inviting farmers to learn by doing was appropriate for generating their interest and developing their capacity. Our strategy thus was IPM *by* farmers, not IPM *for* farmers. Farmer-to-farmer extension was the method selected for the second stage of diffusion of IPM techniques. In the first stage, extension agents trained the first lot of farmers. Then, when enough farmers were trained, so that a critical mass was achieved, second-stage extension began.

3. To achieve these objectives, trainers should be trained first. The most appropriate personnel to serve as the first-stage trainers were the field-level pest observers and the field extension workers. Although the bulk of our institutional training was concentrated on this level of staff, officials occupying higher ranks in both regional and central offices were also trained in IPM techniques so that they came to appreciate its advantages and understand its associated needs. Their commitment helped smooth the implementation of IPM. To assist in the task, the organizational and the personnel capabilities of both formal and nonformal training institutions related to IPM were strengthened.

4. Equally important was the need to institutionalize IPM itself at the farmers' level and within existing institutions. IPM includes planning,

organizing, seeking funds, practical field studies and farmer-to-farmer training, so that farmers become better managers. Agricultural institutions were persuaded to include aspects of IPM in their yearly research and teaching programs.

5. For the longer term, IPM was to be expanded beyond its initial coverage of rice to deal with the pest problems found in other crops, including commercial crops and tree crops. For example, the cotton industry in Indonesia has never made much progress because of pest problems.

PROGRAM SCOPE

Initially, the program was limited to managing and containing rice pests within the rice-based cropping systems in the six main rice-growing provinces: West Java, Central Java, Yogyakarta, East Java, North Sumatra, and South Sulawesi. These provinces contribute around 70 percent of the national rice supply. Once the program was underway, local authorities from other provinces came to see it firsthand. Impressed with the program's performance, they extended it to deal with similar rice pest problems in their own provinces. In the long run, these provinces are expected to produce more rice through intensification and to ease the burden on Java. As more trainers were trained, from 1992 on, the program has been extended to cover six more provinces.

Encouraged by the significant progress made in the rice program, the IPM approach has been extended since November 1991 to cover unirrigated crops (mainly soybean), high-altitude vegetable crops (cabbage, potatoes and chilies) and shallots. For a long time, these crops, referred to collectively as *palawija* crops, were also overdosed with insecticides.

TRAINING

Training was, and remains, the most critical part of the entire program. It involves first the training of trainers, then the training of farmers by these trainers, and finally farmer-to-farmer training. In the first two years of the program (1989–91), we planned to train about 2,000 extension workers, 1,000 field pest observers, and 100,000 farmers. These levels were achieved. Training continued, with around 200,000 farmers receiving IPM training by 1994 and 650,000 by 1996.

The strategy has matured now into its second stage, and an additional 25,000 farmers have received IPM training through farmer-to-farmer training activities. (The numbers cited do not include those trained in additional sessions financed by the districts.) In 1993, around 2,000 high-altitude veg-etable crop farmers were trained in IPM methods. Their motivation was as strong as that of farmers trained in rice IPM, because they were able to reduce the frequency of their pesticide applications from sixteen to twenty times to only two or three times a season (Sudarwohadi 1993). This has drastically cut their production expenses. Nowhere have yields of farmers using IPM fallen, and in some cases they have increased. For example, a study of 2,013 farmers, carried out in the first six provinces during the 1990 wet season, revealed that in many cases the average yield per hectare on fields where IPM methods were used was above 6 tons compared to average yields below 6 tons per hectare on other local fields where IPM was not being practiced (BAPPENAS 1990).

The Process of Training

During the first year of the program (crop year 1989–90), twenty-two senior field pest observers were trained in IPM for one full year in a pilot training module conducted at a department of agriculture field training facility (FTF) located in Yogyakarta. In addition to providing laboratory, dormitory, classroom and recreation facilities, a two-hectare rice field was also made available for implementing and demonstrating IPM practices. After their first four months, trainees went back to their subdistrict offices, where they were required to train a group of twenty-five farmers in IPM over a four-month period. The trainees then received four more months of institution-based training.

Those who completed this training were called first-level field leaders (FL1s). Each FTF located in the provinces was assigned two FL1s to serve as the chief trainers. In addition, ninety field pest observers with some experience were given two weeks of rice IPM training at the main FTF in Yogyakarta. Designated as second-level field leaders (FL2s), they were sent to assist FL1s in the decentralized training programs. Care was taken to ensure that the training given in these provincial FTFs was as good as that provided in Yogyakarta.

FL1s in the provincial field training facilities supervised the IPM train-ing of field pest observers selected from among those deployed in the con-cerned provinces. Each year a FTF could train fifty or sixty more field pest observers (FL2s), including some training on nonrice IPM. These FL2s were then assigned to serve as trainers of farmers at farmer field schools (FFS), which were located throughout the rice-producing areas of the par-ticipating province. Each trainer (FL2) is assisted by two field extension workers (PPLs) who have attended a two-week IPM training session at a provincial FTF. These three people, as a team, are expected to train 100 rice farmers during each rice season, which lasts for twelve weeks. Each farmer course consists of twenty-five farmers, and each team is responsible for conducting IPM training at four farmer schools.

Participants in the field schools were drawn as much as possible from the membership of existing farmer groups. A series of meetings was held with a farmer group to explain the purpose, duration and method of the field school. Since farmer groups nominally have between 75 and 150 members, the persons selected by the group to participate would represent it and be responsible afterwards as resource persons and trainers for the group. The criteria used by the group were highly inclusive: no age, physical, educational or gender requirements were set. Those selected should be active farmers (whether owners, renters or sharecroppers was not deemed important) and be willing to attend for the full twelve weeks.

Incentives offered to farmers include the school's offering a certificate of graduation to farmers who participated in the entire course and who passed the final "field ballot box test" on IPM field skills. This has turned out to be highly valued since the majority of participating farmers did not have even primary school certificates (average formal education was four years of primary schooling). Farmers participating in the initial programs, where IPM field workers were also learning the methods, were given compensation of Rp. 1,000 (US$0.50) per session, reimbursing roughly half of the income they could have earned if they were not attending the school. Subsequent regular field schools offered only a subsidized snack, costing the program Rp. 7,500 (US$4.00) per group per session.

Organizing farmers is a key function. It was general knowledge that many farmer groups existed only on paper, so one of the roles of the field schools was to reinvigorate farmer groups as viable organizations possessing a core of well-trained farmers. After the field school, a number of follow-up programs have been organized by program field workers, including IPM field days for horizontal communication, IPM people's theater, farmer-to-farmer training, farmer seminars, training in participatory planning, and farmer field studies. The field school program is just the entry point for developing a farmers' network, linking local organizations and improving their access, leverage and capability.

During the extension training season, field workers usually conduct field schools on Monday through Thursday. On Fridays, the field workers meet at the rural extension center with the field leaders to discuss their progress and plan for the next week. In addition, monthly meetings are held, bringing together all the area field workers and field leaders for a technical workshop. Experiences are reported and analyzed using techniques such as SWOT (strengths-weaknesses-opportunities-threats) and force-field analysis. Technical input sessions address specific problems, and plans for the next month are established. We have found that in order to keep field leaders and field workers committed, the entire system must keep *learning*! New methods are developed, tested, improved; new approaches are pioneered, new field studies attempted, new crops tackled. Only if the system keeps evolving and learning does it stay committed and clear on its goal.

Training Methodology

This is participatory learning by doing. The participants are asked to look at things for themselves, to discover, to carry out experiments, to discuss with fellow participants, to analyze and to derive from all this practical recommendations for action. Participants are encouraged to be attentive to the reality in the field. Once they learn to practice and understand what they are doing, it is expected that they will not easily forget what they have learned. Participants express their own views freely and engage their fellow farmers and the trainers in active debate. No clear distinction is made between the trainer and the trainees; in most cases, the trainers serve as facilitators.

The rice fields are thus the "blackboard" on which the lesson is written. Demonstration rice fields are divided into two halves. On one half, farmers plant rice using the techniques that they have normally practiced. On the other half, they plant rice following the IPM techniques being assessed. The IPM strategy being taught begins with measures that can produce the most healthy plants, best able to resist pest and disease attacks: selecting good seeds of pest-resistant varieties, proper soil preparation, appropriate plant spacing, timely watering and weeding and balanced use of fertilizers, both purchased and compost. The IPM methods then taught include

1. maximizing the use of existing natural enemies of the insect pests;

2. periodic monitoring of pests and diseases to permit timely, optimizing actions;

3. using physical rather than chemical control methods wherever possible, for example, against rats; and

4. applying chemical insecticide only when periodic monitoring of the balance between pests and natural enemies indicates that the latter are insufficient in number. For example, if farmers find an average of five brown planthoppers or some other pest species and two or three of its natural predators, such as ladybugs or spiders, they may decide not to apply insecticides because they have

learned that this many natural enemies can easily destroy this number of pests.

The twenty-five participants are divided into five subgroups of five persons each. Each subgroup has its own name, coined by the members themselves, usually adopting the names of insects (butterfly subgroup, ladybug subgroup). One participant is chosen by each subgroup to act as its spokesperson.

To begin each session, the trainers outline the program of the day. Usually, the day starts with observing plant growth, the amount and flow of irrigation water, the weed situation and weather conditions, then observing and counting the presence of pests and their natural enemies on sample plants. Each subgroup records its findings. This field observation lasts one to two hours.

Each subgroup then retires to a shady place to plan its presentation to be made before the whole group. To assist with their presentations, members draw pictures of the rice plants, the water level, the weeds, the sunshine or absence of it and the numbers of insect pests and natural enemies. They write down, in short sentences, what they think is important in their analyses. Finally they write recommendations such as: the plants need more nitrogen fertilizer or more water; they need to be weeded; no need to apply insecticides because the numbers of natural enemies are still in balance with the numbers of the insect pests; or postpone applying insecticide until next week, based on observation.

The spokesperson of each subgroup presents these analyses and findings to the whole group. This is followed by intense discussion. Sometimes heated debates ensue, for example, on whether or not the situation warrants insecticide application, or about the names and functions of a newly discovered insect. Trainers facilitate discussion but do not lead it; when group members do not agree on something, the trainer will explain in more detail and ask the participants to discuss the matter further among themselves.

After this session, other topics such as the effect of insecticides on natural enemies or the action of predators species, such as spiders, on an insect pest species, are demonstrated with the help of simple experiments. Some time is spent demonstrating instances in which concerted group action is more fruitful than individual action. These training sessions are conducted in a relaxed but serious setting, important for making the participants feel free to express their own ideas.

Follow-Up

In many previous training programs for agriculture development, trainees reverted to their old practices at the end of the program period. To prevent this from happening in the IPM program, in 1992 we began in selected areas a program called institutionalization of IPM. We returned to those groups of farmers who had already availed themselves of farmer schooling during the first or second year of the program to test what they had learned and were doing in the fields.

The objective of the institutionalization program is to find out how the farmers are still practicing IPM and to encouraged them to undertake further improvements in their farm economy, including preparing production plans for the next crop season (what crop species/varieties to plant, calculating the amounts of the various production inputs to use), looking for financial resources, evaluating past experiences, devising simple field studies to make production inputs more efficient, trying to introduce IPM for their *palawija* crops and stimulating farmer-to-farmer IPM training.

Over 9,900 farmers participated in these follow-up programs, a better name for which might be farmer-led IPM program development. For example, in some field schools in the district of Cianjur, West Java, the participating farmers told us that they did not need to add phosphorus chemical fertilizers to their rice fields, after they experimentally demonstrated that there was no difference in yield between the phosphorus-treated fields and fields with no phosphorus. This modification of the program to local conditions meant an increase in production efficiency with fewer purchased inputs. A few of them expressed a desire to demonstrate their experiences to other farmer groups interested in IPM.

IPM is therefore becoming broader than simply a pest control program. It is considered to be a way to develop human resources, that is, the farmers themselves. This was the underlying objective of the original presidential decree. Through IPM, farmers are expected to become better farm managers and decisionmakers in their enterprises. IPM is not only about controlling pests. We view the program as making an essential and integrated contribution to the total production process.

RESULTS TO DATE

Since the national IPM program began, there have been no serious pest outbreaks of the severity or extent that the country witnessed in the preceding years. Indonesia has managed to save huge amounts of foreign exchange due to the considerable reduction in chemical pesticide use throughout our rice-growing areas.

Field surveys of 2,013 farmers in seventy-two districts carried out in 1991, two years after the program began, indicated that average insecticide applications were significantly reduced (Pincus 1991). A second set of impact studies carried out in 1993, based upon a sample of 3,335 farmers, indicated that this trend has been maintained. Overall, we estimate that the use of chemical pesticides has been reduced by over half (see Table 12.2). What is most important is that farmers' reduced use of pesticides—with their outlay on these expensive purchased inputs cut correspondingly—has had *no adverse effect on yields*.

The use of those pesticides banned by the 1986 decree was reduced by 78 percent in 1991 and by 81 percent in 1993, showing that persuasion and education are more effective than legislation when dealing with remote and outlying areas. Because of the reduction in pesticide use, the risk of environmental contamination has been greatly reduced. Biological life, such as natural enemies of pests, nontargeted and beneficial species, now has a better chance of survival.

The second stage of the strategy—farmer-to-farmer extension—has begun to occur, enhancing the impact of the initial government-led thrust. Those farmers who have been trained in IPM are training their neighbors. The IPM program has also contributed a new learning methodology to the toolkit of our extension workers. The participatory learning process practiced in the IPM farmer field schools will now be used to accelerate other extension programs.

INTERNATIONAL RESOURCES

For the first two years (1989–91), the program was supported with USAID funding that was later extended to 1992. From crop year 1992–93, the program has received World Bank funding, first as a reallocation from an existing extension training project, and later as a regular stand-alone project. The government is determined to extend the program until 1998 in order to arrive at a critical number of trained farmers—about 800,000 to 1,000,000. World Bank funding supports this objective, with 650,000 trained by 1996.

There has been close collaboration with international agencies from the start, in particular with the FAO Regional IPM Program, starting from the early 1980s. The FAO program, based in Manila, has assisted in the development of training materials, monitoring, special studies and strategy formulation. Also, its facilitation of international exchange of technology and extension practices has allowed the countries of the region to learn from each other. The International Rice Research Institute has helped by supplying us with modern rice varieties that are resistant to a number of pests, particularly to the brown planthopper.

Table 12.2 Mean Number of Pesticide Applications per Field

Region	First Impact Study			Second Impact Study		
	Before	After	Change (%)	Before	After	Change (%)
South Sulawesi	2.33	0.48	−79	3.42	1.46	−57
N. Sumatra/Aceh	5.17	1.72	−67	3.78	1.07	−72
West Sumatra	—	—	—	2.57	0.43	−83
West Java	2.39	1.04	−57	2.52	1.29	−49
Central Java/Yogyakarta	2.23	1.37	−39	2.41	1.28	−47
East Java	2.31	1.17	−49	2.35	1.23	−48
Bali/Lombok	—	—	—	2.18	0.90	−59
Average	**2.58**	**1.13**	**−56**	**2.65**	**1.17**	**−56**

Source: Jonathan Pincus, Farmer field school survey: Impact of IPM training on farmers' pest control behavior (Jakarta: Integrated Pest Management National Program, 1991).

Collaboration with the Japan International Cooperation Agency (JICA) resulted in strengthening regional plant protection and field laboratories and in providing support for field studies on pest dynamics. Dutch technical assistance helped strengthen our capabilities in rice gallmidge research and has financed studies concerning pests of high-altitude vegetable crops. Since 1993, a Clemson University team, supported by USAID grants, has also collaborated in researching biological control measures for *palawija* crops.

Neighboring countries are becoming interested in how Indonesia has implemented its rice IPM program. Policymakers and field officers from Sri Lanka, Bangladesh, India, Malaysia, Thailand, Vietnam and the Philippines have come to Indonesia to see our program firsthand. Many countries have sent their field technicians to Indonesia to undergo a three-week IPM training. We have also sent some of our staff to conduct training sessions in some of these countries.

PROSPECTS AND CHALLENGES

Much progress has thus been achieved in applying IPM in Indonesian rice production. However, the 250,000 farmers who have so far started practicing IPM represent a fraction of the 19 million farming families in the country. This is why the IPM program has to be continued until at least 1998 to reach the critical number of at least 800,000 trained farmers. We believe that with this number, the second stage of diffusion will be able to proceed effectively.

Faster progress will be possible if the current strategy is supplemented with additional policy and research support. The existing pesticide regulations should be strengthened with respect to their status, coverage and enforcement. Steps should be taken to regulate the more than 750 pesticide formulations still legally sold in Indonesia. Use of some additional pesticides belonging to highly toxic categories should also be forbidden, with more emphasis on developing and using pesticides that have more intrinsic specificity and are less harmful for the environment. The new approach can also be expanded faster if IPM is made known to more farmers through effective messages communicated through newspapers, radio and television, to increase awareness of environmental and health consequences of pesticide problems. We have come a long way, but there are still many miles to go.

NOTES

Thanks to Russ Dilts, FAO technical assistance team leader, National IPM Program of Indonesia, for his critical reading of this manuscript and his helpful suggestions.

1. This policy was somewhat controversial, because BAPPENAS was supposed to be only concerned with planning, not with implementation, and IPM has previously been the domain of the Department of Agriculture (DOA). BAPPENAS' role in implementing IPM was meant to be only temporary, bypassing the slow-moving bureaucracy and long delays that could happen if IPM was managed by DOA. There was still a strong belief among certain Agriculture officials that chemical pesticides were the most reliable, effective and easy method of pest control. Also, any officials who were closely associated with chemical companies might promote the continued intensive use of pesticides. Later when the program was established and running, it was transferred to the DOA at the beginning of the 1994–95 fiscal year.

SOCIAL SERVICES: HEALTH, NUTRITION, FAMILY PLANNING, AND WATER SUPPLY

13 The Population and Community Development Association in Thailand

Mechai Viravaidya

When I returned to Thailand in 1965 after studying in Australia, I learned in a very unusual and personal way the value of publicity. A relative of mine asked an unusual favor. She was chaperoning a young Thai woman who had just won the Miss Universe beauty pageant to a number of congratulatory functions, and she wanted me to accompany them. I accepted, not knowing that the Thai people would go crazy about this. Because I went everywhere with them and was frequently photographed, I also became a kind of celebrity.

Shortly thereafter, I got a job with the National Economic and Social Development Board (NESDB), where several years later I became chief of the evaluation section. This often required me to travel up-country to the rural areas to assess and report on development progress. Everywhere I went, there were so many children; I could see that population growth was just eating away at whatever progress we made in terms of our development. A study asked people, "Do you have enough for your children—enough education, enough facilities, everything you need as an adult?" The answer was almost always "no." A World Bank study calculated that annual population growth was about 3.3 percent at the time, but there was no population policy or program.

We needed either to speed up the development process or slow down population growth, or both. I was not in much of a position to speed up a bureaucracy's attempt at development. But I was able to see some of its problems. One was a tremendous lack of communication between the government and the people. The NESDB was the planning authority in Thailand and part of the prime minister's office, but implementation was in the hands of the line ministries who did not communicate their development objectives to the people. When most government officials went out to the countryside, they simply talked with other government officials to find out what was going on. I, however, spent a lot of time talking to the farmers, which was not very common in those days. Farmers had some very different views from those of the government.

Introducing improvements was made more difficult by the fact that people in the rural areas did not have a role in shaping development;

everything was supposedly done for them by the government. Unfortunately, I had trouble convincing the bureaucracy that this was a problem. I wrote several reports on the situation, but they didn't get published, possibly because they presented views too directly. So I decided to write a weekly column in a leading Bangkok newspaper. I used the column to write about Thailand's development problems: the sparse conditions in the countryside, the difficulties faced by farmers and the fact that development thinking in the country was heavily influenced by people who weren't aware of what the country really needed. Aside from development, I wrote about population, corruption, the environment and rural poverty—issues otherwise being ignored.

Although it was controversial, or maybe because it was, the column was widely read. At this time I was also teaching at Thammasat University, which has since become known for its commitment to democracy, and I also had a nightly radio show. Later I played leading roles in a series of soap operas based on best-selling novels. The magic of it all was that these opportunities came quite by accident, but they were important for helping me learn about communication. These various channels of communication enabled me to reach quite a wide audience, people who normally did not communicate with one another. I reached the intellectuals, planners and politicians through the newspaper column, while the radio program brought ideas to the average educated person. The soap operas put me in touch with the common person on the street. These experiences working with the media were invaluable once I turned my efforts more directly to the pressing matters of family planning and poverty reduction.

Surprisingly, given the heterogeneity of my audience, virtually nobody challenged me. At functions and at dinners at which I spoke, or on the street, the reaction was the opposite. Many told me they agreed that the problems I spoke about were the urgent questions of the day, although they had been obscured by an authoritarian government. Sadly, no moves were being made to rectify the problems being highlighted. People were concerned, but most were not doing anything constructive to help. It was clear that people accomplished nothing by sitting around and talking about problems. Some action needed to be taken, so I moved into the nonprofit sector to work on certain projects, since I could not be very original within the government.

GETTING STARTED AT THE COMMUNITY LEVEL AND GETTING ATTENTION

In 1971, the government approved a national family planning policy, but its impact was limited. After serving two years as secretary-general of the

Family Planning Association of Thailand, I founded an organization called the Community-Based Family Planning Service (CBFPS) in 1974. I was convinced that we had to change people's attitudes about the number of children they should have and to establish a contraceptive delivery system in rural villages. Such a change would contribute to some long-term good, or at least get us out of the deep hole being dug by massive population growth.

The government's top-down approach to rural people as well as its regular health service delivery infrastructure was not achieving the reduction in the birth rate that was needed in rural areas, so a different approach was called for. I realized that family planning was a sensitive subject, one that was not supposed to be discussed. But if we took into account the Thai people's attraction to *sanuk* (having fun), we could overcome their traditional reluctance to confront embarrassing or controversial issues in public. So, I used humor to bring the condom and contraceptives out of the closet and into the open.

Gradually, we made condoms as familiar as playthings. Once, when I was speaking to 2,000 teachers on the importance of lowering the birth rate, I showed them a condom. Suddenly I had an impulse to blow it up like a balloon. It was like magic. One minute they were sitting there looking stiff and self-conscious, and the next they were roaring with laughter. Condoms could become multicolored balloons; they could be filled with water and thrown; we had condom blow-up contests and water balloon festivals. If you take the ring off the end, I pointed out, they can make wonderful hair bands. To encourage Thai men to have vasectomies, we organized vasectomy festivals on the King's birthday, at which time men could receive the service for free. I liked to joke that Winston Churchill's "V for victory" sign during World War II really meant "stop at two." Today, this is one of the many messages emblazoned on T-shirts that our association sells, along with other humorous slogans, images and condom memorabilia such as condom flowers, condom coffee mugs and key chains.

My experience with the mass media enabled me to promote the family planning campaign far and wide, with the approach adapted for different audiences. The message was brought into schools, factories, shops, even taxis, which helped to spread awareness in the cities. At the time, though, the great majority of the population lived in villages in the countryside. This required a different response. To make the campaign succeed, we had to get both information and contraceptive means to the people, plus we definitely needed a structure that allowed people to participate.

In those days, contraceptives were distributed by doctors, nurses and midwives at government hospitals and health centers, which served only about 20 percent of villages. I became convinced that any solution to the population problem had to begin at the village level. The people had to feel a sense of participation, of not being directed by some far-away government. For leadership we looked to the people who mattered to villagers—teachers, monks and other village leaders—to disseminate the information. For distributing contraceptives, we looked to those who were well situated in terms of village traffic, such as shopkeepers. They were ordinary villagers, but they were essential in helping us make contraceptives readily accessible to communities in more than 25 percent of the country. To help spread the message, we also trained 320,000 rural school teachers within five years.

Each distributor of contraceptives was chosen carefully after reviewing the person's standing in the community, support for family planning and record-keeping ability. These persons received more training in record keeping and were given basic family planning information, such as about contraceptive use. CBFPS trained them and gave them a big depot sign to hang outside their shops. They returned home with supplies of birth control pills and condoms that they could sell in their villages for a small commission. Each of our field workers looked after about 100 distributors and went around once a month to check records, collect the money from contraceptives sold and deliver new supplies.

This network relied on the distributor's hard work, good faith and pride in being selected as the distributor. The payment of a commission added incentive, but nobody agreed to distribute contraceptives in order to get rich. Instead, most distributors regarded it as a high honor to be chosen. Eventually the network encompassed over 16,200 villagers who distributed contraceptives and information. We tried to go everywhere, but we went first to areas where the need was greatest. The northeast was the poorest area and had the highest fertility rate, so most of our efforts went there at first. But we also worked in the north, which was also poor, in part of the center and part of the south. It was a national campaign. By its fifth year, the program was totally self-financing. The money from the sale of contraceptives donated by the International Planned Parenthood Federation and U.S. Agency for International Development was recycled to cover all costs of operating the network.

Surprisingly, there was not much opposition even though the campaign was very visible, and it started having quite a wide impact. To allay the concerns of monks, we cited a teaching of the Buddha that "many births cause suffering." We never had any political problems and not much in the way of general opposition either. The very few people who opposed us I never confronted. I always listened to their suggestions and comments and thanked them. I apologized for the things they did not like and then just continued the way we had been doing things.

Perhaps we minimized any widespread opposition by not talking about sex education. Instead, we talked only about population and family planning, saying that parents should be the ones to discuss sex education with their kids. In that way, people never thought of us as violating the family's responsibility. We also made the subject lighthearted and festive rather than something clinical and dull, as it was usually taught or talked about. The important thing was to make people think about it.

INDICATORS OF SUCCESS AND THE NEED TO EXPAND OBJECTIVES

Objectively, the national family planning campaign in Thailand can be judged a success. Our NGO program is widely credited with helping the government reduce the nation's population growth rate from about 3.3 percent in the early 1970s, to 1.8 percent by 1982, to 1.2 percent in 1994. Concurrent with this decrease has been a dramatic increase in the number of eligible couples practicing family planning, from 11 percent in 1971, to over 60 percent by the early 1980s, to over 78 percent today.

Thailand's success is the envy of many other developing nations that are struggling with high birth rates. The key to success was good cooperation between the government and NGO sector—the ministry of public health supported our efforts, and we contributed to the achievements of the national family planning program; a wide range of contraceptive choices; grassroots participation; and full voluntarism (no coercion). In isolated and very poor areas, where education, incomes and family planning acceptance were low, we introduced a system of community incentives, in about 50 villages. In some of the most remote villages, we set up a community fund into which was paid $200 for every vasectomy performed, $175 per female sterilization, $100 per IUD, and $75 for using the pill. These funds were available for loans to village members whether or not they participated in family planning, with loans made and collected by an elected village committee. These revolving funds were mostly very well managed and maintained. Elsewhere we paid into a community fund $5 for every month that a woman was not pregnant. In order not to privilege some more than others, every woman, old or young, could "contribute" $60 a year to the community fund this way. We also offered households where the wife was not pregnant agricultural credit at a favorable rate. If the bank rate was 10 percent, contraceptive users could borrow at half that rate, while other villagers could borrow at 10 percent—still much lower than the 60 to 130 percent paid to private moneylenders.

Our practice was to promote family planning as something that is in people's interest, not something we would try to "bribe" them to accept.

Material incentives cannot explain the fundamental changes in attitude which the campaigns brought about. Our bold and often humorous approaches have helped turn one of the most private subjects into something that people can now discuss openly with little embarrassment. We can take much satisfaction in this transition in attitudes and behavior.

However, we also came to realize that we should not try to solve population growth problems in isolation, since our real goal was to improve people's lives. The more deeply we got involved in our family planning campaign, the clearer it became that this, by itself, would not be enough to develop the rural areas and reduce poverty in Thailand's many villages. Accordingly, in 1977, the name of CBFPS was changed to the Population and Community Development Association (PDA for short). This reflected our broader goal, and PDA began establishing programs on a district-by-district basis. From our work with villagers on family planning, we learned that their health was one of the best ways of convincing them to have fewer children. Parents would have fewer children if they knew that the ones they did have would be healthier and would be more likely to survive and thrive. This led us to look more closely at the need and opportunities to improve rural health by preventing illnesses.

IMPROVING VILLAGE WATER SUPPLIES

One of the main obstacles to improving health was a severe lack of water resources in the villages. Most poor villagers simply did not have enough water, especially drinking water. Because of inadequate supply, particularly during the dry season, many families were forced to drink unsafe water. In response, PDA set up a water tank program based on the idea of capturing rainwater from the roofs of houses and storing it in large water jars and water tanks. Particularly in the northeast, rain does not fall throughout the year, but only in some months. This made getting ground water difficult, and piped water was out of the question because neither villagers nor the government could afford this. The water tank program proved to be both practical and feasible, however, as an alternative source to ground water. We worked with households to build water tanks about three meters tall and two meters wide, with a capacity of about 11,000 liters of water. This was enough to supply drinking and domestic water for a family for the seven-month period of water shortage.

Where did the money to finance the tanks come from? At first, we got grants from the German foundation, Agro Action. Construction costs were reduced by forming groups of fifteen families to cooperate in contributing the labor. Within fifteen days a group could install fifteen tanks.

We made the program self-sustaining by requiring that every family that got a water tank would sponsor another family, repaying the money for its own water tank over a period of time. The money stayed in the district as a kind of revolving fund. If a grant enabled us to construct 1,000 tanks over ten years, the number of tanks could be increased to 7,000 under this system. This multiplying effect made the program quite effective. It improved hygiene and reduced disease, while saving households (especially women) time and greatly improving quality of life.

A water committee was set up in each village to handle collection of the money owed to the revolving fund. Most everyone was surprised that there were so few defaults. This was partly because if a villager did not repay his or her loan, this would prevent a neighbor from getting a water tank. PDA's efforts were initiated to expand upon government efforts to bring water to rural areas. Where it was apparent that the government would not be able to reach certain remote communities, we stepped in to help, but not by giving things away. We always required some amount of local contribution. Our program ended up building more water tanks than all of the government's programs, thanks to the workings of community management and self-help.

ELABORATING A MORE COMPREHENSIVE RURAL DEVELOPMENT STRATEGY

We started thinking about how to launch still larger projects that could help an even greater number of people. If PDA could get funding for 100,000 home water tanks, which would cost about US$35 million at that time, within ten years our program could get over 700,000 tanks installed, which would have covered the entire northeast part of the country. We fashioned a three-step approach to village development. First, we started with family planning efforts, which we followed up with water and sanitation programs. Then we introduced what we called community-based integrated rural development. This also had three steps: first, improve technology for the villagers; second, resolve resources constraints and increase commodity production; and third, market their products.

By now, most people had accepted that too many children made them poor, and they were ready to stop adding to the number of mouths they already had to feed. The new question became: how to make life better for them, giving them a chance to get their fair share of life's necessities? PDA became involved with them, giving technical and economic assistance and also advice and cooperative-like marketing opportunities. First we selected farmers from one district at a time, allotting about 20 million baht (US$1 million) per district, mostly derived from foreign grants, to be invested in household-level improvement. We had three models in mind: intensive, which provided about 6,000 baht (US$300) per household; moderate, costing about 4,000 baht (US$200) per household; and light, which cost 3,000 baht (US$150).

The basic activities were animal raising, all forms of agriculture and some kinds of water resource development, for example, constructing wells or ponds in the village. To improve agriculture, we started by providing better seeds and fertilizer and by helping villagers begin fish raising. For animal rearing, villagers raised chickens, ducks, geese and rabbits. We encouraged them to plan to use one activity to benefit another, capturing whatever synergies were possible. For instance, geese can be introduced just before the villagers harvest their rice. After the harvest, the young geese consume the grains left behind in the field, getting a good healthy start, after which they can manage by foraging and scavenging around the village.

We also tried to promote appropriate technology at the village level by emphasizing renewable energy, simple farm tools and reduction of energy waste. We encouraged people to use animal waste rather than charcoal for cooking by converting it into biogas. Another innovation was recycling chicken droppings to be fed to the pigs, with the pigs' manure in turn fed to fish, and residues then used to produce biogas. Fertilizer could also be obtained from this process. We also experimented with other technologies such as using solar energy to dry foodstuffs.

Sometimes the techniques villagers were already using were basically sound, but small changes could earn them more money. We introduced a lot of small improvements. For instance, many villagers were already raising chickens, which were a main source of nutrition for rural households. In the past, as many as 90 percent of the chickens might die from disease. We learned this was due largely to in-breeding. By getting villages to exchange their roosters, and by introducing vaccination, survival rates dramatically increased. The villagers also went into commercial production, both for egg laying and selling poultry meat. Later, we encouraged them to expand into pig raising, which was more complex, due to the different types of diseases. This also involved determining, on a village by village basis, how many families could best raise pigs and how many would raise chickens.

While PDA encouraged villagers to become organized, it has not set up PDA organizations at village level. A variety of special-purpose organizations have been established for managing activities sparked by PDA, such as the village committees organizing water tank construction and handling repayment. We wanted to be sure that villagers perceived the organizations as *their* organizations. So a variety of cooperatives, farmer groups, associations and handicraft companies have sprung up, encouraged, and in some cases financially backstopped, by PDA. The main task for PDA staff, including the managers and directors, was, and continues to be, spending time sitting and talking with people, to know their needs and concerns and capabilities and what they are willing to commit themselves to for their own and their children's betterment.

PDA has aimed to achieve income increases of about 30 percent a year, and it has used routine evaluations to gauge the effect of what has become one of the most integrated development programs for Thai villages. We went beyond measuring income to assess whether project activities were succeeding. We also sought to learn the perceptions of the people. We asked them if their lives were now better, and if so, in what ways? Our measurement device, called the "Thai bamboo ladder," started from zero and went up to ten. We asked questions such as: "What is the ideal situation you would like to see in your community?" They would answer, "Enough water, a school for my children, good health, no robberies, and a fair price for my crops." We called this the ideal, which we valued at ten.

We then asked what was the worst possible situation they could imagine themselves in, and this was termed zero on our scale. Then we asked them where they thought they were on the ladder at the time. Some said five; others said six or seven. We asked them to indicate where they were before PDA got involved in their village, and some pointed to two or three. Finally, we asked them where they thought they would be in three or four years' time, and they pointed to eight or even nine. This revealed to us how the villagers evaluated their own progress within their own value system, and that they looked forward to improvements—a brighter future in their community.

One of the most important steps was to let villagers know where they could look for help. PDA taught the villagers to identify their needs and to figure out ways to get them met, through their own means and with our help. PDA set up special centers in a number of districts that were particularly poorly served where villagers could come to get supplies and learn valuable information. Some information was especially important for helping farmers market their produce at a fair price instead of getting cheated by middlemen. This gave them more control over their economic performance. We tried to make the villagers strong enough to stand up to the businesspeople, not trying to cut them out, but providing the villagers with real alternatives.

A PEOPLE-CENTERED APPROACH

Another key was participation. We didn't work with villagers as their masters but rather as their equals. This was crucial to their sense of self-worth and represented a tremendous social change in their lives, building their confidence and initiative over time while our staff worked with them. The great majority of the villagers were honest with us because they knew that if they cheated us, they were really cheating themselves. This contributed to much progress since heretofore changing villagers' impressions about development assistance had always been difficult. To us, development did not necessarily mean more roads, more electricity or more whatever—it meant changing people's attitudes and behavior, to help them become more capable of self-help.

Participation also means no handouts. PDA firmly believes that handouts breed passivity and indifference, and that villagers will be more committed to the activities and possessions that they have an investment in. When PDA moved heavily into water resource development—tackling one of the greatest threats to livelihood for farmers—villagers paid for their water jars and water tanks after purchase through a loan program. The same principle generally applied to villagers who started to raise chickens or pigs and used money from a community fund to buy their first animals and materials to start the business. When they repaid the loan, the money went into a common revolving fund that stayed in the community and funded other villagers looking for loans for their needs.

In retrospect, we see that PDA's approach to development did help villagers to become more self-sufficient within two to four years, although in some poorer areas, development took longer. The key was to get the villagers started on the path to a better life through their own efforts. This then continued until they had both met their basic needs and established a firm footing of economic security. For instance, when building up water resources to enable the villagers to farm year-round, PDA sought also to deal with urgent issues such as the need for off-season income to provide for families' needs while new systems were being planned or built and when their farming income ran out.

Many villagers had already turned to small cottage industries as an alternative. PDA took the cue and built many new programs based on existing village skills and knowledge. For example, the cloth-making industry offered good opportunities. But it was important that villagers not only know how to make cloth, but, more importantly, how to make it with attractive designs so that it could be marketed in urban areas or exported for higher prices. The same was true for villagers making Thai handicrafts to sell. We encouraged households to go beyond producing primary commodities and to add value to their own work. Instead of selling only fresh bananas, they learned to market dried bananas all year round. Food processing and vegetable pickling helped them earn income and add value to garden crops. We also taught them how to make cheap baskets and bricks. In place of the traditional approach of only growing just rice and other farm produce, they learned how to produce other things, to be more imaginative.

The underlying benefit of increasing off-season employment and income generation in rural communities is that it gives people a greater economic stake in their communities. If villagers can derive more benefit in their community, such as from a business, they are more inclined to stay there instead of moving elsewhere, or migrating to Bangkok to seek jobs before and after the harvest. They will try instead to improve the situation around their homes and businesses. Basically, we tried to turn small farmers into small businesspeople, and to open up cooperatives where the farmers could gain. PDA continues to promote this strategy of broad-based villager participation, similar to what was expressed twenty years ago when the organization was founded. Our approach requires looking to the people themselves for solutions, going into villages and finding out what people want and what their ideas are in dealing with their problems.

PDA has evolved from its rather modest origins—in a crowded, cluttered converted shop house on a little street off the busy thoroughfare known as Sukhumvit, to occupy currently an eight-story office building and compound containing a restaurant, cafeteria, health and sterilization clinic, handicraft store and staff housing. In addition, it has expanded and opened fourteen field offices in the north and northeast, from which the various project activities are launched. From a staff of 25 in 1974, PDA has grown to having 600 staff.

This expansion has not come without much time, effort and, of course, money. The total annual budget reached US$12 million a year at its peak, when PDA was involved in a lot of refugee work. The present level is closer to US$9 million, but this supports probably more development work than at the peak of funding. To share its experiences, PDA has now established an Asian Center for Population and Development, which has already given training to over 2,000 people from forty-seven countries.

Most PDA projects have been funded by Western donor agencies, foundations and governments, which have come to trust the PDA's community-based implementation approach, its experience in managing large-scale programs, and its commitment to benefiting the rural poor majority. PDA funds up to 40 percent of its annual expenditures through a variety of private businesses, some under the auspices of the Population and Community Development Company Ltd. (PDC). PDA holdings include the now-famous "Cabbages and Condoms" restaurant chain, started in Bangkok, with four branches in Thailand and one in Beijing, China. Plans are being drawn up to expand into other parts of the world. PDA also has a handicrafts store in Bangkok, which Mobil Oil and Oxfam helped to start, as well as numerous development companies located at its field offices. PDA profits go entirely to help fund PDA's work. Apartment rents, honorariums and fees that I often receive for speaking or serving as director of companies also go toward PDA's activities.

Noting the steady decline in foreign development aid and knowing that Thailand's rural development needs are still far from being met, PDA has diversified to meet future needs through the Thai Business Initiative for Rural Development (TBIRD). This was conceived in the late 1980s and was further developed during a year I spent as a visiting scholar at the Harvard Institute for International Development. The program recruits private businesses to finance the costs of development in individual rural villages. At the same time, employees of the companies work with the villagers to teach them basic finance, marketing and other business skills they will need to sustain themselves in the future.

Although the principal aim of the scheme is to provide villagers with local economic opportunities and a decent sustainable income, a corollary aim is to cultivate the private sector to assume part of the costs of rural development in Thailand, especially as foreign aid declines. Since its launching in 1989 with pioneering commitments by Volvo and Bangkok Glass, the program has grown to include projects in over 120 villages in the north. It increases the effectiveness of donor aid by recruiting private companies to bear much of the actual costs of rural development work in villages, making tax-deductible contributions through PDA. Companies have helped villagers to start an array of cottage industries, including silk weaving and basket making. Many of these are now independent and self-sustaining.

TBIRD has also been able to recruit companies to relocate part of their production base to rural areas, taking machinery to the people rather than vice versa. The most successful venture so far is that of Bata, the Canadian shoe manufacturer; 45 percent of its school shoes—six million—are produced in factories owned by rural cooperatives established with the help of PDA. Bata's success has helped convince other companies also to move production to the rural areas. Now the government is encouraging other companies to follow suit, for producing garments and leather goods, processing semiprecious stones and assembling electronic components. Not only has this stopped outmigration from villages where production has started up, but young men and women are returning home to their villages from Bangkok.

In 1996, a system of minimarkets is being established in villages, where village shopkeepers are organized to own 40 percent of a central supply company. In turn, these shopkeepers are encouraged to hold equity capital in the new factories being relocated to rural villages. All shopkeepers and factory owners will contribute 10 percent of profits to village activities for the less privileged. Some Bangkok companies have agreed to allocate 3–5 percent of their profits, of directors' fees and of directors' and staff bonuses toward expanding PDA activities. Through continuing innovations in programmatic focus and in financing mechanisms, PDA is achieving multiplier effects well beyond those that were first launched with its water jar program years ago. Of course such development efforts are all the more successful when the villagers are able to participate as owners and can watch the value of their investments grow over time.

NOTE

I would like to thank Pamela Mar, program officer with the Thai Business Initiative for Rural Development, for her assistance in preparing this chapter.

14 The Iringa Nutrition Project: Child Survival and Development in Tanzania

Anirudh Krishna with Urban Jonsson and Wilbald Lorri

Toward the end of the 1970s, in spite of the efforts of government, religious organizations and external agencies, levels of mortality, illness and malnutrition among infants and young children in Tanzania remained at unacceptably high levels. The national government accorded high priority to the advancement of health, and by the end of the 1970s it had built and staffed large numbers of new health facilities across the country. Yet Tanzania's infant mortality rate of 130 and its under-five mortality rate of 225 per 1,000 live births were among the highest rates in sub-Saharan Africa. An estimated 7 percent of all children under five were severely malnourished (weighing less than 60 percent of an acceptable minimum for that age), and an additional 43 percent were moderately undernourished (between 60 to 80 percent of standard weight). Thus, about half of all Tanzanian children under five—over two million children—suffered from moderate to high levels of malnutrition. Large numbers of children suffered from malaria, diarrhea and measles, which were also the most frequent causes of death.

There was, within the country and outside, a clear recognition for the need to develop a new strategy that would deal effectively and quickly with these problems. Organizational as well as technical innovations would be necessary. These would first be tested on a subnational scale, but, to be meaningful for the rest of the country, the new approach would have to introduce solutions within the limits of administrative capabilities and available resources. Begun in 1983, the Iringa Nutrition Project (INP) managed to enlarge significantly the pool of available resources by attracting a high degree of community involvement. The results were impressive. Within four years, the pilot project had reduced the prevalence of severe malnutrition among children under five years of age in the Iringa region from 6.3 to 1.8 percent. Other statistics were almost as dramatic as a new approach to child survival and development was demonstrated and then extended to other parts of the country. The strategy drew on administrative and political organization as well as on community resources and personnel.

PROGRAM EVOLUTION

The approach was arrived at after diagnostic studies and small research projects had been conducted on behalf of the government by the Tanzania Food and Nutrition Center (TFNC). TFNC, throughout the 1970s, undertook a number of surveys to help develop a nutrition surveillance system. Discussions and workshops organized by TFNC to discuss the results of these studies led to the formulation of a conceptual framework that identified problems and potential solutions for malnutrition. This distinguished *immediate* causes: inadequate dietary intake, disease; *underlying* causes: insufficient household security, inadequate maternal and child care, insufficient basic health services and unhealthy environment; and *basic* causes: formal and nonformal institutions, political, economic and ideological superstructures.

Immediate causes needed to be addressed through better delivery of services, and underlying causes by capacity-building through information and education; long-term solutions to basic causes were to be found in community organization, joint action, mobilization of resources and advocacy. It was clear that no standardized package of technical interventions could adequately address all of these causes and lead to effective solutions. Since decisions on nutrition-related issues were seen as essentially family based, with existing and potential contributions from the village community, the new strategy focused on small community groups.

However, even as local communities were made the pivot of the new strategy, the strategy itself, at least in its initial stages, was driven from above. Members of village communities were trained by government or government-selected institutions. A cadre of animators was mobilized to inform and educate village communities about the problems and the potential for community-based solutions. And the process was set in motion by high-level commitments within the central government, with the president himself playing a leading role. The remarkable feature of the strategy is that as the program went forward, local communities took control of an ever larger share of program activities, with government staff continuing to perform essential facilitative and supportive functions.

STRATEGY

Iringa, one of the twenty regions of the country, was selected as the site for implementing a pilot project because its diverse agroecological zones that could provide a broad base of experience. Compared to other regions, it had higher levels of malnutrition and scored poorly on other demographic indicators. However, the region had a relatively stronger administrative infrastructure, so implementation could be easier. The fact that Iringa is one of the few food-surplus regions in the country was also an important consideration, since program designers had to solve problems of distribution and consumption rather than supply.

A detailed proposal for funding was submitted to the joint WHO/UNICEF nutrition support program funded by the Italian government. Large numbers of regional and field-level staff from a number of departments participated in preparing the project, which aimed at reducing malnutrition, morbidity and mortality among infants and young children, ensuring better child growth and improving maternal nutrition. A parallel objective was to improve local capabilities at all levels of society to assess, analyze and deal with nutrition problems.

Priority areas for innovation were identified as household food security, health services and child care, but rather than promote a defined set of interventions, project planners preferred to initiate a process for community-based solutions. A conceptual framework was developed to help communities assess and analyze their health and nutrition problems, identify underlying causes, and, having done so, undertake necessary remedial actions locally with little or no financial assistance from outside. This became known as the Triple-A cycle of assessment, analysis and action.

The program utilized existing administrative structures, linking them from the village to the ward, district, regional and national levels. A national steering committee with representatives from the prime minister's office, the line ministries, TFNC and donor agencies provided overall policy guidance.

Initially, INP covered a population of 46,000 children under the age of five, located in 168 villages. The program was launched by the prime minister at a mass public meeting held in Iringa town in December 1983. Follow-up village meetings, in each of the 168 villages, were facilitated by trained workers. A film, "Hidden Hunger," which highlighted the wide prevalence of malnutrition, its major causes and potential solutions was shown at each village meeting. Village representatives were selected for training, and a schedule of quarterly village health days, a major programmatic innovation, commenced.

After a midterm evaluation conducted in 1986 sharpened the program's approach, the area of operations was expanded to cover the entire Iringa region, and some 450 villages with 150,000 children were added to the original 168. The Child Survival and Development Program (CSD) which followed and drew on the experience gained in Iringa extended this approach to cover other regions of the country. By the end of 1991, close to two million children under five were registered in the UNICEF-aided CSD program.

Additional donor agencies—the World Bank, IFAD, SIDA, GTZ and NORAD—began supporting nutrition programs in other parts of the country along the CSD lines developed in Iringa. By 1996 the program is expected to cover virtually the entire country.

Dramatic improvements, similar to those in Iringa, have been observed and maintained in the expansion programs, which by 1993 covered half of Tanzania's population. "At the end of 1992, severe malnutrition rates in the nine mainland regions with three or more years of CSD program experience had fallen in some places from as high as 8 percent and 6.9 percent [before the program] to 1.8 percent and 1.6 percent [post-intervention]" (UNICEF 1993). These remarkable results were achieved even though, as a consequence of deep and continuing recession in the country, budgetary support of national health policies was cut from 7 percent of government expenditure in 1979 to 4 percent by 1987. In real terms, this represented a reduction of about 70 percent. The experience in Iringa and Tanzania has provided the foundations for a new nutrition strategy that was adopted by UNICEF in 1990 for promotion around the world.

PROGRAM APPROACH

Critical elements in the approach developed by INP, later expanded to other regions, include:

- A participatory process that enables communities to recognize, analyze and find solutions to commonly shared problems, through the Triple-A cycle described below.

- A powerful catalyst for community mobilization in the form of weight-for-age information used in growth monitoring. At the individual and community levels, weight-for-age data generated at village health days served as an effective spur to action by providing objective evidence of a child's need and/or a parent's neglect. At higher administrative levels it served as a simple-to-manage, sufficiently informative index for monitoring progress and for targeting support for actions taken at subordinate levels.

- Building capacity at the local level by training village health workers (VHWs), paraprofessionals with limited basic education who reside in the villages. This enabled local people to carry out growth monitoring and to analyze the data themselves, to handle child care and feeding centers and to construct buildings and latrines. VHWs with basic training could diagnose health problems and dispense drugs, thereby alleviating the critical shortage of trained medical personnel in the countryside.

- Developing and building upon the synergy between top-down and bottom-up dynamics. While government officials and party workers at all levels were expected to give full support to program initiatives, the initiatives themselves were proposed and articulated by village communities acting through their village health committees.

- Acting simultaneously for the achievement of short-term results that would maintain the momentum of local enthusiasm, for example, child immunization, while efforts were made to address more basic causes through longer-term solutions, for example, empowering women.

- Enabling local communities to develop program activities most appropriate to local concerns and understanding of the nutrition problem. Among the solutions selected by communities are infrastructure projects such as piped water supply, construction of health centers, income-generating activities and a host of agricultural, animal husbandry and environmental initiatives. Flexibility, with built-in capacity to change with circumstances as they vary over time and space, was an important characteristic of the program.

- Assisted self–reliance. Communities are encouraged to look for solutions mostly within the limits of what resources they can themselves provide. Overall, it is expected that two-thirds of total resources will be contributed by the villagers themselves, mostly in the form of labor for construction projects (Jonsson et al. 1991, 197).

Program Focus

The village community is the locus of program interventions. The Triple-A cycle for social mobilization consists of: (a) *assessing* the child nutrition problems facing a household or community, (b) *analyzing* the causes underlying these problems and (c) developing *actions* to resolve the problems. Assessment of results is fed back into the cycle. Village leaders, village health workers and extension agents from various government departments are trained to use the Triple-A cycle and engage villagers in it.

The focal point of the program is the village health day observed at a public location in each village at least once every three months (in many villages, monthly). There are health and nutrition lectures and demonstrations, but the main activity is the growth monitoring for all children under five. Weight-for-age information collected on these days provides the basis for assessing local children's health problems and leads to the next steps in the Triple-A cycle. Villagers discuss and analyze local health needs and formulate the actions that can be taken by individuals and by the community. Outsiders—extension agents, ward- and district-level officials and party workers—attend the village meetings, but they do not set the agenda.

INDIVIDUAL AND COMMUNITY ACTIONS

Weight-for-age information gathered at village health days is used for individual follow-ups of severely underweight children. The household of any severely underweight child is visited by the village health worker and other members of the village community. At times, the team may include party officials from village, ward and division levels or extension workers from health, agriculture or social welfare departments. "The purpose of the visit is a combination of nutrition education, micro-level problem analysis and social or political persuasion to produce behavioral changes" (Pelletier 1991). Follow-up visits ensure that the household has adopted the desired and agreed changes in behavior and attitudes. Improvement is monitored at successive village health days.

Information provided by program staff addresses all three necessary conditions for good nutrition, that is, household food security, caring practices and access to basic health services and a healthy environment. Particular emphasis has been given to improved complementary feeding practices, especially increased feeding frequency and high nutrient/energy density of the diet, plus reduced workload for pregnant and lactating women.

Poor households that have no means of supporting themselves are often assisted by the village with food provided from the community plot or through community donations. While the village supports needy individual households, district-level administrators identify and provide support to the most adversely affected villages; regional-level program staff monitor and backstop the district.

At each level, weight-for-age is the basic index of performance used, not only as it relates to nutritional status, but also as an indicator of the overall level of socioeconomic progress. Weight-for-age information also serves as a basis for stimulating competition between villages, which helps knit them together as joint action groups. Annual prizes are awarded to the best-performing villages.

HIGHER ADMINISTRATIVE LEVELS

Each quarter, the village health committee passes on to the ward a simple one-page report containing weight-for-age information on all participating children as well as a description of actions being taken at the village level. The report describes the support that is required from government sectors at higher levels to complement local efforts. The reports sent from the villages are discussed at the ward, district and regional levels. At each level, decisions are taken on how best to support particular villages, and tasks are assigned to certain departments. The regularity of meetings and the constant flow of readily processable information makes for greater accountability within the system. Each level of administration must report and justify to the next higher level all actions it takes in each quarter.

ADMINISTRATIVE STRUCTURE

The program has built upon the existing administrative infrastructure. Government and party workers at all levels are responsible for meeting program objectives. At the village level in Tanzania, all households have previously been grouped into ten-family groups. Leaders of all such groups along with the village party chairman and an elected village secretary, make up the village council. The village health committee functions as a subcommittee of this council. Village health workers provided by the communities are trained and then linked to public agencies operating at the community level. Extension staff and their supervisors at the ward, division and district levels are integrated into CSD activities through implementation committees that function at these levels.

Although the program operates under the banner of nutrition and child health, a wide variety of activities have been undertaken that reflect the diversity of solutions devised by different village councils. Recognizing the multisectoral nature of most local problems, interagency coordination has been instituted at the district level to ensure more effective responses to local development initiatives.

Horizontalization of agency operations at the district level has been achieved by placing the CSD-related activities of all line and sector agencies under the control of a coordinator for child survival and development. The coordinator for a district may be selected from among the staff of any of the participating line agencies, but once appointed, he or she is responsible to the planning office at the center, which exercises supraministerial authority in coordinating the activities of the separate line agencies. Thus there is close coordination between higher and lower levels of program administration. Staff are encouraged to visit problem villages and to see things firsthand. Personnel at all levels have been familiarized with the conceptual framework that is used to analyze causes and propose solutions to malnutrition and related problems.

TRAINING

Several institutions including TFNC and the University of Dar es Salaam are actively involved in this important function, which has two broad purposes. The conceptual and analytical component, in which all levels of government staff and village workers are exposed to the objectives and approach of the program, trains them to analyze causes and search for community-based solutions; a skill component gives certain cadres specialized training on technical or administrative activities for which they are responsible. Training for civil servants includes sensitizing them to local needs, problems and priorities.

The village health workers, traditional birth attendants and traditional healers, various ward, division and district officers and extension workers in agriculture, education, health and community development are all trained in this integrated approach to reducing malnutrition. The chairman, the secretary and other members of the village health committee are trained to use the Triple-A cycle. Training sessions provide, in addition to information, opportunity for dialogue and feedback.

Formal training at TFNC and regional centers is supplemented by a variety of other formats and tools. A quarterly newsletter is produced using material from trained village correspondents. Village communities are encouraged to participate in role-playing exercises. Increasingly since 1990, trained social animators have helped in mobilizing village communities. Meetings of the national steering committee—and of regional steering committees, which have taken over management responsibilities as the program has expanded—are often held in villages, with the active participation of all levels of program stakeholders. The meetings themselves act as an important forum for training and orientation. Close involvement of the TFNC helped in the development of Iringa's initial conceptual approach and in documenting and benefiting from the structured learning that resulted from the operational research conducted during implementation.

SELF-RELIANCE

External subsidies have been gradually reduced as the program has expanded. The guiding principle is to find solutions that can be accomplished with local resources before asking higher levels for assistance. A decentralization policy in operation since the mid-1980s authorizes village councils to collect levies and enact bylaws to support program objectives. Thus, programming at the village level has been facilitated by financial decentralization. Districts can also raise resources through levies and bylaws. Local authorities are now expected to finance development plans that have been formulated at the local level, although this is not always feasible. Community contributions have increased; the goal is to provide two-thirds of total program funding, although few districts have attained this level of self-financing so far. In most villages, salaries and the training costs of health workers are borne by the community.

COSTS AND PROGRAM SUSTAINABILITY

The cost of operating the CSD program has been dramatically reduced. UNICEF estimates the annual recurring costs of operating the program is now US$3–5 per child per year, far lower than the US$12–17 required in the early days of the Iringa pilot program. Staff costs are the largest category of expenditure (nearly 40 percent), and vehicles and transportation account for a further 26 percent (Jonsson et al. 1991). The higher costs in the initial phases of the program reflect the expense of high-level personnel, initial training and some infrastructure. A conscious effort has been made to reduce these costs substantially in the later phases.

While the expenditure per child in Tanzania is on par with CSD programs elsewhere, indeed somewhat lower than most, Tanzania ranks far higher in the proportion of resources contributed by the community. What is most impressive is the wide range of local talent and local resources that have been elicited as a result of program interventions. In terms of its second objective—empowering individuals and communities to act on their own behalf—the program has been successful well beyond initial expectations.

Recent changes in the economic and political situation in Tanzania—liberalization and structural adjustment and the emergence of a multi-party system—will have an effect, as yet unclear, on the long-term prospects for the program. The weakening of existing political and administrative structures, from the national to the village level, has diminished some of the institutional support that elicited and then reinforced community management. However, the breakdown of the single-party system, which initially spurred this effort, need not result in diminished political concern for child health and nutrition since all political parties continue to support investment in human development.

By moving ahead rapidly, the program has awakened strong hopes and aroused much interest across most sections of the population. In some cases, local authorities at regional and district levels have started CSD programming in anticipation of government action (UNICEF 1993). Too much has been invested now by local residents and donors alike to make a precipitous decline likely. Over the last dozen years, an effective and efficient set of procedures and incentives has been developed. An expanded program will deal not only with severe nutrition but also the relatively neglected problems of the moderately malnourished, as well as targeting efforts to address other issues associated with rural poverty.

Rural communities and their residents have always had some problem-solving capacities as a result of their need to develop the means for survival and cope with adverse conditions. However, they seldom dealt with nutrition problems directly. When poor people become aware of the presence and importance of malnutrition, they normally try to focus some of their efforts on improving the nutritional situation, such as changing their uses of available resources to remedy shortcomings, and orienting decisions and efforts to achieve desired nutritional outcomes. Most of the time, however, these activities remain far from ideal.

A systematic process consists of a correct *assessment* of problems, followed by an appropriate *analysis* of their causes. Then, based on this understanding, *actions* are taken to correct the less-than-ideal situation. This process continues to include *reassessment* so that iterative self-evaluation leads to self-directed improvement, producing continuously better results, that is, more desirable outcomes.

Such decisionmaking and action existed indigenously in Iringa, but they were mostly intermittent and seldom institutionally supported. There was no need for prepackaged approaches; indeed these would likely be inappropriate and unsuccessful. Rather there was need for outsiders to play a catalytic role in formulating and institutionalizing a process of continually identifying and solving problems, where rural people themselves would be the key actors, not passive beneficiaries of transfers of resources and provision of services. Some conceptual framework showing causes and how they relate to each other is therefore essential for systematic improvement. In Iringa, the Triple-A approach was continuously refined to be more accurate, comprehensible and applicable.

UNICEF's support has focused on training facilitators to support community mobilization. They work with village health workers and traditional birth attendants, who are respected members of the community. These locally based partners in improving village health are often volunteers or are at least recommended by friends and neighbors. They are paid by the community, while facilitators from outside are generally paid by the government or a nongovernmental organization.

The relationship between facilitators and community mobilizers determines the extent to which outside support becomes catalytic and empowering, rather than creating a new dependency, which leads to unsustainable programs. The selection and training of facilitators and community mobilizers is therefore crucial. Too often, facilitators are taught to train mobilizers on what to do. This is not likely to lead to capacity building. For facilitators to empower community mobilizers, participatory training methods must be used, and power must shift from the outside supporters to the facilitators and mobilizers working as a team for the goal of community empowerment.

For community mobilizers to be effective, there need to be community organizations. In our Iringa experience, the presence of any form of community organization was an important determinant of long-term success. Where such organizations do not exist, they need to be created. It is important, however, that these organizations represent the poorer sectors of the community as much as or more than those who are less poor. Women's groups or organizations are most likely to become committed and efficient actors on behalf of improved nutrition and for resolving other problems as well. The involvement of women through the whole program and at all levels has been crucial for rapid progress. Equally important, however, is avoiding the perception and attitude that solving the nutrition problem is solely the responsibility of women. Successful programs are gender-conscious rather than women-focused.

Establishing community-based monitoring systems was essential for accelerating the improvement of decisionmaking processes. These systems, however, should be demand-driven, that is, poor people must first become aware of the problem and have an approximate understanding of its causes, so that they can know what new information will improve their decisionmaking.

Several recent studies of successful nutrition-oriented programs have confirmed the importance of the factors described above for explaining the successes of programs in other countries. For example, the nutrition improvements achieved in Thailand show many similarities with the developments launched in Iringa in Tanzania. That these principles evolved independently lends credibility to their validity as generalizable approaches to improvement in social services and human development that is empowering and self-sustaining.

NOTE

Anirudh Krishna drafted this chapter based on documentation from the Iringa Project and the Cornell Food and Nutrition Policy Program after Urban Jonsson, a key project advisor and an adjunct professor of nutrition at Cornell, indicated that he would not have time to write such a chapter himself. He did, however, read Krishna's draft and shared it with his colleagues, B. Ljungqvist and Olivia Yambi, who were also involved with launching the Iringa project. They also endorsed this account, and Jonsson added some reflections to the chapter in October 1995. In November 1995, we became acquainted with Wilbald Lorri, also involved with the Iringa project from the start and now managing director of the Tanzania Food and Nutrition Centre. He agreed to review and augment our analysis of the Iringa case. We also thank his colleagues, Benedict Jeje and Hidaya Missano, who read and concurred with the presentation.

15 The Self-Help Rural Water Supply Program in Malawi

Anirudh Krishna with Lindesay H. Robertson

The gravity-fed rural piped water program in Malawi, one of the earliest examples of participatory rural development from sub-Saharan Africa, has been referred to as "one of the best organized piped water projects in Africa" (Hill and Mtawali 1989) and "the most outstanding rural piped water program in Africa, if not the world" (Warner et al. 1986). Forty-seven piped water schemes serving over one million people have been completed since the system of organization, incentives and technology was first developed in the late 1960s. More projects are under construction. Gravity-flow systems now serve up to 30 percent of the 8.5 million people of Malawi, 88 percent of whom live in small villages scattered throughout the country.

The situation in this region prior to the installation of the piped water schemes was summed up by two Malawian respondents, quoted by Liebenow (1981):

#1: The absence of water during the dry season meant that my mother had to get up before dawn and start the search for water before we took off for school. Often she had to travel many miles to a river bed and dig through the sand with a metal cup until she came to the water level. It often took hours of digging and dipping until she had enough water for the cooking and drinking. There was never enough for bathing or washing our clothes even though we insist on bathing daily during the rainy season.

#2: It was not until I went off to boarding school that I realized that I did not actually have to suffer from dysentery during the dry months. I though it was a natural state of affairs associated with the change of weather. We used to drink green brackish water like that over there [pointing to a stagnant pool].

The situation was thus quite similar to that faced by poor rural inhabitants in many parts of the developing world. However, within fifteen years, beginning in 1968, gravity-fed systems were providing a safe and reliable water supply to nearly one million such people. Thousands more were applying to be included and offering voluntary labor contributions to

228

install similar systems in their villages, with support, encouragement and sometimes direction from the local party leadership.

Local communities were responsible for constructing water facilities in their villages. To be eligible for inclusion under the scheme, they had to agree to make substantial voluntary contributions. Technical supervision and construction materials were provided by the government, and financial assistance was made available by a range of international donors.

These systems bring piped water to villages from a year-round source, spring or stream, located in the mountains. Since the source is located far above the line of habitation, the water is free of pollutants. Water from the source flows by gravity to public taps located at convenient points in the villages, after passing through screens and sedimentation tanks that allow suspended particles to be removed. Experience shows that these schemes have proven to be extremely reliable. Since the source of water is perennial, reliability is a function of construction quality and system maintenance. On both these counts, the systems constructed have performed well. Their good performance was both a result of and a motivating factor for high levels of community involvement.

New schemes are undertaken in an area only at the request of the local communities. They are not only involved in system design and planning; they are required to supply nearly all the labor for construction and to carry out continuing maintenance after construction. Maintenance has been of a high order, with more than 90 percent of disruptions set right within two days, according to Warner et al. (1986). The women of these areas no longer have to walk long distances to fetch water, and the incidence of disease has been much reduced (Chauhan 1983). Liebenow (1981) reported a considerable movement of Malawians into the areas newly served by piped water.

The program developed an appropriate technology that matched local needs and local resource endowments. Project costs to government have been kept low by the large amounts of voluntary effort made available by local communities. This has contributed to the rapid spread and durability of the systems, and, more importantly, to a strong sense of local ownership. Communities not only feel responsible for maintenance and upkeep; they have been equipped to perform these tasks by being provided with training, basic equipment and ready access to technical advice.

The expanded role for local people is possible in part because the technology is simple and relatively easy to handle. This, however, was no coincidence. Simplicity of technical solutions provides no automatic formula for successful rural development. Project managers had to devise an appropriate fit between technology, resource endowments, local institutions and system-level capabilities. Tracing the dynamic interplay between technology and local institutional development, guided by program management, offers lessons for development practitioners from the Malawi water supply case.

EVOLUTION OF THE SYSTEM — THE PILOT PROJECTS

A 1968 community development project intended to serve sixteen villages in the Chingale area identified gravity-fed, piped water schemes as a possible technical solution to the chronic problem of water shortage in the region. Robertson, the engineer with the project, had been recently recruited to the Ministry of Community Development and Social Welfare to work in this area. As he had lived for ten years in Malawi as a missionary before joining the government, he had already considerable experience working with rural communities. A good account of this whole program has been written up by HABITAT (1989).

A perennial stream on the lower slope of Zomba Mountain offered a year-round source of potable water. Once a source of water was identified, the hardest thing was to convince Chingale community representatives that water could flow the full distance—ten kilometers and even uphill in some stretches—to the villages. Local people formed a water supply committee that mobilized voluntary labor to dig trenches for the pipeline. This committee was also made responsible for the subsequent maintenance of the system. The government agency provided material inputs—pipes, fittings and cement—and made available technical supervision. The supply was distributed through twenty-five taps serving 3,000 villagers, providing each of them up to 27 liters of clean water a day, throughout the year. The total cost to the government was US$7,200, less than $3 per capita, primarily covering the cost of the 25 kilometers of pipe needed to carry and distribute the water.

The success of the Chingale project persuaded the Ministry of Community Development and Social Welfare to extend the same approach to the Chambe area in Mulanje district. As a first step, village leaders were taken to Chingale to meet the local water supply committees and to inspect the project. They were convinced of the benefits from the system, and on returning to their villages, persuaded other residents that it would be worthwhile to undertake a similar project and to make the contributions that would be required of their community. A public meeting was then convened where the government engineer offered materials and technical advice, if local residents would agree to supply the labor and subsequent management. They agreed, and the government posted an engineer with five community development assistants in the expanded project area.

Construction began in 1969 and was completed in 1970 at a cost of about US$80,000. Water supplied through 180 public taps served a population of

30,000 living in sixty villages. Again, the government's cost was under $3 per capita. Since this project was much larger than the Chingale project and took longer to complete, there were times during the construction period when local enthusiasm flagged and work slowed or stopped. Organizers then realized that close communication between project staff, community leaders and local people could be better achieved by organizing the work in smaller project areas.

SCALING-UP

The success of the two initial projects led to greater official and donor-agency interest in gravity-fed systems and a groundswell of local interest emerged. Other village communities, once they perceived the benefits of the new water schemes and understood the commitments required of them, began to offer labor contributions if similar projects were taken up in their areas. However, "the government decided on a policy of controlled growth . . . because of the limited number of trained people . . . too rapid development could result in unsuccessful projects (Hill and Mtawali 1989, 60). At the time, only two more projects were taken up in the Chambe area. Gradually, more projects were taken up in other parts of the country.

A rural piped water section was established within the Ministry of Community Development and Social Welfare. Six major and five minor projects serving over 400,000 persons were started over the next ten years, with donor agencies providing funds for materials and staff salaries. Among the donors were DANIDA, CIDA, Oxfam, UNICEF, the Dutch protestant and the Dutch Catholic aid organizations, and the Christian Service Committee of the Churches of Malawi. The program received a major boost in 1980 when the U.S. Agency for International Development (USAID) undertook to finance a five-year expansion of the program (later extended to eight years). By 1985, twelve out of eighteen new USAID-assisted schemes had been completed, serving an additional 265,000 people.

The later generation of projects, while primarily focused on gravity-fed rural water supply, also included complementary activities related to health education and sanitation. Additional project activities included construction of pit latrines, washing slabs and refuse pits, and training in basic health and sanitation. Field personnel from the department of health worked with village-level planning units, which previously included only technical and engineering personnel as government representatives. The principles and procedures of assisted self-help that evolved during the pilot water supply projects were extended to apply to these new activities as well.

The concern for steady but controlled expansion enabled project management to analyze and benefit from experience and to change specific aspects where problems had occurred earlier. For example, the cement-asbestos pipes used in earlier projects were increasingly replaced by locally produced PVC pipes that were easier to handle. Maintenance, initially the sole responsibility of the village community, is now shared with the government, which accepts responsibility for repair jobs that are technically beyond the abilities of village paraprofessionals (Glennie 1983).

SELF-HELP AND COMMUNITY ORGANIZATION

The key to the projects' success is the involvement of the whole community, and the setting up of a village community organization that can handle the large amount of work to be done and ensure that everyone does his or her share (Robertson 1981). The first step in community organization is to hold a public meeting to discuss the project. Members of parliament, party leaders, government functionaries and local residents attend the meeting. The area chief asks his people if they want the project and are willing to work for it. If they agree, the village assembly appoints a project committee to organize work on the project. A network of local committees is formed to correspond with the physical system of the pipeline that will carry water from the hill sources to the communities. It is important that these committees are not appointed by the government, and that they derive support from the people, chiefs and party leaders.

The functions of local committees differ during the construction phase and the maintenance phase. During the construction phase, a main water committee, consisting of community leaders from each village to be served, is responsible for overall program management. It plans the work and allocates tasks among participating villages. Section committees or branch committees are elected in each village located along various sections of the pipe. These are responsible for organizing the voluntary labor contributed by households in each village to perform the work according to the program already agreed upon. Village committees select standpipe sites in their respective villages, organize self-help labor from each village in work groups and try to ensure a good turnout.

In the maintenance phase, the main water committee, repair teams, tap committees and village health committees all operate. The main water committee, which carries over from the construction phase, supervises the repair teams and reports all situations requiring major repairs to government staff, who are locally deployed and respond quickly to any committee calls for assistance. All routine inspections, maintenance, replacement and repairs are undertaken by the village repair teams. Tap committees at the village level are responsible for keeping the tap site clean, for replacing tap washers, and for reporting other problems to the village repair team.

A majority of members on most tap committees are women, as is true for many of the village committees. All funds that are required for local repairs, and those needed to compensate members of repair teams, are raised from the village community. Members of repair teams are trained in basic maintenance and repair skills by government staff. In fact, training has been a major focus of the program because "unskilled and semiskilled voluntary labor—no matter how well motivated and energetic—can accomplish little unless skills are introduced" (Liebenow 1981).

Committee members receive training so that they can provide informed supervision to volunteer laborers. Tasks requiring skilled labor are not entrusted to local committees. Instead, project authorities recruit and train from among local residents a cadre of specialized technical personnel. Complex construction tasks are turned over to teams of these personnel. But wherever possible, tasks have been redesigned to make them more appropriate for unskilled or semiskilled village teams, even if this has sometimes resulted in small technical compromises.

The main project committee operates under the district development committee, which is chaired by the district commissioner and includes members of parliament, party leaders, district-level heads of government agencies, and other elected representatives. This main project committee oversees the network of village-level committees, which in turn guide the self-help efforts of communities.

The allocation of tasks between local communities and the government agency follows the principle of comparative advantage. Thus, government is responsible for undertaking feasibility studies and aerial surveys, for supervising construction to maintain quality, for arranging funds to cover the material costs, for training and for helping communities establish the committees that manage local inputs. Local communities are primarily responsible for digging the trenches and the foundations for intake and sedimentation tanks, for helping carry pipes and other materials, for laying the pipeline, and for providing sand, stones, other materials and tools that are available at little cost to them. They also have responsibility for routine maintenance.

STRUCTURES AND PROCESSES

A request for a new scheme from any community is channeled to the responsible government department through the district development committee. To ensure proper coordination among the various government agencies that deal with rural water supply, at the start of the United Nation's Decade of Water in 1980, a department of lands, valuation and water was created within the Office of the President and given sole responsibility for all water schemes.[1] Any new proposal is examined according to two criteria: the first, technical feasibility, concerns the availability of a source of potable water at an altitude high enough to allow a gravity-flow system to work; the second, social feasibility, is concerned with the degree of local interest evident in the villages to be served for taking responsibility to manage and maintain a collaborative undertaking. In choosing between alternative locations that are otherwise similar, government planners give preference to areas that have a high potential for agriculture development and a small population base that could be expanded if there were a reliable source of drinking water.

A flexible approach to planning and implementation has enabled variations in the general strategy to suit particular local circumstances. Project staff in charge of field implementation are responsible, in association with local leaders, for designing the scheme and for scheduling construction activities. They are given full responsibility and authority for dealing with local people and for addressing their preferences and priorities. When recruiting project staff, technical qualifications are given roughly the same weight as attitudinal attributes, such as willingness to live in remote rural areas and ability to cooperate and work with poor rural people.

Technical assistants live in the villages, working under the direction of more experienced project staff, before they are given independent responsibility for an area. At this time, they are organized into small teams, headed by a supervisor who regularly visits them in their place of work. Team spirit is promoted by regular meetings, open consultations, sporting and social events and by nurturing interteam competition.

The work schedule is organized so that most of the labor inputs can be made during the slack agricultural period. Activities that require relatively small amounts of voluntary labor, such as surveying or specialized construction tasks, are undertaken when seasonal agricultural demands for labor are highest, that is, when planting or harvesting are being done by local residents, most of whom are farmers.

Construction commences from the source, with the intake and main line being built first. Water is sent down the pipes as each new section is added. This gives visual evidence to the volunteer workers that, through their efforts, the mountain water is being brought closer to their villages. To ensure a smooth flow of work, tools are pre-positioned by department staff before the work groups arrive each morning. The same attention to detail ensures that pipes are delivered on time to the trenches that are ready to receive them.

All of this planning helps to foster and maintain people's enthusiasm, which is crucial to the spirit of local self-help. The completion of a branch line to a village is marked by a ceremony in which the system is symbolically handed over to the village committee to maintain. Local participation in the maintenance phase is made easier by people's involvement during the construction phase. The knowledge that local residents acquire while participating in the construction phase also ensures that the exact location of the pipe can be quickly detected in case of a break.

COSTS

Over time, the costs of the gravity-fed water supply schemes grew from about US$3.00 per capita at the outset to about US$7.60 by 1987 (though some of the increase is no doubt due to inflation).[2] Schemes constructed under a USAID program, supplying 36 liters per person per day to over 400,000 persons in the late 1980s, had construction costs of US$14.60 per capita, still a very favorable rate of expenditure (HABITAT 1989, 21). Gravity-fed systems remain considerably cheaper than available alternatives. Moreover, if reliability of supply and ease of maintenance are considered, the gravity schemes come out even further ahead, being much simpler to operate and maintain than the alternatives. The estimated costs of maintenance for the USAID schemes was figured to be US$.15 per person per year, half of which is covered by communities.

However, assessing the direct labor costs of construction in strictly monetary terms undervalues the longer-term benefits that result from voluntary community involvement. It is difficult to explain the high levels of system reliability and sustainability without appreciating the strong sense of community ownership that has marked each stage of the program. This sense is largely the result of cost and management sharing. Thus, village residents regularly inspect and maintain these systems and devote considerable energies in keeping them in good working order. The government agency can meet its responsibilities for doing all major repairs because the need for such repair has, to a large extent, been obviated by regular maintenance at the village level. Compare this with the familiar experience of water supply systems—and other infrastructural investments—constructed with full financing and complete management control provided by governments or donor agencies. Most of these have not lasted long and needed frequent large outlays on rehabilitation and repair.

LESSONS

The Malawi gravity-fed rural water supply schemes, one of the earliest examples of popular participation in large-scale, government-sponsored development projects in Africa, developed a methodology for participatory development that has delivered sustainable benefits over a wide scale of operation. Several elements of successful project design and management identified by observers of rural development during the last two decades are found in the Malawi program, which was elaborated gradually during the late 1960s and early 1970s. These lessons continue to be relevant today:

- Devising appropriate technical and social-organizational solutions through a pilot-project learning process built capacity as the program expanded gradually.

- Developing local ownership was a three-step process: (i) demonstrating the benefits of the new system by organizing site visits for local leaders, (ii) requiring that local communities make matching contributions and (iii) treating local communities as partners at all stages of the program—design, implementation and maintenance.

- Sharing responsibility between the government and local communities based on their respective comparative advantages meant communities were expected to perform only the tasks they could manage, given appropriate training, resources and organizational support.

- Devolving authority for planning and implementation to field-based staff enabled field-level personnel to fine-tune program design and bring it more in line with local preferences, making it possible for village communities to exercise greater control.

- Working with existing patterns of local organization considered appropriate to local cultural conditions and working with recognized local leadership, both traditional and political, permitted the program to expand quickly and yet leave behind effective local management capacity.

- Political factors can be very important in either positive or negative ways. In the early years, the Malawi Congress Party was a constructive actor at the branch (village) level, bridging between traditional leaders and the self-help committees. As often happens, over two decades of rule, the Party became alienated from its roots and was eventually overthrown. In the later years, Party actions undermined some of the spirit of self-help. What role politics will play in the future remains uncertain, but it must always be considered.

The Malawi rural water program shows what can be accomplished, both quickly and at relatively low cost, when a system of assistance is put in place that encourages and supports self-help and self-management. The validity of its main elements is confirmed by an extensive evaluation for the World Bank using many quantified measures of 120 other rural water supply programs around the world (Narayan 1995).

Recalling a conversation he overheard some years ago, Robertson suggests that certain aspects involving motivations and values, not addressed in the World Bank study, should be considered. For example, a donor representative was surprised to learn that the local chairman of a self-help water project lived outside the project area, and thus his village would not receive any water from the investment of labor he was managing.

"You mean to say," the visitor asked incredulously, "that you do all this work without getting get paid for it, and you don't even get any water from the project yourself? How is this?"

"That is quite easy to answer," came the reply. "The people in these villages are my brothers and sisters. When they drink good water, I drink."

The spirit of self-help that was roused in Malawi was thus not simply a selfish one, although people's efforts were amply and well rewarded; it was also a public-serving one. This aspect of development should not be forgotten. When all the pieces can fit together, there is a tremendous potential for change and improvement among rural people. The task of development is to fit all the pieces together.

The early water projects in Malawi ironed out the wrinkles not just in the technology but also in people's attitudes. Local leaders emerged who came forward with their ideas. Field staff realized that they could contribute important insights and recommendations, and they took pride in doing so. As the program proceeded, policy and ways of doing things were not dictated from the top, but grew out of solutions to day-to-day problems, through the sharing of ideas among various contributors— field staff, villagers, technical management—all working together. U.S. Peace Corps, British Voluntary Service Organization (VSO) and other volunteers adapted easily to this philosophy, and like-minded donors appreciated it, so the program became established and grew. It is still growing.

NOTES

Because this is one of the most impressive and instructive cases of scaled-up, sustainable rural development, especially in Africa, we tried for many months to reach Lindesay Robertson, the initial project engineer and a key actor in this program. When no connections could be made through Malawi, Krishna drafted this chapter, drawing on Robertson's own report on this program (1981) and on several other studies and evaluations included in the bibliography. Fortunately, before this volume was finished, we made contact with Robertson in Scotland, where he has retired. He reviewed the draft chapter and confirmed its accuracy, contributing at our request some of his own observations to this account.

1. Before 1980, during the formative years of the project, the rural piped water section was within the Ministry of Community Development and Social Welfare. Subsequently, in 1984, the rural water department was transferred to the Ministry of Works. Thus the rural piped water work was able to establish its identity and modus operandi—working in a participatory manner with local communities—before it was absorbed into a more "technical" department.

2. A USAID evaluation estimated that of the per capita cost of providing water in the late 1980s, US$6.60 was for materials, and the per capita community labor was valued at only US$1.00 (Warner et al. 1986). This certainly undervalues voluntary labor contributions. Even at the low Malawian wage rate on which this calculation is based, it is difficult to see how labor inputs—on the order of two to three weeks of work for every adult (man or woman) in a village—can be translated into such a small amount. Moreover, the calculation includes only the direct costs and does not take account of overheads, including supervision and training, or of the time expended by local residents in discussing and planning and in forging agreement among themselves. The latter are not cost-free activities; there is a high opportunity cost of time for the poor, who must manage a day-to-day existence as casual wage earners supplementing whatever their meager plots of land produce. The wages lost through spending two to three weeks in volunteer labor have to be made up by working extra hours at another time.

NATURAL RESOURCES: AGROFORESTRY, WATERSHED, AND WILDLIFE MANAGEMENT

16 A Haitian Peasant Tree Chronicle: Adaptive Evolution and Institutional Intrusion

Gerald F. Murray

During ten years of operation, between 1981 and 1991, the Agroforestry Outreach Project (AOP) made it possible for some 200,000 peasant households throughout the ecologically and politically ravaged country of Haiti to plant over sixty million fast-growing wood tree seedlings on their land. The unexpected participation of as much as 20 percent of the entire rural population in this tree-planting effort vastly exceeded what anyone had anticipated. Several articles and reports (for example, Conway 1986; Murray 1984, 1987; Lowenthal 1989) have discussed the project's conceptual and methodological underpinnings; how it used anthropological theory and ethnographic methods to reformulate the relationship between trees and people in a manner acceptable to Haitian villagers, and how it employed nongovernmental channels to implement the project, bypassing Duvalierist ministries to assure that donor funds would reach intended beneficiaries in the form of income-generating seedlings.

After ten years of effective operation, the project was renewed for yet another five years. But it was brought to a sudden halt by bureaucratic interventions in 1991. Even though it was partially resurrected in early 1995, it is important to examine the vulnerability of such an undertaking to institutional oscillations. Although tens of thousands of rural households benefited from the AOP's provision of trees, this case shows that even well-functioning projects can be damaged by institutional meddling.

BACKGROUND

Three basic assumptions underlay AOP design: (a) that the rural smallholding population was the sector most likely to spearhead tree planting in Haiti; (b) that this effort had to build on microeconomic considerations, specifically on peasants' need for income, rather than on the macroecological concerns that shape the thinking of most development agencies and environmentalists; and (c) that externally funded projects can facilitate substantial behavioral change, if designed on the basis of ethnographic insights into smallholder socioeconomics.

The initial project document (Murray 1979) identified institutional factors—project design and implementation—rather than village-level barriers as the source of previous failures. Given appropriate incentives and opportunities, it was argued, Haitian villagers would plant trees in great numbers. Having contributed preliminary studies and helped design the project, I was invited by the U.S. Agency for International Development (USAID) to launch and direct it for the first two years. The project's rapid output argued for the correctness of its core hypotheses. However, even a well-functioning project that meshes with local cultural subsystems, is ahead of schedule in producing targeted outputs, and evolves still more effective procedures over time can be sabotaged.

In Haiti the usual whipping boy for such an institutional critique is its government. In this case, such lashes would be off target. The AOP was designed to be insulated both from the institutionalized predation of Duvalierist ministries and the institutional chaos of the post-Duvalier years. The intruding institution was, paradoxically, the provider of generous support over the previous decade, USAID.

Although some unfortunate behaviors on the part of individual USAID officials are chronicled here, the agency's overall track record in Haiti was generally far better than that of most other bilateral or multilateral agencies of equivalent size. During the years of disorder and public sector paralysis that followed Duvalier's ouster in 1986, most large donor agencies, led by their mandates and/or their philosophies to channel their funds through the government of Haiti, reacted to the political chaos by sitting on their hands, shaking their heads, sharpening their pencils, doing studies, or closing their offices and evacuating their expatriate personnel. USAID, in contrast, was one of the few donors in Haiti that continued, despite political chaos, to fund ground-level activities in health, nutrition, tree planting and job creation. A simplistic USAID-bashing critique would therefore be unwarranted. This account identifies the extraneous management factors that can cause an institution's program decisions to oscillate between inspired deftness and ill-informed bludgeoning. The oscillations continue, as the agency now appears to be moving back to a more supportive role.[1]

AOP did not regreen the entire Haitian landscape, a goal that might require either centuries of time or preternatural interventions far beyond the capacity of a development project, but it did induce two hundred thousand households throughout rural Haiti to incorporate serious tree planting (several hundred trees per household) into their economic survival strategies. Although the hefty funding required to resurrect the project has yet to materialize, two of the thirty-five nurseries are back in operation, generating a trickle of trees that will hopefully swell again to the volume of the 1980s. Even though this present trend is promising, the structural vulnerability of efforts such as AOP to institutional swings, by a donor or a sponsoring government, is in itself a major problem that warrant systematic analysis.

UNDERLYING PROJECT THEORY

During the nineteenth century, the interest of foreigners in the trees of Haiti was exclusively extractive. Haitian regimes allied themselves with foreign companies to remove much of the precious hardwood from Haiti's forests. In the twentieth century this orientation was reversed. Starting in the late 1940s, foreign agencies began financing reforestation projects among Haitian peasants. Generally, these projects were inspired by ideologies of statism, environmentalism and protectionism. The Haitian state was to promote and own the trees planted; the trees would be planted principally to restore and protect the environment, and, once planted, the trees themselves would have to be protected from peasant woodcutters and charcoal makers.

Villagers identified the Creole term *rebwazman* (reforestation) with coercive interventions by the Haitian state—supported by foreign money—to force them to cover part of their land with unwanted trees, whose subsequent removal could result in penalties. Rumors spread throughout villages that the state or the foreign project would subsequently expropriate the land once the trees were mature. Given these factors, it should be no surprise that tree-planting projects in Haiti had little success.

Based on anthropological reconstructions of cultural evolutionary processes and on my own ethnographic research on Haitian peasant communities, I proposed that USAID try to reverse all three of these principles. First, state control of wood would be replaced by peasant ownership and usufruct rights; second, the macroecological needs of the environment would be served not directly but instead indirectly, by meeting the microeconomic needs of smallholding cultivators; and third, fast-growing wood trees would be planted, not for protection's sake, but explicitly for harvesting and selling wood, thereby encouraging widespread planting. Together these ideas led to a major paradigmatic and programmatic shift in USAID's strategy for Haiti.

The evolutionary theory underlying the project strategy was based on an analogy between the current wood crisis and the much earlier food crisis of our mesolithic ancestors that led to the ancient neolithic transition from foraging to a domesticated mode of food production. Our hunter-gatherer predecessors did not solve the increasing scarcities of wild meat and vegetation through protectionist or conservationist tactics. Rather, they responded by shifting gradually into a domesticated mode of food procurement (Murray 1987). The contemporary tree dilemma, both globally and in Haiti, viewed within the same theoretical framework, proposes a transition from an extractive mode of procurement to a domesticated mode of production. Designing tree-planting projects that regard wood as a renewable crop to be harvested and used would better suit the orientation of the Haitian peasants, among whom I had worked, and also correspond to the prehistoric strategy adopted by our neolithic ancestors to deal with the decline of natural sources of vegetation.

This was the historical rationale for the proposed tree-planting strategy. But projects have to function in the existential present. The major contemporary assumption was that present Haitian farmers, operating in the ethnographic here-and-now, are energetic and economically rational decisionmakers oriented principally toward the market in their land use decisions. They previously rejected tree projects, it was hypothesized, because projects failed to link tree promotion to local market opportunities, toward which the economic energies of Haitian peasants have been so heavily oriented for the past two centuries.

Since Haitian households had only smallholdings to cultivate, wood trees would have to be incorporated into existing farming systems that were already under stress. Peasants would not plant forests, but only wood lots or tree stands. Thus, the idea of *agroforestry*—the combination of food crops and trees on the same plot, or at least on the same holding—replaced that of *reforestation* as the guiding concept of the project. Second, in view of the involvement of Haitian peasants in local markets, the planting of trees was explicitly and publicly promoted as an *income-generating* rather than as an ecological or subsistence strategy. Project messages thus promoted, rather than castigated, the cutting and selling of wood.

The project was planned with three core components, each of which had to be carefully programmed and thought out: a *technical* strategy that would produce trees, a *benefit-flow* strategy ensuring that the economic resources from tree planting would go to the farmers and not to some other social group, and an *institutional delivery* strategy to guarantee that donor funds would not get siphoned off by other actors with their own personal or institutional agendas.

Previous projects had focused largely on the technical dimension and mostly ignored local benefits. Ownership of the trees planted had been assigned, in some projects, to a vague village entity or to the state itself, while in other projects it was left undefined. Either way, farmers were not sure that they were really the owners of the trees, and many were apprehensive about eventual expropriation of their land once it was planted with alien trees. Being told that trees should be protected, not cut, further raised apprehensions. Ownership ambiguity, ecological sermonizing and hidden threats dampened potential farmer interest in planting trees.

To counteract this, AOP explicitly and publicly assured full ownership of the trees to the individual farmers planting them. Indeed, the project took the locally unprecedented step of encouraging farmers to cut their trees, without asking project permission first, to harvest the wood and sell it as lumber or charcoal whenever the trees were mature and the trees' owner needed cash. Presenting fast-growing wood as a privately owned, harvestable crop was a new message to most of these farmers.

Equally critical to ensuring benefit flows was the institutional delivery strategy. Despite the predatory attitude of the Duvalier regime toward development funds, USAID and other agencies routinely channeled the bulk of their grants and loans through one or another government ministry. As a result, tree-planting funds routed through the ministry of agriculture produced very few trees. This institutional route was tactfully but purposefully circumvented in the project design.

An alternative delivery structure based exclusively on nongovernmental organizations (NGOs) was adopted, despite protest from Duvalierist officials and from several highly placed USAID officials in Haiti who saw their task, abstractly, as that of "building institutions." Stripped of its sloganeering veneer, this approach often amounted to dutifully pumping new infusions of U.S. money into predatory Haitian state bureaucracies. After some bloody in-house battles within USAID and some courageous backroom maneuvering by some junior USAID officials, an innovative project was approved in which not one nickel would go to Duvalierist bureaucracies. The part of the program that I initially managed was a grant of $4 million, made to a U.S.-based NGO which undertook to enter into agreements with local NGOs all over Haiti. These organizations actually organized the outplanting and follow-up on the trees.

The operational foundation of the project was the Haitian peasant household that agreed to plant several hundred fast-growing trees on its own land. AOP entered into an arrangement with villagers, an informal contract, by which households would supply two of the factors of production, and AOP would supply the third. Farmers who wished to participate would have to make some of their own land available for the trees and would have to supply all the labor. The project would provide the capital in the form of free seedlings. The project would also provide technical assistance, suggesting different ways to incorporate trees into existing farms—distinct woodlots, border plantings on cropped fields, rows of trees within fields, full intercropping with other crops. These were simple recommendations. Decisions about how they would plant their trees on their own land were left to farmers.

The early results of the project have been described in numerous publications and reports generated by the project itself.[2] These reports document that farmer response to this new option far exceeded even the most optimistic project projections. Many, perhaps most, government projects have time delays and cost overruns. This project faced the opposite dilemma: once Haitian peasants were convinced that the trees would be theirs—and not the state's or the project's—and that they could harvest the wood when and as they needed it, villagers requested and planted four to five times more trees than the original estimates. Also, the project found ways of supplying the seedlings for much less than the original estimated cost, which enabled it to increase its output as demand expanded.

As a result, the four-year goal of getting four million trees planted had already been reached by the end of year two; by the end of year four, some twenty million tree seedlings had been distributed, rather than the four million originally envisioned over five years. Survival rates, at first low, particularly in the drier areas, soon rose to technically acceptable levels—in the 60 percent range after twelve months. As news of the project spread, peasant demand for the seedlings kept increasing.

PROJECT EVOLUTION

Because it surpassed early goals, the project was renewed and extended for a decade. When my contract terminated toward the end of year two, another anthropologist assumed project directorship. During its ten-year life, the project experienced two types of pressure for change: positive internal ones that nudged it onto more adaptive pathways, and destructive ones stemming from intruding external forces. Both kinds of pressures occurred from the beginning.

Adaptive Internal Evolution

Throughout its life, the project adhered to its original principles of private tree ownership and of peasant rights to harvest the wood for income-generating purposes. But other aspects of AOP shifted and evolved. A major shift was the eventual decentralization of seedling production. Seedlings were originally supplied by a large nursery near Port-au-Prince and shipped by truck to communities in distant parts of the island. This initial dependence on one central nursery had been reluctantly adopted as a temporary means to launch the project rapidly. Within a few years, happily, seedling production became decentralized and regionalized, as a network of over thirty well-run nurseries was established all over Haiti, managed by many of the same Haitian NGOs that were organizing the outplanting of the trees. Large numbers of farmer-run backyard nurseries were also started to supplement the NGO nurseries.

Second, an increase in the variety of trees made available to farmers, including locally known species, moved them away from reliance on a few exotic species. Third, although for logistical reasons the project had to supply standard packages of seedlings to farmers, the mixes of trees supplied to individual farmers became more tailored to local demand, and a few nurseries actually began taking orders from individual farmers for specific numbers of seedlings of selected species.

Fourth, the number of seedlings delivered to individuals was reduced from 500 to 250 or less. This was done partly to permit the project to reach more farmers, since the demand for seedlings had outstripped the project's capacity to produce them. But many farmers were not able to plant 500 seedlings at once. On the basis of our conversations with farmers during project design, we had calculated that even small farmers would have access to enough space on their holdings for this number. If planted in a two-meter by two-meter grid, 500 seedlings would require only one-fifth of a hectare. But we had not factored in competing demands on farmers' labor.

At nurseries, seedlings could easily be removed from their containers (special root trainers that produced easily transportable microseedlings) and shipped to a region within a few days of the onset of the annual rains. But to prevent spoilage, they had to be planted within a few days by the farmers who received them. Farmers were also planting their other crops at precisely this time, and many farmers were leaving some of their 500 seedlings unplanted. Providing smaller numbers of trees at one time permitted AOP to reach more farmers, and it meant that more care was given to the seedlings themselves.

A fifth shift was the emergence of alley-cropping and hedgerows as a major project activity. Initially, AOP focused on wood trees as a future harvestable wood crop, placing little emphasis on soil conservation. Once hedgerows and alley-cropping began to be introduced, using *leucaena* and other appropriate species, which trapped soil that would otherwise wash downhill and which increased crop production near the hedgerows through nitrogen fixation, both soil conservation and increased agricultural production emerged as important project contributions. AOP thus evolved from being a promoter of wood trees to being a genuine agroforestry project.

Other positive shifts were administrative. In its first years, the project covered four regions; this number was increased to five. Initially, regional directors were all expatriates. Even though all expatriate staff were required to become fluent in Creole, English continued to be the language of in-house project meetings and project documents. Within a few years, however, Haitians worked themselves up into positions of increasing responsibility, and Creole became the language of meetings and of project documents. While this shift to Creole as the project language did not increase the flow of trees, it was symbolically important for the Haitianization of the project.

Negative External Pressures

Adverse influences were also encountered, although, at least in the beginning, they were resisted. A dynamic staff person backstopping AOP in the Washington home office of the implementing NGO provided important support to the field operations, and fortunately, she stayed with the project for ten years. Perhaps by virtue of his own institutional responsibilities, however, the NGO's executive officer when the project commenced, a former USAID mission director, gave the impression of being less concerned with what the NGO could do for the project than vice versa. There were pressures to acquiesce in questionable but technically legal (and perhaps quite common) courtesies to friends and colleagues of the CEO. Fortunately, the importuning was withdrawn when the field office resisted.[3]

USAID/Haiti itself began shackling the project with cost-inflating accretions of marginal value to the central goal of the project. A separate multimillion dollar research project, whose major beneficiaries were, in my opinion, U.S. professors, contractors and graduate students, was foisted on AOP, although many interesting studies of high quality came out of this (for example, Balzano 1986, 1989; Ashley 1986; Grosenick 1986). Fortunately, the funds for this research were not extracted from AOP's operational budget but were added on by USAID; thus, the research did not reduce or impede the flow of trees. But it did absorb funds that might have been better used for direct project outputs, and it added an aura of bureaucratic, business-as-usual opportunism to a project whose managers had, up to that time, been proud of cutting costs and beating deadlines.

Despite these external pressures, for ten years the project functioned well. Appreciating this, the USAID mission in Haiti extended AOP for a year beyond its original termination date, and then extended it for another five years, through 1991. During the turbulent years following Duvalier's removal in 1986, when political chaos brought most government programs to a halt, AOP continued largely unaffected, because of its nongovernmental implementation and because of the increasing demand by Haitian peasants for what the project offered. After a highly positive end-of-project evaluation in 1991, AOP was renewed again for another five-year period under a new name. Shortly thereafter, disaster struck.

This occurred with the arrival of a new USAID mission director who began dismantling what his predecessors had supported successfully. Even though a cooperative agreement had been signed between USAID and the participating NGOs to continue the project for another five years, the new director simply revoked the agreement and forbade the grantees to distribute any more free seedlings. Peasants, he said, were no longer to be spoiled with subsidies; they should pay full market costs for any seedlings which they received from any USAID project. However, this opposition to subsidies was apparently limited to Haitian farmers because it did not apply to the government officials and foreign contractors whose salaries and air-conditioned vehicles are routinely subsidized by the agency.

This arbitrary change in policy undermined the foundations of the project as it was then operating—essentially a voluntary exchange with farmers who, if they supplied land and labor, were provided several hundred seedlings free of charge. This arrangement was identical in many ways with that prevailing in the United States. When working with much more prosperous farmers in its own country, the American government already knew that it would have to underwrite most or all of the cost of seedlings if it wanted to get wood trees planted on private farms. Project implementers knew that suddenly requiring Haitian peasants to pay cash for seedlings would bring the project to a halt.

The participating NGOs protested and argued against this policy change. The project had received outstanding outside evaluations; it had been the jewel in the mission's portfolio during the 1980s and had achieved growing international attention as a showcase project. Haitian farmers were certainly less able than American farmers to pay for tree seedlings, particularly given their economic distress following years of international embargo against Haiti after the ouster of Duvalier. The mission director, however, ignored every evaluation, every message, every plea—and imposed his new policy. The result was the shutdown of thirty-five nurseries around Haiti, which were putting out nearly eight million forest trees per year onto degraded Haitian peasant land, at a time when efforts should have been accelerated to restore Haiti's devastated environment. Ironically, this USAID decision was taken at a time when the U.S.-imposed embargo was forcing Haitians to accelerate their charcoal production in rural areas.

The project itself was not officially terminated. Rather it was converted into a more conventional hillside farming project which emphasized alley-cropping, backyard tree nurseries, and other improved land use behaviors,

most of which AOP had already introduced as supplements to tree planting. These activities now became the main focus, as tree planting was rele-
gated to the margins, and the unique system of agroforestry extension
developed in the 1980s was abandoned. The number of trees planted per
year plummeted from eight million to several hundred thousand. The survival monitoring, a central part of AOP, was dropped. The number of
farmers reached by the project per year declined from tens of thousands to
a fraction of that number. What did not decrease, of course, was the cost of
the project. Under AOP we were spending about $70 per rural participant.
The cost in the new project is closer to $750 per participant, but only a frac-
tion of this reached villagers in terms of any palpable material benefits.

The return of Aristide in late 1994, plus the widely unlamented depar-
ture of that mission director from Haiti, opened the door to reexamining
USAID's environmental projects. High-level authorities in USAID/Wash-
ington, apparently acting in response to a nudge from the White House,
put together a special environmental task force for Haiti in November
1994. I was invited to join the task force as an outside member and was
given a green light to assist in putting together proposals for the resurrec-
tion of AOP. The anticipated resumption of significant development assistance to Haiti has not materialized, so most of the activities that the task
force proposed remain on paper. But one small activity has been reestab-
lished, the reopening of several root-trainer nurseries. Tree dissemination
is receiving less than a million dollars, not the twelve million dollars that
was requested and justified. But the system is slowly being primed again,
and reactivation of the tree flow is feasible.

LEARNING FROM EXPERIENCE

The willingness of Haitian villagers to plant trees, and the ability of donor
and implementing institutions to launch and support this process, clearly
constitutes a major reason for hope. This chronicle should end, however,
with neither promotional hype nor with lamentations about evil bureaucrats, but rather with some causal analysis. The flow of trees onto Haitian
farms during the 1980s was engendered by a cluster of three causal factors
that may never again fully coalesce: a mass of energetic and economically
rational peasants, oriented toward local markets, willing to experiment
with new land use practices that would strengthen their position in those
markets; a network of operational NGOs capable of linking these peasants to external sources of funding and new technologies; and a funding
agency (in this case, USAID) willing, at least for a decade, to experiment
with new modes of implementation.

Whereas it took three clusters of actors to make the project work, it required only one causal agent to dismantle it. The crisis that suspended the program was attributable neither to the peasants nor to participating NGOs. Their opinions, preferences and capabilities were ignored. And although recent USAID reports diplomatically allude to Haiti's political crisis as responsible in some way for the now-lamented termination of AOP (it is considered poor taste to criticize former mission directors openly), in fact the demise of AOP was produced by factors internal to USAID.

Will the project reassert itself? The prognosis is modest. The first two causal factors—rational, energetic farmers and competent NGOs—are still alive and well in Haiti. Hundreds of thousands of Haitian farmers have now shifted into the production, rather than simple extraction, of wood. My advocacy of the NGO route to reach these farmers implies no naive view of the inherent goodness of NGOs. The extractive opportunism of many new NGOs, and their inclusion under the same generic NGO label as older and more serious institutions, casts a pall over the entire NGO strategy now favored by many donors.[4] But in the short-term perspective of contemporary Haiti and the long-term perspective of development in general, NGO behavior has been less detrimental than that of governmental institutions, either donor bureaucracies or recipient bureaucracies.[5]

The Achilles heel in the AOP approach is to be found in the third causal factor, reliance on unpredictable external donors. Here prospects look bleak. Despite the reopening of two AOP nurseries with USAID funding, current USAID Haiti mission discourse at the time of my most recent visit (January 1996) is once again to reroute funding of all agrarian activities through their "proper" home, that is, the ministry of agriculture. The NGOs, without whom USAID could have done nothing during the Duvalier and post-Duvalier years, are being sidelined as unsustainable fly-by-night amateurs undertaking activities better managed by the presumed-to-be-more-sustainable government of Haiti.[6]

Given the erratic behavior of external donors, is there any way of breaking dependence on external funds? Why not encourage farmers to produce their own seedlings? This is a philosophically attractive option. Unfortunately, the peasant backyard nurseries that have moved in this direction have achieved only limited output. Experience in many countries indicates that wood trees will be planted in substantial numbers only through the delivery of free, or at least highly subsidized seedlings. In Haiti, farmers will often pay for fruit or coffee seedlings, but they will rarely, if ever, pay for wood-tree seedlings. Nor will they produce them in the quantities required to have a significant local ecological or economic impact. They will, however, plant and care for tens of millions of seedlings if they are provided in some way similar to that of AOP.

Continuing dependence on external funders and seedling producers will make many observers uneasy. There is a widespread sense in the development community that a good project is one that will continue without any outside support after a specified period of assistance, and, to achieve this, subsidies must be kept to a minimum during the life of the project. To accommodate this sentiment, a compromise proposal is often heard: Stop total subsidization of seedlings. Have farmers pay a small, symbolic amount for the seedlings. "That way they'll appreciate the seedlings more and take better care of them."

Not only is there no evidence to support this assertion, but attempts to serve two masters simultaneously are likely to end up serving neither. A project run this way would not be sustainable because it would not generate enough funds to be fully self-financing, and neither would it produce enough volume to make a substantial environmental impact. A project that recovers only a fraction of its seedling production costs through small payments is no more "sustainable" than one giving the seedlings away. And when confronted with short-term and long-term investment options, most cash-needy Haitian farmers will not spend anything on wood-tree seedlings. The main achievement of any compromise measure would be to reduce the seedling flow to a fraction of what it could be if planners would simply define wood-tree seedlings as a justifiable project contribution to a larger societal good, that is, the reforestation of denuded hills and valleys.

The millennia of extractive wood mining that have gone on around the planet, and the centuries of that behavior in Haiti itself, have created an orientation to the wood tree that will not change overnight. As a result of AOP, tens of thousands of farmers now view the wood tree as a welcome income-generating crop, rather than as a gift of nature to be quickly cut before someone else does. Trees are not yet culturally construed in the same category as traditional crops. Because of the length of time that wood trees take to produce a harvest, the ambiguities concerning financial yields per hectare, and a number of other factors, trees are not yet treated by Haitian farmers as an ordinary crop in which they are willing to invest capital. They will allocate land and labor to this new crop, but not cash. And my field visits to tree-planting projects in Central and South America and West and East Africa lead me to suspect that this reluctance to invest capital may affect wood tree projects elsewhere as well. In retrospect, AOP's strategy of meeting rural people halfway on this issue was fully on target.

Other objections may be that the approach is not sustainable, or that farmers stop planting trees as soon as project funding stops. Research has shown that, in fact, project participants do find ways to produce more trees—protecting and managing regrowth, transplanting pioneer seedlings—even after the project leaves a community. But the objection is true in that the volume of planting achieved under AOP is certainly *not* achievable without continued donor support. For how long? Probably until such time as the volume of arboreal biomass outplanted in Haiti (or any country) has reached a stage where farmers can, without jeopardizing their traditional agrarian activities, harvest and manage their own domestically controlled and marketable spontaneous regrowth on a sustained yield basis, without any further dependence on project nurseries. This will take a long time.

Although Haiti's macroproblems give reason for pessimism, the experience reported here justifies optimism for the specific domain of tree planting. The key is a negotiated compromise between the macroecological concerns of foreign donors, environmentalists and government planners, on one hand, and the microeconomic needs of poor Haitian smallholders, on the other. AOP arranged such a coincidence of interests. Despite recent setbacks, it appears worthwhile to seek the resources to begin again in Haiti and, making culture-specific adjustments as appropriate, to attempt extrapolation elsewhere.

NOTES

1. In late 1994, after the return of Aristide, I was invited back to Haiti twice by USAID/Washington as a member of a special Environmental Task Force. One of its major objectives was to reinstate the previous flow to the countryside of peasant-planted and peasant-owned trees. The current mission management in Haiti commissioned a retrospective evaluation of AOP. The verdict was quite positive (Smucker and Timyan 1995).

2. Over three dozen references that deal exclusively with AOP are available, and numerous others allude to AOP. In addition to ones cited earlier are: Ashley (1986); Balzano (1986, 1989); Bannister and Josiah (1993); Buffum (1986); Buffum and King (1985); Conway (1986); Grosenick (1986); Jickling and White (1992); Lauwerysen (1985); Lowenthal (1989); Smucker (1982); Smucker and Timyan (1995); White and Jickling (1993).

3. On one occasion while I was visiting Washington, the executive introduced me to a gentleman with a "strong background in information-gathering" whom he thought we should bring down to Haiti as a consultant, on project funds, to write up public relations blurbs about our project for other potential donors. I was later told (but could not, of course, verify) that the gentleman in question was a former CIA employee interested in consultancies. I thanked both the executive and his friend for their concern and assured them that we already had the required in-house writing skills in Haiti to promote the project. The executive was not pleased with my inflexibility and lack of imagination but dropped the matter.

4. In a report which I did previously for USAID in El Salvador, I proposed a distinction between ONGOs and FONGOs: ONGOs are Operational **NGOs**

with a track record of genuine service delivery, while FONGOs are Foraging **NGOs**—middle- or upper-class urban hunter-gatherers searching for development funds to finance their salaries, vehicles, computers, photocopiers and fax machines, of marginal relevance to the future welfare of the rural poor.

5. As of July 1995 both the World Bank and the Interamerican Development Bank, impressed with the efficiency of USAID's pioneering NGO strategy are trying a mixed model in which the Haitian Government will receive their funds but with the understanding that it will contract with NGOs to implement the activities. Both the peasant sector and the serious NGO sector have had too many bad first-hand experiences with the governmental sector to receive that proposition with anything but skepticism.

6. One of these so-called "fly-by-nighters" which played a major role under AOP in getting millions of trees planted was the Roman Catholic Church. Compared to it, the Haitian ministry of agriculture and USAID are transient actors on the world stage. The inflated discourse heard in USAID and other development agencies about government as the only source of "institutional sustainability" could be viewed as harmless postulation were it not being used as a rationale for diverting international funds from impoverished villagers to urban elites.

17 Participatory Watershed Development and Soil Conservation in Rajasthan, India

Anirudh Krishna

A massive government initiative for integrated watershed development was started in early 1991 in India's northwestern state of Rajasthan. In January of that year, the state government created a new, multidisciplinary department of watershed development and soil conservation (WD&SC). By 1993, the new department was carrying out work on more than 100,000 hectares; about 2,000 staff trained in the multiple tasks of integrated watershed development were working with a large number of community organizations, using a variety of low-cost, area-specific technologies.

Integrating technology, social organization and administrative arrangements was crucial to program progress. WD&SC devised an appropriate mix of these elements at most of the 250 locations where it was working. Specific solutions varied among locations, but certain elements were common, particularly cheap, replicable and locally renewable technologies. These were developed in cooperation with local residents participating through users committees (UCs) facilitated by department staff. Procedures for sharing costs and benefits among local residents—and between them and the government agency—emerged, with different formulas for sharing costs and benefits adopted in the various locations.

Decentralization of decisionmaking, dissemination of information, building confidence among staff and local people, and an iterative process of experimentation and learning facilitated the emergence of locally appropriate technologies and organizational patterns. In 1993, WD&SC Rajasthan received a certificate of merit from the National Productivity Council of the government of India, in recognition of its development of appropriate technologies and of the high levels of community participation in its activities in the Cheetakhera watershed. In 1994, this national award went to another Rajasthan watershed, the Losing watershed in Udaipur district. Developments up to 1995, four years after work began, are examined here; no doubt better and more robust solutions are emerging as the work continues. The author directed the new department for its first three years. We know that even rapid initial progress may not lead to long-term success. But this case is presented because it shows that a complex and conservative bureaucratic system can be quickly reoriented toward more participatory and interdisciplinary approaches.

RAJASTHAN: WHY WATERSHED DEVELOPMENT?

More than any other state in India, Rajasthan depends on rainfall for meeting its biomass needs. With a land area of 34 million hectares, Rajasthan is almost twice the size of Bangladesh and larger than Italy or New Zealand. Eighty percent of the state's fifty-five million people live in rural areas and depend on agriculture. Animal husbandry supplements incomes, providing protection during the bad years when crops fail.

Increasing population (2.5 percent per annum) places a great strain on natural resources. Even more rapid increase in the cattle population has led to intense pressure on grazing lands. Animal units per 100 hectares increased from 39 in 1951 to 105 in 1988. Common lands and forests account for 45 percent of all land and provide up to one-quarter of the incomes of the rural poor. Deterioration of these lands has reduced the availability of fodder and fuelwood.

Only 13 percent of the cultivated area is irrigated, mostly by wells and tubewells. Their recharge and sustainability depends primarily on rainfall, so the whole area, except for the 5 percent that is canal irrigated (1.6 million hectares), depends on rainfall. In arid areas and some semiarid areas, groundwater is found only at a great depth, and then often with a high dissolved salt content. In the arid western part of the state, mean annual rainfall is only 250 millimeters, with 500 millimeters in the semiarid central part, and at most about 1,000 millimeters in the southeast. Ninety percent of rainfall occurs between July and September.

Harvests are inadequate to meet local needs in three out of every five years due to insufficient and/or untimely rainfall, which is associated with severe food, fodder and drinking water shortages. Frequent droughts lead to periodic temporary outmigration of human and cattle populations, creating a permanent situation of food, fodder and energy insecurity.

Watershed development to capture and use all available rainfall is therefore of critical importance for Rajasthan. However, apart from a few small-scale projects implemented by scattered nongovernmental organizations (NGOs) or university programs, no work of this sort had been done before 1991. The state government had separate line agencies dealing with soil conservation, forestry and crops, each working in isolation. There were hardly any local people involved in these programs, except as daily wage laborers. All field work was fully subsidized and planned from above. The scarcity of funds for maintenance, coupled with little local ownership, resulted in high rates of deterioration of those physical facilities built by the state.

Performance of staff and of departments was measured mostly against expenditure and quantified targets. Apart from professional pride and peer appreciation, there was little organizational incentive to make staff work for quality or sustainability. An abundance of development initiatives since the early 1950s that failed to accomplish more than localized improvements had produced cynicism and a lack of faith among the people of the state.

Traditions among government development agencies were not well suited to provide any support for the new department's quest for integration, participation and sustainability. On the other hand, since no other agency had the capacity to carry out watershed development on more than a fraction of the large area requiring this type of treatment (nearly 25 million hectares), the state had to play the central role, at least to begin with.

MAKING A BEGINNING

The immediate impetus for the state government to set up a new department was an offer of large amounts of program funds on soft terms (mostly grant) from the central government and from the World Bank. Rs. 1,360 million (about US$45 million) was made available from the central government to finance projects under its National Watershed Development Program for Rainfed Areas (NWDPRA) over a five-year period, 1991–95. NWDPRA provides full funding in each subdistrict for the treatment of one small watershed, covering between 1,500 and 2,000 hectares, in which less than 30 percent of the arable area is irrigated. The scheme envisages a maximum expenditure, including overhead, of Rs. 3,500 (US$115) per hectare. An additional Rs. 740 million (US$25 million) was provided from the World Bank under its Integrated Watershed Development (Plains) Project (IWDP). Under IWDP, one project area of 25–30,000 hectares was selected in each of four districts.

The term watershed in Rajasthan refers to an area of between 1,000 to 2,000 hectares that drains at a common point. For planning purposes, each watershed is divided into between five and eight microwatersheds. Under the new programs, work was to be taken up simultaneously on 250 watersheds located throughout the state. Each watershed was to be worked on for a period of five to seven years, after which time no further funding would be available for that area. The programs, designed as they were by the World Bank and the central government, were broadly predetermined and formulated mostly in a top-down mode. However, there was some flexibility in program parameters, and it was here that the department looked to find space for innovation.

The ninety-five watersheds coming under the World Bank-assisted IWDP were located in four large clusters covering a total of 100,000 hectares. Work was to proceed slowly, with less than 20 percent of the area planned to be covered in the initial three-year pilot phase. The 133 watersheds under the central government-funded NWDPRA, totalling 350,000 hectares, were scattered all over the state. They were supposed to be fully upgraded within four years. Another 100,000 hectares were added to this total when the state government, after observing positive first-year results, decided that the soil conservation works of all other state-funded programs would also have to follow the new integrated pattern.

There was great pressure on WD&SC to begin in a bigger way than we would ideally have liked. Rajasthan was not the only state eligible for funding under IWDP and NWDPRA. The latter especially was intended for projects in rain-fed areas throughout the country. In an effort to spur states to action, both funding agencies made their allocations among states on the basis of prior-year expenditures. There was no way that the new department could retain the good will of the state government without out-competing other states in obtaining larger amounts of grant funds.

The bureaucratic need to justify our large initial staff base created additional pressure to step up the pace. The soil conservation wing of the agriculture department took the lead in preparing the documentation for the new lines of credit. This unit, with its staff of about one thousand, was transferred into and formed the nucleus of the new department. Staff from other line departments could be taken on deputation as required. But as neither retrenchment nor redeployment of existing staff were feasible options, the new department would for some time have a preponderance of soil conservationists in its ranks.

The targets meant that we needed to treat *ten times* the area that had been covered in any previous year under soil conservation schemes in Rajasthan. Although we could not meet this objective in the first year or two, the initial pace of work definitely needed to be very fast, much faster than we would have liked. Apart from having speedy implementation as an imperative, no other external guidance was available. Program objectives were broadly defined:

> to conserve, upgrade and utilize natural resource endowments; to ensure perpetual availability of food, fodder, fiber, timber and biomass in a sustainable manner; to generate employment in the rural sector; to improve ecological balance and the production environment; to reduce inequalities between irrigated and rainfed areas; to improve cash flows for residents of the rainfed areas.

Certain new techniques of dryland watershed development had been successfully implemented by NGOs and university research stations in many parts of the country. But when the government sought to extend the benefits of watershed development to larger areas, the technical dimensions of the task were emphasized at the expense of the administrative and, especially, the social organization dimensions. Although participatory development was an avowed goal of both the World Bank and the government programs, there was no provision in either program for any activity or expenditure related to social organization.

Having come into existence at the end of January 1991, the department had only four months of lead time for the first year of field implementation before the monsoon began to gear up. All planting work (conservation hedges, vegetative fences, trees and pastures) had to coincide with the first monsoon showers. All preparatory work (digging pits and trenches, arranging for planting material, training) had to be completed in advance, while simultaneously forging links with local communities. Finally, staff from different disciplines had to learn to work together.

Thus there was little time available to draft a comprehensive strategy. We had to plunge right in, get our hands dirty and refine our methods as we went along. This was both a drawback and an advantage. Since even the most senior officials had little prior conception of the innovations required, there was a general willingness to experiment. This led to "a widespread unleashing of the creative talent of field staff," as one visiting government official described the process.

We held four three-day conferences in February and March 1991, with the leaders of the ninety-seven field units and their supervisors attending. We discussed among ourselves the objectives and programming needs for the new task of watershed development in an open, semistructured manner, with everyone contributing, regardless of seniority. Field officials were given a simple message: "Start with what you know, what resources you have or can find, what people want; do small-scale experiments of whatever you think might work."

It was agreed that no penalties would be imposed for experiments that failed in spite of all honest intention and care, an application of the principle of "embracing error" proposed by Korten (1980). Supervisory staff would play a facilitative role, liaising with researchers, NGOs and field units in an effort to identify and make available alternative best practices from whatever source.

To have a sound technical basis, the National Remote Sensing Agency prepared detailed base maps of each watershed using aerial and satellite imagery. Our workshop came up with the idea of employing village youth for conducting technical surveys and engaging unemployed engineers of the area for training and supervising these surveyors. A range of new methods was devised innovatively and field-tested by staff acting on their own initiative. Methods that worked were made available to other colleagues.

At the end of the first-year planting season, extensive debriefing sessions were held. Significant progress had been made in developing many area-specific technologies. Indigenous practices had been actively sought out, and in many areas local practices were found that had potential for wider application. Staff who had toured projects of other state governments and NGOs contributed additional new ideas.

How best to begin working with communities was still a matter of some ambivalence and uncertainty. We had tried to overcome villagers' feelings of apathy and disinterest by going out freely among them. Staff participated in village discussions that were set up to achieve some common understanding of the problems and to debate potential solutions.

In many locations the first problem was how to initiate dialogue. Some of us thought that showing a film would be a good way to start a discussion, but relevant films were not easily available. Our first film, provided by the World Bank, was not about watershed development, nor even about Rajasthan. The film described farmers' experience with vetiver grass—in Fiji! But it was useful nevertheless. People came to see the film and stayed to talk about the problems of dryland farming. They organized users committees, about which more later, and began to accept shared responsibility for implementation.

Still, we had more questions than answers: how far should staff go in helping village residents establish users committees or suggest regulations for the use of common lands? Was there a menu of models to discuss with the people of an area? We hoped NGOs could advise us on these points and perhaps provide some staff training. We organized a series of workshops with NGOs, meeting as well with two social science research institutions. It was disappointing to find that researchers, NGOs and government were all suspicious of each other. Each preferred to work separately, in spite of having a common concern, rather like the nine blind men with the elephant.

DEVELOPING A STRATEGY

In spite of the obstacles, considerable progress was made the first year. We developed a common vocabulary that helped unite our multidisciplinary staff. Encouraging field results generated considerable enthusiasm among staff and local residents alike. A variety of practices were experimented with, and as much as ten-fold increases in fodder yields from village common lands were observed in most locations. Early visible results were important in demonstrating to staff and village residents alike that significant gains could be made with the new program. This encouraged local residents to make available to the program larger tracts of common lands.

In many instances in the first year, staff and UC members had been forced to beg permission from doubtful villagers to work on even half a hectare of common land, out of the 400 to 600 hectares that could be found in most villages. However, within three months, the planted fodder grasses had grown tall and were available for harvesting by all villagers. Such evidence went a long way in establishing trust. Slowly, bonds of friendship began to develop among field staff and local residents.

Increases in grain yields on treated private lands also provided evidence of increasing productivity. However, uneven results were observed among different locations, and some officials and many communities did not respond very well to the new style of functioning. Tables 17.1 and 17.2 present first-year results for fodder production on common lands and for food grain production on privately owned lands in response to various conservation and improvement measures.

We organized a large training effort between November and February when there was a respite from field activity. This included study tours by staff and UC representatives together visiting successful projects implemented by other state governments and NGOs; in-house training of project personnel led by senior staff and innovators; specialized technical training for staff and paraprofessionals conducted by the state agriculture university and other institutions; and workshops and seminars for project staff and UC members.

The results of first-year implementation were discussed in participatory management meetings, where each level of staff could help shape the strategy that would guide the department's operations. We concluded that our basic challenge was to integrate, in new and sustainable ways, the three key elements of our strategy: technical, social and administrative.

Technical Strategy

Technology had to be developed that could improve agriculture, forestry, animal husbandry, horticulture and any other activities that could sustainably exploit the area's natural resources. For any large-scale adoption, technologies needed to be cheap and easily accessible to local residents, since we needed to improve and conserve over twenty-five million hectares. This could not be done by relying primarily on government or even donor support. Department resources could not cover such a huge area in even

Table 17.1 Change in Fodder Production on Common Lands as Result
of Program Interventions

Treatments	Eklingnath watershed kg/ha	Kotri watershed kg/ha
No treatment (control)	25	35
Protection only (fencing)	75	65
Agave with contour V-ditch	210	385
Vetiver grass with contour V-ditch	167	460
Cenchrus with contour V-ditch	200	470
Chiseling at two-meter contour intervals	259	406

Source: Evaluation by College of Technology and Engineering, Rajasthan Agricultural University (1992).

fifty years of operation. Our mission therefore was to arrive at replicable technologies that could be adapted and adopted by residents over a wide area, acting on their account and with little assistance from outside.

Our surveys indicated that farmers were not willing to expend more than forty workdays per hectare for soil and moisture conservation measures. We aimed for a set of practices costing no more than Rs. 1,000 (US$33) per hectare to guard against erosion and further degradation, since investments to improve production methods would have to be made on top of any for conservation. It was too much to expect that investing such a small amount would permanently transform low-input, high-risk subsistence agriculture. Clearly, the technology needed to be renewable and also simple, drawing as far as possible on local skills and raw materials. Thus, local initiatives were more important than central ones in the program's search for appropriate technological solutions.

Social Strategy

Social organization was initially difficult to establish. Motivating area residents to come together in village organizations that could play a leading role in watershed development took a lot of effort by Department staff. At a minimum, local organizations were needed for the management of common lands, which comprised 40–50 percent of the area in each watershed and which were the main source of fuelwood and fodder.

We found that the attitudes prevailing in the villages were not very supportive of cooperative endeavor. Traditional forms of social organization were mostly broken down, and the resulting vacuum had not been filled

Table 17.2 Change in Food Grain Production on Private Lands as Result of Program Interventions

Treatments	Sorghum, Kotri watershed kg/ha	Pearl millet, Barna watershed kg/ha
No treatment (control)	156	600
Field bunding	385	875
Vetiver grass barriers	456	925
Cenchrus barriers	n/a	717

Source: Evaluation by College of Technology and Engineering, Rajasthan Agricultural University (1992).

well by modern institutions such as the *panchayat* (local government) system. This phenomenon appeared to have multiple causes. Village people referred sadly to the rifts created by party politics, to the breakdown of social and religious sanctions, to an expanding population that forces larger numbers of people to compete for ever scarcer resources, and to commercialization that widens the gap between rich and poor. These dynamics were often exacerbated in interactions with government agencies.

Many of the initial disinclinations and apprehensions of local people were eased when we successfully delivered some early, visible results. People have seen too many examples of failed government projects. Faith had to be restored before enthusiasm could be stoked. Since restoring faith needs situation-specific solutions and since social dynamics vary widely from village to village, there was an overwhelming need for decisions to be made at the points that are closest to the field reality.

Administrative Strategy

Administration of such a far-flung effort required new approaches. To devise new technologies and social organization and get them accepted required decentralization of authority to the field level. Since this is a major inversion in a bureaucracy steeped in top-down tradition, we realized that staff would not automatically have the confidence to exercise authority. Many would be afraid; all would need reassurance. Integrating staff drawn from different line departments into a unified and cohesive team was another major task. Integrated watershed development required more than installing soil and water conservation treatments; improved production systems had to be introduced on treated lands. Drawing staff from the departments of agriculture, forest, animal husbandry and horticulture meant that much training was necessary to broaden thinking and competencies.

Another important administrative task was motivating staff. The use of pay or promotion-related rewards and penalties was made virtually impossible by systemwide civil service rules. Peer pressure was weak since staff were drawn from six different parent departments and, at least initially, retained divided loyalties. Yet without high levels of motivation, staff could not be expected to act with the amount of responsibility required in a decentralized system.

ATTEMPTING SOLUTIONS

A number of policy decisions, resulting from an iterative search for appropriate solutions, were made during the first two years. These decisions cleared the way for field staff to innovate and develop more helpful technologies and working methods. Close contact was maintained between field and headquarters so that lessons learned at any one point could be quickly shared with others.

In the area of technology, three major decisions were made. First, vegetative conservation methods were to be used wherever possible in preference to mechanical methods such as earthen dams and concrete structures. Even where heavy structures had to be constructed on account of high stream velocities or at the lower ends of drainage lines, these structures were planted around with shrubs, tree saplings and grasses that would grow to enmesh them in a few years. Before the structure had time to disintegrate, it would be held in place by the vegetation growing all around it. Conservation barriers on fields were almost always made from grasses. Although *vetiver* grass was preferred, primarily because we knew about it and could get planting material to any watershed needing it, field units were free to experiment with other local species.

Second, UC members and educated unemployed youth selected by the villages were invited to attend integrated technical training of two months' duration. Increasingly, we turned over project activities to these paraprofessionals.

Third, a technical manual was prepared and updated each year, describing the range of technical solutions that had been developed in the department and elsewhere. Staff were encouraged to develop yet more technical solutions and to see their name in print.

On the social organization front, we made additional major decisions. We agreed to work with and through UCs, which were set up by holding informal elections among area residents in each watershed. UCs set priorities for developing common lands, arranged for works, and determined the criteria for sharing products (mostly grass in the first and each subsequent year, and trees at the end of a longer period). They were responsible for protecting the trees and pastures. Even though members could prevent their own cattle from roaming in the planted areas, there was no way to control stray animals or those coming in from neighboring villages. Thus, fences had to be erected. These were mostly made by planting thorny shrubs and native cacti (*euphorbia*). Watchmen were often deployed by UCs, and fines were instituted to deal with offenders.

Since we found no existing organization in most villages, we had to induce local residents to create new ones. No fixed formats were prescribed for the structure of UCs or for their procedures of work, although openness, accountability and representative membership were all stressed. All transactions were conducted in the open and on fixed days of the week. UC members, elected by village residents and liable to recall, were paid by the program for their time.

The task of social mobilization was the most difficult one for us and required the greatest effort by the administration. At the end of two years, we managed to have effective local organizations to work with in about half of our locations (with half of these performing extremely well). Over time the association became more fruitful. UCs in several locations took over primary responsibility for all tasks of implementation and maintenance. We collaborated with UCs on planning and paid out program funds after measuring field results.

We also decided that local residents would have to contribute 10 percent of the cost of activities in the form of cash or labor. Field units thought that local residents would be unwilling to contribute any higher proportion, being familiar only with government programs subsidized 100 percent. Thus, it was decided to begin with 10 percent and to raise it as the benefits of the work became clearer and more widespread. Many of us felt that local residents would take management responsibility only when they have contributed some part of program costs, however small it may be to begin with. Also, when government staff must rely upon local contributions, they cannot ignore or belittle the concerns voiced by residents. The latter will demand to be kept informed and will pay only for those activities that they approve. Thus, without cost sharing, we felt that participation would remain more nominal than real.

While enforcing cost sharing, we addressed the equity concern in two ways—by limiting our program expenditures to a fixed amount per participating family and by insisting that all participants make some labor contributions. Large farmers also availed themselves of program benefits, but in proportion to the size of their landholdings, their benefits were modest. On the whole, the strategy was more successful than if we had tried to debar large farmers entirely, thereby making enemies of them from day one. This has been the experience of many public programs, which are widely perceived as less than legitimate if they serve only a part of the public.

Three more decisions expedited progress administratively.

First, tasks in the watersheds were not subdivided and assigned by technical discipline. Instead, each field-level staff member, without regard to his or her discipline, was made responsible for one microwatershed and for all the planning and implementation tasks in that microwatershed. This way, each staff member could develop close links with the residents of a particular area, getting to know the people and their problems more intimately than would have been possible from a narrow technical perspective. To support this decision, some cross-disciplinary training was undertaken; for example, engineers were trained in basic forestry and pasture management, and agronomists were trained in conducting topographical surveys.

We hoped to break down barriers between technical disciplines to encourage teamwork among field staff. Field units had between seven and ten staff members representing a mix of disciplines. They were jointly responsible for a group of watersheds. (This strategy parallels the approach to field organization adopted in the Gal Oya project in Sri Lanka, discussed in Chapter 11.) Unit staff relied upon one another for technical advice and, equally important, for moral support. Integrated two-week training courses were organized to help unit-level staff get a sense of the big picture, of the larger objectives of what they were doing, of the means available and of the current state of knowledge (and ignorance). Although individual effort was recognized, progress was measured for the unit as a whole. Substantial authority was delegated to the field units for planning and implementation.

The second decision was to draw up five-year plans of development for each watershed through discussions between staff and area residents. Supervisory staff and the head office had relatively little say in finalizing these plans. Further, five-year plans were not cast in concrete. First-year implementation was to be on a small scale so that staff and area residents could gain familiarity with new methods. Plans could be revised by field staff whenever it was felt that new knowledge could be beneficially incorporated. To facilitate rapid, two-way communication, sixteen staff from the head office were selected to work as link officers between the field and head office, acting as roving ambassadors for the project. They were each assigned a part of the state where they were responsible for passing problems and progress reports up from the field and suggestions down from the head office.

Third, a state-level steering committee was created, chaired by the agriculture secretary. Heads of all concerned line departments—forests, horticulture, animal husbandry, rural development—as well as representatives of the finance and personnel departments were members. State and national-level research institutions are also represented. The committee was authorized to set policy on behalf of the state government, thereby avoiding the delays and frustrations that might have arisen if each agency had to be dealt with separately. Issues of coordination among line departments were thus resolved quickly across the table.

RESULTS

These decisions resulted in a reasonably rapid spread and development of a large range of technical and social innovations. Encouraging field results—in terms of increased productivity, reduced soil and moisture loss, increased local incomes, and enhanced supplies of grain, fodder and fuelwood—have continued to be observed as the department has expanded work to cover larger areas each year (see Table 17.3).

Productivity increases have resulted from the work on arable lands, with grain yields increasing in some places as much as 100 to 150 percent. Farmers have been encouraged to try newer and more drought-resistant varieties of rain-fed crops, to experiment with new species of crops, to adopt better agronomic practices (contour cultivation, strip cropping, early plowing) and to work with improved farm implements. Among the practices promoted by the program, farmers express much interest in mixed horticulture, where a variety of fruit trees are planted in alleys wide enough to let a plough pass between them. Crops can be grown in the space between the alleys until the trees are tall and begin to deliver fruit.

Silvi-pastoral plantation on common lands is another activity that local people have undertaken with growing enthusiasm, acting through their UCs. In the first year, village people were suspicious of any suggestion to take up any work on common lands. Their experience with previous government projects led them to believe that if they allowed a government agency to fence the village commons, they would no longer have the right to enter the land and enjoy its produce. These suspicions diminished when they discovered that the new project worked differently. Since all the work, including the vegetative fencing, was to be done by UCs, and since the grass produced each year was to be harvested by local people following whatever rules their UC decided, there was no loss of control to an outside agency. In 1991, village people were hesitant and watchful, but by 1993, over 30,000 hectares of common lands were being fenced and treated annually. Representative increases in yield are shown in Table 17.4.

In addition to improved varieties of grass and legumes, over one million trees were planted on common lands to serve as a common pool of fuelwood.

Table 17.3 Growth in Expenditure and Area Treated

Year	Expenditure on Watershed Treatments Rs. million	Area Treated hectares
1990–91	160.2	33,057
1991–92	221.1	48,524
1992–93	376.1	129,686
1993–94	463.6	164,689

Tree species were selected by the UCs, which themselves contracted to raise the seedlings in decentralized village nurseries. Members of UCs and the nursery personnel they selected were trained in various aspects of nursery and planting techniques. Careful attention to seed selection, nursery practices, land preparation and timely planting have resulted in survival rates as high as 89 percent, with mean survival rates about 70 percent.

Improvements in quantity and quality of work, although heartening, were never all that was required to achieve the program's mission. The medium-term objective in each watershed was to work ourselves out of a job after developing low-cost technologies and promoting the acquisition of skills by local people. Thus, along with survival rates and the rate of expansion, other indicators also needed to be monitored. The per hectare cost of work was one important measure because it indicated how close or how far we were from our goal of developing cheaply replicable technology. Progress toward the other major objective—self-reliance among watershed residents—is more difficult to measure. To some extent, however, a diminishing trend in staff costs serves as a proxy for greater local self-reliance.

Table 17.5 gives gross figures for the entire state. These do not show the disparities that exist among different watersheds. A range of factors explain the differences in level of performance between staff and UCs of different locations: background and age of UC leadership, technical expertise and commitment of local paraprofessionals, people skills and devotion to the task shown by department staff. These factors are hard to measure, but we must try harder to get a handle on them.

In our hurry to get on with the job of implementation, we paid insufficient attention to process documentation. Beyond maintaining records that were required to account for expenditure, and to explain why certain techniques were preferred over others, most field officers did not keep any other written accounts of the action research conducted by them. This has

Table 17.4 Increase in Fodder Production[1] on Pasture Plots (1991–93)

	Kotri watershed kg/ha			Barna watershed kg/ha		
Conservation Technique	1991	1992	1993	1991	1992	1993
Protection only (fencing)	65	550	880	300	490	510
Vetiver grass planted with contour V-ditches	460	1,610	1,652	686	1,920	2,050
Cenchrus with contour V-ditches	470	1,390	1,840	1,133	2,130	2,250
Chiseling at two-meter intervals	406	1,730	1,270	1,166	2,060	2,200

[1] Sun-dried grass.

proved to be a constraint as the department seeks funds for future projects. Donor agencies, academics and senior bureaucrats want data, having little time or inclination to visit the field and see things for themselves.

Evaluation has relied on four methods: examining the relevance and short-term results of program activities through quarterly meetings held at the village level; process evaluation conducted every six months by an internal team and an impact evaluation conducted annually by an external consultant; technology evaluation by a committee of staff drawn from other departments; and long-term evaluation of physical impacts by comparing satellite images of a cross-section of watersheds over three-year intervals.

Close research support has helped in the development of appropriate technology. While experimenting with and extending new techniques, a good link has been maintained between department staff and the research stations of the Rajasthan Agriculture University. Technical advice has also been sought and obtained from other state and national institutes. Collaborative action research is being conducted with the Central Arid Zone Research Institute and the International Crops Research Institute for the Semi-Arid Tropics (ICRISAT). At the local level, field units are collaborating with NGOs, most notably for organizing seed banks, and with university research stations.

ISSUES FOR FUTURE RESOLUTION

Although the WD&SC program has made a strong start in Rajasthan, there are some aspects which are still a cause of concern, either because progress has been slow or because the solutions found are not yet fully reassuring.

Table 17.5 Summary Trends in Project

Fiscal year	Staff Expenditure as % of Total Annual Outlay	Cost per Hectare Rs.
1990–91	16.6	4,848
1991–92	15.8	4,556
1992–93	13.9	2,968
1993–94	12.8	2,815

The Question of Subsidy

Even after four years of development, most villagers still say that, although the work can result in large yield increases, they are unwilling to take up even the most attractive practices (horticulture, agroforestry) if they themselves have to contribute more than 25–40 percent of the total cost. This is partly a reflection of poverty and of a diminishing concern for the land, but forty years of wholly subsidized development programs are equally responsible. A government program that is not fully subsidized is looked at with suspicion: "Are the staff making off with some part of the money?" These doubts, hinting at that age-old malady of corruption, are largely misplaced with regard to this program. The scope for malpractices has been considerably reduced by conducting all transactions in the open, and by UCs publicizing all plans and reporting all accounts fully to the village assembly in monthly meetings.

However, the questions once posed still need to be answered. In the three years that I was the director, we faced such questions more than once —from state legislators, district-level politicians and the press. Many of these doubts, occasioned as they were by our new, unprecedented method of work, have died down as methods have been improved and as more people see their advantages. Subsidy levels are being brought down in a new generation of projects being taken up from the current year. The withdrawal from subsidy will, however, remain a slow process to be pursued incrementally over the years.

Political Support

The need for political support became more obvious as the work progressed, as benefits are often a bone of contention between opposing village groups. Since not much else was going on in many of these villages, the UC became a ready forum for expressing rivalries. Politicians at various levels would be roped into taking sides in village conflicts; often, work stopped until allegations could be investigated and put to rest. Our attempts to inform and educate area legislators and the field visits we arranged for cabinet ministers and party leaders were, at best, makeshift solutions.

Sustainable solutions can result only from linking village-level UCs with higher-level political structures. This has been an area of weakness. Some recent developments, however, hold out reasons for hope. In local government elections conducted in 1995, many UC leaders were elected to office in recognition of the development initiatives they had led. Even though the impact of this election could heighten rather than allay political tensions, few leaders, we hope, will want to impede a program that has such evident popular support.

Legal and Political Status for UCs

UCs need to gain legal status as corporate bodies. Although they are managing all work done on common lands, the land itself continues to be vested not with the UCs, but with government departments (revenue and forest) and with village *panchayats*. These legally constituted bodies for a single village or a group of villages are vested with some quasi-judicial powers, but their ability to undertake joint resource management is limited. The departments and *panchayats* were, in most cases, happy to hand over land use rights to UCs. But the transfer can become legally valid only when UCs are formally registered as cooperatives or as companies under existing laws.

Each of these laws requires that UCs conform to some fairly rigid organizational structure, that they adopt standardized rules and procedures, and that they open their books for government inspectors. WD&SC was unsuccessful, in the initial years, in effecting any compromise acceptable both to the UCs and to the bodies that administer these laws. This is an important matter because most village people suggest that after the department's involvement is over, three or four years from now, they would be unlikely themselves to make the effort required to keep these institutions alive.

Linkages with NGOs

One source of support for UCs in the postproject phase could arise from networking with NGOs. In 1991 we tried, without much success, to establish links with NGOs of the state. However, in later years, initiatives taken by staff at the field level have been more successful. Some of these initiatives were followed up by the head office and have resulted in the formulation of a proposal which envisages NGOs, WD&SC and UCs working in collaboration on a new set of projects. One such project financed in part by the Swiss Development Cooperation started in 1995. It will, we hope, pave the way for a new generation of collaborative endeavors.

Helping the Landless

Watershed development programs, as they exist in Rajasthan today, have little direct concern with the problems of the landless. Apart from the development of common lands as sources of fodder and fuelwood, there is some provision in NWDPRA for grant-cum-loan–based assistance to landless persons to start small-scale village enterprises. This is hardly a sufficient amount, and especially in the early years of the program, the department did little to utilize these funds effectively. In recent years, however, UCs have begun selecting landless residents for training in activities such as mushroom cultivation, rabbit rearing, basketmaking and fabrication of ferro-cement construction materials. They are also being helped by the department to build links with technical institutions, markets and banks.

Many of these problem areas reflect the limitations of a top-down project, whose preprogrammed provisions constrain action on many unanticipated, but nevertheless important, issues that come up during implementation. Prior to this program, Rajasthan had little or no experience with large-scale, integrated watershed development interventions in rain-fed areas with small farmers, and much has been learned about what to do and what not to do. The programs have resulted in substantial staff training, in major improvements in participatory management and community-based planning, in the identification of many technical problems and in the solution of a few of them, and in the creation of a large pool of technical and managerial talent across the countryside. More significant achievements will, we hope, be recorded as the lessons of the first few years are absorbed and as methodologies are further refined.

NOTE

An earlier version of this chapter was prepared for *New Horizons: The Economic, Social and Environmental Impacts of Participatory Watershed Development*, a project organized by the International Institute for Environment and Development in London.

18 The CAMPFIRE Program: Community-Based Wildlife Resource Management in Zimbabwe

Simon Metcalfe

The Communal Areas Management Program For Indigenous Resources, known by the acronym CAMPFIRE, evolved as an undertaking to reconcile the different interests of government and community authorities concerning control over wildlife resources. In twentieth-century Zimbabwe, the ascendancy of bureaucratic rules over traditional conventions is real but not always very deep. Nowhere is this more obvious than when reviewing the relationship of African governments to the wildlife resources in their domain.

Under colonial rule, which lasted, effectively, until 1980 in Zimbabwe, a policy that separated rural people from their customary use rights over natural resources may have seemed tenable. However, governments that depend on popular rural support to remain in power have to address the issue of natural resource ownership; they must make clear who is responsible for wildlife, both for meeting the costs of its management and for allocating the benefits of its conservation.

Zimbabwe recognizes three kinds of land ownership: communal, private and state. Almost half of Zimbabwe is classified as communal land, generally semiarid and less arable areas that were left under African community control. A commercial elite privately controls one-third of the country for "modern" agriculture and for large-scale cattle and game ranching. The protected wild and forest areas under state control, which comprise 15 percent of the country, are also found mainly in semiarid areas adjacent to the communal lands.

Until the 1970s wildlife conservation was the sole responsibility of the state. The beneficiaries of its maintenance were mainly foreign tourists and hunters, the resident white Zimbabweans, biologists and ecologists. Many of the protected areas were established at the expense of local people, who lost both land (forage resources) and rights of access to wildlife. At the same time, communities received totally inadequate compensation for the damages inflicted by elephants trampling crops and carnivores killing livestock. These and other wildlife animals, such as buffalo, crocodiles and hippos, endangered human life in several remote rural communities.

The conflicts of interest between conservationists and rural communities emerged more clearly after the transition to elected self-government. As part of a new wildlife management policy, ecologists with the Department of National Parks and Wildlife Management (DNPWLM) introduced the concept of "sustainable use" and encouraged an integration of conservation and development objectives. Social scientists sought to draw on rural development experience elsewhere, pointing to the importance of community participation and institutional development. The genesis of CAMPFIRE arose from the various insights offered by ecologists, rural sociologists and rural development specialists.

Its legal basis was anticipated in 1975 when the DNPWLM first permitted private landowners to manage and use the wildlife on their lands. An amendment two years after independence (1982) gave legal backing for the innovations that CAMPFIRE was to introduce. Zimbabwe was the first country in Africa and still is one of the few (besides Botswana and Namibia) to have a statute with such scope as the 1975 Parks and Wildlife Act, as amended in 1982.

With a background in urban social and community work in England during the 1970s, I returned to Zimbabwe, after a decade's absence, to work on primary health care and community development projects for Save the Children Fund–U.K. between 1980 and 1987. While learning something of the complexities of rural development, I became personally acquainted with the Zambezi valley districts of Binga and Nyaminyami, both of which encompass vast wildlands.

During 1985, I became aware of CAMPFIRE's potential through contacts with Marshall Murphree of the Center for Applied Social Sciences (CASS) at the University of Zimbabwe. I suggested to the Nyaminyami district council the advantages of the CAMPFIRE approach. Consequently, the council asked me to coordinate a district development conference that would include all the local and institutional stakeholders involved in development to debate thoroughly the resource-use issues facing that district.

In June 1986, over eighty people from outside the district were put up in tents, and for three days a debate—literally "in the bush"—took place, with many district participants contributing. I advertised the conference widely, raising funds to put a four-page development supplement into the national newspaper. For a brief moment, Nyaminyami was the focus of a vigorous development debate. We had participation from CAMPFIRE advocates, national parks department personnel and university staff with a wide-ranging agenda.

Russell Taylor, an ecologist from DNPWLM, and Marshall Murphree of CASS both spoke of the potential for wildlife to become the backbone of the district's production system. This meeting of key technical, community and administrative parties set in motion a process that led to Nyaminyami district's being the first district to be granted authority over the wildlife on its land. In 1988, I joined the Zimbabwe Trust, a nongovernmental organization, or NGO, and was able to focus full time on supporting the initiation of the Nyaminyami Wildlife Management Trust and on spreading the CAMPFIRE program generally.

MANAGEMENT SYSTEMS

Management of wildlife resources on communal land differs from that on state and private land, at least in part because of the greater time and effort it takes to make effective decisions. Management transaction costs can be very high, especially when difficult decisions have to be made and consensus is not easily forthcoming. Whenever a community-based decision is likely to produce winners and losers, misrepresentations and evasions can occur. This is understandable because social harmony is a high priority in rural communities, even if it is maintained at the expense of ecological and economic viability.

The potential for community-based decisions to become compromises with suboptimizing management has historically provided a rationale for technical personnel and local authorities to intervene. Thus, because of the difficulty of community decisionmaking, one of CAMPFIRE's primary organizing principles is that the unit of wildlife management should be as small as possible. It is assumed that primary social groups require less complicated institutional arrangements to manage group resources and are therefore better able to monitor and enforce their decisions.

The 1975 Parks and Wildlife Act allowed authority to be devolved from the state to a district-based local authority. In Zimbabwe, local authorities were already empowered to plan and manage communal lands. The relationship among local government authorities, traditional tribal authorities and CAMPFIRE advocates has been critical in the program's evolution. District organization is a three-tiered structure composed of the district and the lower levels of the ward and the village (see Figure 18.1). These closely parallel the traditional organizational structures of the chieftaincy, the headmanship, and the *kraal* (compound).

CAMPFIRE's preference that the village, or sometimes the ward, should be the main management unit for wildlife was not supported by the statute, which formally empowered the district government. Thus CAMPFIRE had to deal with problems arising from the relationships between different tiers of local government, customary roles and approaches, and

Figure 18.1   Levels of Statutory Decisionmaking and Activity

1. National Level
Parliament (political)
Government agencies (administrative and technical)

‖

2. District Level
Rural District Council (political)
District Development Committee (administrative and technical)

‖

3. Ward Level
A set of village communities having cooperative/commercial relations;
often corresponds to the seat of a traditional leader (chief or headman),
a market center, or a subdistrict center.

‖

4. Village Level
A relatively self-contained, socioeconomic-residential unit; residents
usually closely related with established families and elders.

Source: Adapted from Norman Uphoff, *Local Institutional Development: An Analytical Sourcebook with Cases* (West Hartford, Conn.: Kumarian Press, 1986), p. 11.

wildlife dynamics. The village must account for its resource use to the district, but, reciprocally, the district is accountable to the village. This two-way accountability has been central to achieving intercommunity coordination and sustainable resource use.

The ministry of local government coordinates the district and its subunits through a pyramidal hierarchy with the usual centralizing tendencies. Although the law makes the district council the local land authority, land is customarily regarded as the property of the ancestors who are responsible for the natural resources of a particular area. Access to land and natural resources is traditionally mediated through chiefs, headmen and the heads of *kraals* or spirit mediums who act as the guardians of the land.

Traditional authority is strong because it allies the heads of the most influential local families, the local elite, into a customarily legitimized hierarchy. If they withhold support, traditional authorities can thwart land use plans by granting competing access to land. The council loses popularity if it tries to evict persons who are seen by most as having a legitimate right to the resource. This either/or situation had to be transcended if CAMPFIRE was to create an alliance of authority over—and management responsibility for—wildlife use.

It was a brave act for DNPWLM, a small department in the ministry of environment, to challenge the tenurial structure of communal land and take on the superstar agency, the ministry of local government, rural and urban development. Even if the national parks department might have been weak at cabinet level, its actions got an appreciative reception in rural districts and communities.

CAMPFIRE'S IMPLEMENTATION

CAMPFIRE began operating in 1989 with a de facto granting of authority over wildlife to two districts: Nyaminyami (previously named Kariba) and Guruve. De jure promulgation of "appropriate authority" did not take place until 1990, when DNPWLM negotiated an understanding on CAMPFIRE with the ministry of local government. This sequence meant that DNPWLM launched an important new policy without first reaching a consensus with all other ministries at the national level. District administrators, as agents of local government, were won over to the program and became advocates for it to their head offices. They played a vital role by enabling CAMPFIRE to move ahead, ensuring that bureaucracy would not destroy a program that promised new advances but that could have been stalemated.

The backgrounds of Nyaminyami and Guruve, and the ways CAMP-FIRE developed in each district, were quite different, reinforcing that the program would be an experiment in adaptive management. Although it followed some basic principles (Murphree 1991), CAMPFIRE's implementation was never seen as following a blueprint.

"Appropriate authority" to manage wildlife locally was granted to district councils under the 1975 act, provided that they could satisfy DNPWLM concerning their "intent and capacity" to use authority beneficially. Over time, the intent criterion came to mean that a council accepted CAMPFIRE principles, DNPWLM guidelines for quota setting and the basic formula for distribution of benefits. (This formula proposes that at least 50 percent of revenues from wildlife be allocated to communities for their direct benefit, 35 percent for wildlife management costs, and 15 percent at most to be used for district council expenditures.) The capacity criterion remained moot, as few districts had much experience. Unfortunately, the focal management unit, whether district, ward or village, was not clearly identified. Devolution of authority itself became the driving force behind the institutional learning process.

At first, just a handful of agencies promoted CAMPFIRE: the DNPWLM, especially its terrestrial ecologists; the Center for Applied Social Sciences at the university; the World Wide Fund for Nature's (WWF) Multispecies Animal Production Systems Project; and the Zimbabwe Trust, a rural development NGO. The agencies formed themselves into a CAMPFIRE collaborative group.

Once authority over wildlife had been granted to the first two districts in 1989, the collaborative group supported a series of workshops that I organized to promote the program in other districts. District representatives saw that they had much to gain by controlling their wildlife and the revenue from it. By the end of the year, ten more districts were being helped to initiate their own CAMPFIRE programs. In the process, a CAMPFIRE association of wildlife-producing districts was formed. Its first major initiative was to speak out for local interests in the face of a proposed world ivory ban. Figure 18.2 sketches the structure of the CAMPFIRE association and the functions of the collaborating group of agencies supporting the program.

The CAMPFIRE Association was prominent at the 1989 meeting of the Convention on Trade in Endangered Species (CITES) where, following the prior example of the Inuits of North America, it vigorously defended the rights of local peoples to use and trade in wild species under their control. The government of Zimbabwe, through its national parks department, and the CAMPFIRE association were allies in this effort, and this helped forge a closer working relationship. At a later workshop (1992), DNPWLM and the collaborative group agreed that the CAMPFIRE association should be the lead agency for CAMPFIRE and that NGOs should be encouraged to provide the scaffolding to support the building of this institution.

CAMPFIRE AND LAND USE PLANNING

The Zambezi valley, which is Zimbabwe's northern boundary, has long been infested with tsetse fly, resulting in high cattle mortality. Wildlife, which have more natural immunity, did not have to compete with domestic cattle for forage resources. The success of the government's tsetse eradication program in the 1980s, from a national parks department perspective, raised the specter of loss of wildlife habitat. Newspaper headlines at the time summed up the conservation dilemma: "Tsetse control: boon or blight?" (*Zimbabwe Wildlife*, June 1985).

The tsetse control debate polarized opinion. Proponents justified the program by claiming that enhanced cattle and farm production opportunities

Figure 18.2   The CAMPFIRE Association and Collaborating Agencies

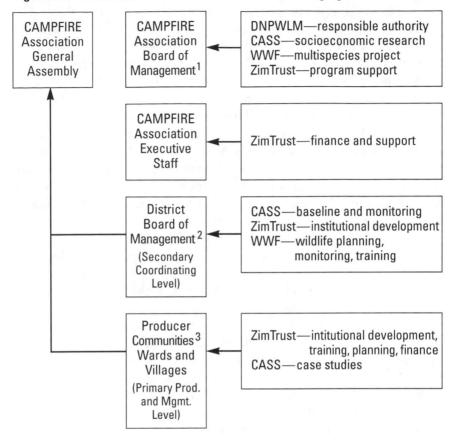

[1] Association policy is established by general assembly at annual meeting where producer communities are represented. Board of management coordinates and overseas execution of policy. Executive staff implement policy on behalf of the membership.

[2] District boards of management provide coordination and management services to ward and village membership.

[3] Producer communities are the primary members of the CAMPFIRE association. Their representatives elect the board of management at annual meeting of general assembly.

following the removal of the fly would enhance development. Groups supporting conservation of game and forests argued that the fly is the ally of conservation, and its removal opened the way for adverse land uses and for settlement getting out of control, leading to habitat destruction and degradation of the land itself.

Land use planning without an enforceable tenure structure leads to an open-access situation that pits technocrats, elected local authorities, politicians and traditional authorities against one another. Local authorities accuse traditional leaders of selling the land unwisely. Traditional authorities say councils are attempting to govern something that is not theirs. The veterinary department says that cattle in some areas must be removed, but politicians are not prepared to enforce evictions. This is part of the wider sociopolitical environment within which CAMPFIRE must operate. CAMPFIRE offers a tenure arrangement for wildlife and other natural resources that allows for their conservation and use by a community, alongside individual cropping and livestock production.

The DNPWLM, supported by CASS, WWF, ZimTrust and the CAMPFIRE Association, proposed that the lowest level of community organization should be the unit responsible for managing wildlife. However, the rural district council was the legally recognized authority for decisions governing land and natural resources, to which all subunits of communal organizations are accountable. The crux of the matter was: who would actually pay the costs for and reap the benefits from wildlife management? In particular, what would be the relative and reciprocal rights and responsibilities between village, ward and district units? Also at issue was the relationship between modern and traditional authorities, and between them and technical agencies.

Given this background, a comparison of CAMPFIRE's development and implementation in two cases highlights some of the contrasts and similarities in the program. The first case shows how the program initially headed in a direction that was inconsistent with the ideas and values undergirding CAMPFIRE. The first case of devolved authority for community management of (and benefit from) wildlife was less participatory than envisioned, although it had some other positive features. This case shows that a learning process can occur even when a somewhat false start is made, provided that the values and goals, with appropriate modifications, are not abandoned.

Nyaminyami District

The Nyaminyami Wildlife Management Trust was a district initiative, not national or community-based. Its main protagonists were the district administration, the district council and its executive officers, DNPWLM, WWF, CASS, and myself for the Zimbabwe Trust. The district had no revenue base and was thus financially, technically and administratively dependent on the central government, especially the ministry of local government. One of the reasons that Save the Children Fund–U.K., the agency I initially represented, was working in Nyaminyami was because it was one of Zimbabwe's poorest districts, as seen from chronic nutritional deficits of children.

The district was marginal, politically and economically. Annual rainfall is around 600 millimeters per annum, with day temperatures averaging 30 degrees Celsius and with midseason droughts frequently ruining crop production. Many of the communities in the district had been forcibly moved to upland areas when the Zambezi valley was inundated by water following the completion of Kariba dam in 1960. Ironically, although the area routinely has a grain deficit, there is abundant protein in the form of wildlife. Although some households had access to fishing on Lake Kariba, no households were legally allowed to use the terrestrial wildlife resources. Professional sport hunting concessions existed, but all receipts went to the central government. Some tourism existed, which involved simply observing and enjoying the wildlife, not taking it, but very little rent was paid to the Council for leases on land for such activities.

The DNPWLM was responsible for setting hunting quotas, negotiating and signing contracts, collecting revenues from trophy hunting, for the problem of animal control, and for antipoaching programs. These latter two programs put the national parks department in an invidious position vis-à-vis the communities because it was perceived as putting more effort into catching poachers than into dealing with problem animals. The communities pointed out that game animals (government property) could destroy their crops and livestock (personal property), even their lives, and generally go unpunished. However, if people destroyed animals by subsistence hunting (considered poaching), they could be harassed, arrested, fined and imprisoned. In practice, the people's management strategy often was to mount a protest against crop destruction and occasionally get an offending elephant or buffalo killed, so those in the immediate vicinity could have a windfall of meat. The department was seen as blocking local development and as an unpopular manifestation of central government.

The driving motivation for getting CAMPFIRE established, and Nyaminyami was no exception, was that it created local ownership and captured some of the value that the private sector was increasingly placing on wildlife. A constraining force was a lack of clarity regarding property rights. Once rights over wildlife were devolved from the state to the district, the latter was empowered, but the communities could do little unless the district further devolved rights and responsibilities to lower levels, whether modern, traditional or preferably both. The private sector requires binding agreements between itself, local authorities and communal people before it will invest. When the council negotiated with a marketing agency, for example, it was unclear whether the council could assuredly deliver the land use that the contract stipulated, such as an undisturbed environment for an eco-tourist activity, since communities could sabotage any agreement they disdained.

At the start of the Nyaminyami Wildlife Management Trust, there was disagreement. The council favored establishing a local government agency, while the national parks department desired a producer-based, group-shareholder approach. Two constitutions were proposed, one with representation of the people through their elected councilors, the other with an annual general meeting of shareholders coming from the wards. The first arrangement would make the trust practically a subcommittee of the council, while the second would create a more autonomous body.

At the trust's first annual general meeting in January 1989, the district administrator, who was also chairman of the trust, endorsed the first approach:

> . . . the Trust would act on behalf of the people . . . and the flow of information and ideas from district level to the village level and *vice versa* would occur through the existing political and developmental structures. . . . It was felt that contrary to widespread belief, the [local government] structure was created not only for political but also for economic and developmental issues, and that it would serve the purpose of mobilizing and engaging the mass of the people in economic and development projects. (emphasis added)

In such a scheme, much would hinge on the vice versa relationship between higher and lower levels of district authority. Wildlife management, economic development and democracy were all tied up in the same structure.

Nyaminyami had impressive wildlife resources, with a population of 2,500 elephants, 7,000 cape buffalo, and 30,000 impala. The district provided habitat for over twenty-four large wildlife species including lion, leopard, crocodile, hippopotamus, sable, eland and kudu. Two large trophy-hunting concessions made use of these resources, and there was a cropping harvest quota for 1,500 impala annually, as well as a number of quality eco-tourist camps.

Given the wealth of the district's wildlife resources, and its top-down approach, Nyaminyami proceeded to establish a substantial wildlife management capacity based on a classic park management model, with personnel who are trained, uniformed, armed and linked by radio communications. No other district in CAMPFIRE has followed this model, however, either because they could not afford to, were not convinced by the approach, or were dissuaded.

With support from WWF's Multispecies Project, Nyaminyami piloted the most sophisticated resource monitoring procedures of all CAMPFIRE districts. For example, the age of all trophy elephants shot has been estimated and their tusks, lengths and weights measured. Problem animal reports have been logged and mapped, and this information has been used to develop a protective fencing strategy. Crop damage has been monitored, estimated and mapped, and a compensation scheme experimented with.

It was discovered, for instance, that compensation claims lacked any built-in mechanism for balancing individual costs against group benefits. As a result, Nyaminyami has canceled individual compensation as a right, and now leaves this up to the wards to settle. For each dollar paid in compensation, the ward's dividend is reduced by that amount, to establish a cost-benefit relationship. Nyaminyami has also developed a lakeshore tourist plan and has learned how to structure a tourist joint venture for itself.

On many levels, Nyaminyami's achievements are laudable, but the communities themselves are hardly participating in the planning and management process. They remain somewhat alienated from both the trust and from the wildlife on which it depends for its existence. Reports of communal snaring of antelope and of unauthorized settlements within restricted areas persist. There is little community organization below the district-run administrative structures, as most authority remains with the board of management.

Despite efforts made by ZimTrust to promote participation, the Nyaminyami council was more prepared to have authority granted to it than to pass this on to the wards and villages. Nyaminyami initially gave each ward an equal dividend from wildlife revenue, despite the fact that animals are not evenly distributed within the district, and it has not allowed communities to use their dividend to pay cash to households. Once the ward has selected a project, such as a grinding mill or a roof for a school, a salaried officer from the council or the trust has organized the project, thus depriving the community of learning how to manage funds and projects themselves. Further, Nyaminyami has spent a rather high percentage of its revenue on management activities, leaving a reduced amount for direct community benefit.

Critics of the Nyaminyami approach argue that if less were spent on salaried management, more resources going to communities might stimulate greater local management. As the trust is still evolving, it is possible that greater participation will eventually occur, creating a more sustainable institution. But Nyaminyami is threatened by immigration pressures and haphazard land use settlement, linked to tsetse control, and unless it can mobilize community commitment, it runs the risk of closing off potential options for wildlife use.

Implementation of CAMPFIRE in Nyaminyami has deviated from the principles articulated by the program's proponents. First, tangible rewards were not given to those who lived with the wildlife, but rather to the higher district administrative level. Second, benefits were not distributed in relation to costs or risks, but rather all wards were given equal dividends. Third, there was no direct correlation between the amount of management effort expended and resulting benefits, as all communities benefited, irrespective of their commitment. Fourth, the unit of proprietorship (the district) did not coincide with the unit of production and management (the communities). Finally, the unit of proprietorship was not as small as practicable, within ecological and sociopolitical constraints, since this was the district rather than wards, villages or traditional authorities. By giving control to the council-run trust, the customary institutions for land management were ignored, and consequently, communities were not really empowered. Rather, control by state institutions just moved closer. With communities' stake and control weakened, in-migration has continued, and wildlife are threatened by habitat fragmentation.

The Masoka Community in Kanyurira Ward, Guruve District

Unlike in Nyaminyami, the CAMPFIRE story in Guruve does not focus mainly on activities at the district level. Instead, there was, from the outset, more vigorous cooperation between community and district institutions. Wildlife is unevenly distributed in the district. The northwestern part of Guruve adjoins a protected safari area, which has a thriving reservoir of wildlife. Prior to the district's being given authority over wildlife resources, Marshall Murphree of CASS had visited Masoka, the largest community in Kanyurira ward, and had helped raise their awareness both of wildlife's potential and of their rights to its benefits. The same contact was not made with wards to the north of Kanyurira. Murphree's selection was opportune. In some other wards, over and above the usual ward-versus-district problems, there are greater differences between traditional and elected authorities. Often several ethnic groups live in a community, including agriculturalists who are dominant over a group who were previously hunter-gatherers. Kanyurira, on the other hand, is a more homogeneous locality.

The Guruve District Council, in the first year of CAMPFIRE, allowed the revenue from wildlife to be distributed according to the natural distribution of big game. Also, it gave Kanyurira, but not the other wards, a free choice of how benefits would be distributed. Kanyurira ward is quite large (400 square kilometers) with a small population, only 60 households (482 people) in 1988. The area is rich in wildlife and for many years has been utilized by professional safari hunters. Before, all wildlife revenues went to the Treasury. In 1988 a CASS study showed community attitudes toward wildlife that were generally negative; local residents were concerned mostly with gaining more community services from government, controlling tsetse fly and encouraging new settlers.

Once there was distribution of direct benefits to the Kanyurira community through CAMPFIRE, wildlife came to be seen a community endowment and something of economic benefit, to be nurtured rather than eliminated. "We see now," said one elder, "that these buffalo are our cattle." The process rekindled a proprietorial attitude toward the ward's wildlife. Living with dangerous wildlife is always a mixed blessing, but some form of usufruct right allows local cost-benefit trade-offs to be made. Once people in Masoka village decided that their wildlife were worth having, the conservation status of these resources improved.

Kanyurira ward residents elected their own ward wildlife committee to actively manage their involvement in the project and the revenues that resulted on behalf of their community. Clear entitlement to the wildlife resources meant that, instead of community members having to be taught conservation awareness from above, they were motivated to learn what they needed to know. As one villager said, "Long back we had a distant relationship with the Guruve district council. Now we have a close one because we have money in our pockets."

At first the council maintained that the community was not capable of administering the wildlife funds, which amounted to some US$20,000. A member of the wildlife committee said, "We wish to be fully in charge of the revenue which accrues to our village. We want to have autonomy from Guruve Council. But I think this will take time because we don't know how to go about it." In fact within a year, the ward had requested and received training in committee operation and fund management from ZimTrust, and the committee was able to maintain its own double-entry ledger book. Given an enabling ownership structure, the community members were highly motivated and rapidly learned what they needed to know.

At the first annual general meeting of the Kanyurira ward wildlife committee in 1990, some women argued that they had been left out of the dividend distribution. As heads of households, even if divorced or widowed, they claimed an entitlement right. The committee had to review its rules of participation. If households were the basic membership units of the community, what qualified as a household? Masoka village decided that a household existed if it had its own kitchen and a family group ate together. This meant, for example, that polygamous marriages were one household if they cooked and ate together, and they therefore received one dividend share. Once given clear rights of resource tenure, economic incentives flowed in ways that encouraged communities to resolve problems for themselves.

At the request of Masoka community, CASS and WWF provided assistance in developing a village-based land use plan that delineated arable and settlement land to be protected by a game fence from wild land. CASS has also undertaken a household survey to help the community monitor demographic changes in Kanyurira over time.

Kanyurira residents have aggressively defended their rights in the face of possible interference from the district council. When it had developed its land use plan, the community charged its councillor and its wildlife committee chairman to take the plan to the district for approval, with these words: "Tell them that these are our animals, and these are our plans. We will not accept any changes imposed by others." The understanding and enforcement of accountability—of the council to the community and of community leaders to their membership—is central to the success of CAMPFIRE in Kanyurira so far.

It is interesting to note how Kanyurira allocates wildlife benefits variably over time. In years when the crop harvest is bad, benefits are allocated to households as cash dividends, while in good years they have been invested in social infrastructure and production activities. One of the district's—and the ministry of local government's—objections to paying cash dividends is that household heads (men) will waste the funds on beer and nullify any development benefit. In fact, community decisionmaking has been very strategic, using resources from wildlife to assure food security in drought years and to promote development in good harvest years, a truly complementary land use.

As community members now have a vested interest in conserving their wildlife, they have rapidly learned how offtake quotas are set, and also how safari operators run their business. Many of the operators' staff are community members, so the village is well-informed of all the hunters' activities. The professional hunter, for his part, works closely with the village wildlife committee and pays respect to traditional leaders. This includes ensuring that the spirit medium is given the expected portions of meat from any animals shot, such as thigh meat of an elephant, from the side on which the elephant falls.

However, a cautionary note from Guruve should be sounded. Many other wards there, in contrast to Kanyurira, have experienced rapid in-migration and reduced wildlife management opportunities. It is unlikely that any community, by itself, can resist outside developmental and migratory pressures unless there is full cooperation between both traditional and modern community institutions—council, government departments and political leaders. However, without a community-based sense of proprietorship, it is even less possible to resist these pressures, which will ultimately undermine wildlife habitat.

CAMPFIRE — THE WIDER CONTEXT

The Kanyurira experience has given CAMPFIRE's backers reason to believe that participatory, community-based management can work as well as, or better than, more administrative management at district level. Structures and practices similar to Kanyurira have been developed with Mahenya community (Chipinge district) and Chikwarakwara (Beitbridge), as well as in several other areas within districts, but most CAMPFIRE programs stand somewhere between the Nyaminyami and Kanyurira cases.

What seems most important is that a defined social group have a real sense of ownership over specific resources within a clearly demarcated geographic area. Ownership provides a basis for giving economic incentives to protect wildlife. Even when the people-to-resource ratio is high, there is incentive to establish local common property institutions. However, it is easier to maintain sustainable resource management if demand is fairly well in balance with supply, that is, if demand is not expanding because of population increases.

By 1995, twenty-six districts were implementing the CAMPFIRE program, covering over half of the country. The remaining districts have not sought to participate because there is too little wildlife on their land to create incentive to seek membership in the program. CAMPFIRE, apart from its specific role in wildlife management, has also been involved in communal resource management innovation, and its institutions exist as prototypes for natural resource common property regimes. With land tenure changes creating a new context for the operation of the technical agencies dealing with natural resources, CAMPFIRE can provide a national policy framework for communal resource management that is participatory and bottom-up. Considering that the department responsible for this shift just a decade ago epitomized top-down management, this is quite a turnaround.

Much of the success of CAMPFIRE can be attributed to a few factors:

- An innovative and bold policy that empowered communities and landowners to benefit from the wildlife in their territory;

- Good marketing of the resource, which can generate more value from wildlife wherever it exists;

- Dynamic and coordinated local agencies, staffed with people committed to the country and the program; and

- Flexible donor support, which nurtures an adaptive programmatic approach rather than attempting to carve the territory up into project fiefdoms, as has happened in some other countries.

When I started working full time on CAMPFIRE in 1988, I was one of a handful of people involved. Today, each district has several people employed in supporting roles, and each village has a wildlife committee. Many pay local people to maintain game fences, patrol for snares, count populations, estimate crop damage and supervise projects. District-level staff and below are generally paid out of CAMPFIRE revenues, which presently total several million U.S. dollars annually. At the national level, CASS has about a dozen postgraduate students researching the program. ZimTrust's institutional development unit plans to have three provincial offices, staffed by up to twenty-four trainers. WWF involvement likewise has grown, and the CAMPFIRE association itself is expanding. Donor funding is used mainly for training, monitoring, research, capital investment and income-generating projects. Virtually all recurrent expenditure is met from wildlife revenue, following the national parks department's guideline that up to 35 percent of gross revenue can be spent on the management of wildlife.

CAMPFIRE has not looked back since it was launched because it has been popular and effective. That does not mean the future is entirely rosy, because various issues of community organization, land tenure, land use planning and effective management still have to be resolved. Compared to the old policy, though, local people are involved, debating the issues themselves and developing their own capabilities to tackle these problems. The agencies that helped implement CAMPFIRE can realistically plan to reduce their involvement within the next decade and allow these community-based institutions, coordinated through the CAMPFIRE association, to carry the program forward. Community-based wildlife management is dynamic and evolving in Zimbabwe's communal areas because local institutions and local capabilities have been the focus and aspiration of the program, from the very start.

19 Reasons for Hope

These experiences from Asia, Africa and Latin America show that the lives of millions of poor and marginal households have been uplifted through their own efforts, assisted by the well-conceived and persistent efforts of "outsiders," whether individuals, government agencies, universities, nongovernmental organizations (NGOs), or donors. These are not experiments, although they usually began with experimentation. They are not "hot-house" programs, although they often started as pilot projects. They started small but sought to have national and even international impacts. As the founder of BRAC says, "Small is beautiful, but large is necessary." Given the immensity and the urgency of the needs of the world's poor, both rural and urban, it is important to expand successful programs. But this expansion must occur at a pace and in ways that are consistent with their organizational capabilities and that can retain the confidence and creativity of all involved. This latter requirement is vitally important and often ignored.

The admonition to think globally and act locally was formulated as advice for the growing environmental crisis that we face around the world. For dealing with the concurrent developmental crisis, it should be reworded slightly: think globally, but begin by acting locally. Successful efforts will not begin on a macro scale, but large-scale programs that operate in the spirit and with the incentives and flexibility of small-scale programs are possible. Scaled-up programs may not be as effective in all respects as their smaller precursors; that would be expecting too much. Indeed, practically all of the programs reported here, including those that we had a hand in, have lost some of their effectiveness and quality in the scaling-up process. But the benefits resulting from economies of scale and from extending programs over larger areas, even with somewhat lower performance levels, represent a great improvement upon the present efforts being made by most governments and private agencies to assist the poor.

We have seen, in the cases reported here, some dramatic and impressive stories. Because of space limitations, however, very little of the tedious, humdrum and routine aspects of program development has been conveyed.

What is important to see is how they usually begin very modestly, starting with an idea and a conviction on the part of one person or a few friends. They were then nurtured by people at many levels of the resulting organizations, people who shared an understanding of how outside resources could be used to bring forth indigenous resources, how to make these combined resources productive, and how to make the provision and use of such resources sustainable by meeting people's needs in realistic, flexible and respectful ways.

NOT MOST FAVORED CONDITIONS

These remarkable advances were for the most part not achieved in countries or regions of countries that are considered to be very favorable for development, considering natural resource endowments or levels of income, education or infrastructure. Two of the cases with the broadest impact—Grameen Bank and BRAC—are from Bangladesh, a country often referred to as a "basket case" when it comes to development, because of the extreme poverty, the population pressures, the oppressiveness of the rural power structure, and the faults and weaknesses in the governmental structure (Blair 1994). NGOs have been able to get around the latter constraint by tackling these developmental barriers with deft strategic moves, eliciting cooperation from millions of the rural poor, particularly women, to alleviate economic, educational and social disabilities, largely by their own combined efforts.

The obstacles to development in Orangi, Pakistan, were not only demographic and economic. In Chapter 2, Akhter Hameed Khan does not go into the political and ethnic tensions that in 1991 made this slum a tinderbox, as former immigrants from India clashed with ethnic Pakistani groups, leaving behind dozens of dead and massive property damage. Community organization could not compete with the heavy weaponry of armed factions to prevent the conflict, but within a matter of months, the lane committees managed to repair much of the damage and to restore a sense of comity to the community, setting up networks to try to contain future outbreaks of violence before it could escalate and spread. Sadly, as these political forces have become national in scope and entangled with drug and other interests, Orangi again became the scene of tragic violence in 1995. How much of the social and physical infrastructure built up in Orangi has been destroyed we do not know. But this underscores how remarkable it was for the pilot project there to build so much cooperation and physical capital in Orangi under such conditions.

The villages in Khaira district of Gujarat State were not the worst off in India, but they were certainly impoverished, with per capita incomes of

$50–100. Eighty-seven percent of the households belonging to the AMUL coops are small, marginal or landless, with 70 percent of the families having only one or two head of cattle to milk each day. Yet this district was the seedbed for cooperatives that have spread now to 170 districts (out of 500) across the country.

Sri Lanka is generally thought to be one of the most attractive and benign countries in the Third World. Yet it was racked by ethnic and political conflicts during the 1980s that took 50,000 to 80,000 lives. Some leaders of both the savings societies and the irrigation associations reported on in Chapters 4 and 11 were subject to death threats during this time, and some of these threats were carried out. The Gal Oya irrigation project, where a system of farmer organization was started for the whole irrigation sector, was considered to be the most disorganized and conflictual in the country. "If we can make progress in Gal Oya, we can make progress anywhere in Sri Lanka," the top official for water management in the irrigation department told reconnaissance team members when planning started for the project.

The Southeast Asia cases, as national programs, did not start with the most unfavorable areas, although they were not the most favorable ones, either. In Africa, the region generally thought to be most difficult for promoting development is the Sahel, which stretches across half a dozen countries of West Africa with little rainfall, very limited natural resources, negligible infrastructure, poor education and health services, and pervasive governmental neglect. Yet a careful assessment of the causes of poverty and environmental degradation led to a highly decentralized, participatory and self-reliant approach to reversing the decline they saw across the region. The obstacles became an impetus for communities to redirect traditional institutions for mutual self-help toward collective action. About one million residents of the Sahel, working together in some 3,000 affiliated groups across six countries, are now using the dry season to diminish its debilitating effects, by constructing facilities to harvest and store water, through new processing enterprises, training and other means.

The Tanzania, Malawi and Zimbabwe cases all deal with areas that are very dry through most of the year and that are underserved by infrastructure throughout the year. Local people quickly took up the opportunities given them by village committees to improve their children's health, to provide potable water and to manage wildlife beneficially as well as sustainably. While the Iringa district in Tanzania was chosen because it had somewhat better administrative infrastructure and more available food supply, this was also a region with child malnutrition more serious than the national average, reflecting social and distributional problems that can be more intractable than simply increasing physical supply.

Haiti, Bolivia and Guatemala, especially the Indian communities in the latter, are some of the poorest and most disadvantaged parts of Latin America. The district of San Martin Jilotepeque described in Chapter 9 was so beset by physical violence by 1979 that the World Neighbors project had to be withdrawn.[1] During the preceding seven years, farmers had increased their yields of maize and beans by roughly six times (from 400 to 2,400 kilograms per hectare), with a project expenditure of less than $50 per family. Equally remarkable in retrospect is their managing to double their yields again over the next fifteen years, to 4,800 kilograms per hectare, without any further outside assistance, using the participatory research and extension methods that World Neighbors had developed with them. Families in comparable areas not participating in the program, who had increased their yields only to 600 kilograms per hectare by 1979 were up to only 1,200 kilograms per hectare by 1994.

Under the very difficult conditions of rural Bolivia, DESEC has been able to help households quadruple their potato production and establish a number of other programs that improve rural people's quality of life. The reforestation efforts in Haiti are truly remarkable both for their scale and speed, in a country experiencing disorder and despair. Twenty million trees were planted by farmers in four years' time, five times more than the project target set for a five-year period. While Mexico is more developed economically and socially than the other three Latin American countries considered, the state of Puebla was not one of the more prosperous areas, and Plan Puebla focused exclusively on smallholders farming in the poorer, unirrigated parts of that state.

The accomplishments reported in this volume thus represent efforts to tackle the worst of rural underdevelopment, and these programs were able to succeed in situations that were not particularly favorable. In fact, an analysis of 150 local organization cases from Asia, Africa and Latin America found that the success of local organizations was, on average, somewhat *inversely* correlated with more favorable environmental conditions such as infrastructure, topography, per capita income and literacy levels (Esman and Uphoff 1984, 99–136). This is not to say that the worst situations will necessarily be the easiest to improve, but rather to underscore that one should not assume that the worst will be impossible or intractable. Good design of programs and high quality of leadership can compensate enough for efforts to be successful under many, if not all, adverse conditions.

Making progress under such circumstances, however, can take time. V. Kurien spent almost twenty years developing the AMUL model with farmers in the Indian state of Gujarat. But there can also be rapid advance. Once the model was well understood, it could be used to spread benefit rapidly to tens of millions of people. Sometimes progress can also be very quick from the start, as seen with the Agroforestry Outreach Project in Haiti and the Gal Oya project in Sri Lanka. The incentives, technology and organization involved need to easily understood, adaptable and modifiable in light of experience, and embraced by the people who, it is hoped, will benefit from them.

THE PERSONAL FACTOR

These cases clearly demonstrates the importance of personality and personal qualities—idealism, interpersonal skills, perseverance, energy and enthusiasm. This partly reflects the methodology for assembling this volume, asking protagonists of successful development programs to write about their experiences. But we think this is not the main or only reason. It is obviously true that large-scale changes require leadership that is out of the ordinary. The great personal contributions of figures now legendary in the development literature like Akhter Hameed Khan, Dr. V. Kurien, Dr. Muhammad Yunus and Khun Mechai are not diminished by observing that the factor of personality can be overestimated as readily as underestimated. Indeed, as seen in Chapter 2 of *Reasons for Success,* those who have had large personal impact underscore the importance of a team approach and having excellent leadership provided at all levels of a program.

All of the accounts in this volume emphasize the importance of the contributions of various levels of program staff—their ability, their commitment, their creativity and their devoted hard work. There is much innovation and even heroism and sacrifice by staff that is known only to villagers and other staff which is not only left anonymous here but usually is not documented anywhere. Even when the results of programs are reported, the names and actions of the individuals who made the process successful on the ground are seldom known. As a matter of courtesy and appreciation but also because it is true, the authors of the exemplary cases in this book praise their colleagues and support staff, as well as project participants' contributions, crediting them with making the programs a success.

COMMON ELEMENTS

An unstated hypothesis motivated our planning and production of this volume. We were curious to know whether there would be much commonality among the cases, or whether they would all be unique. While each case is obviously and impressively one-of-a-kind, we are sure that readers were struck time and again, as we were when editing the chapters, by how much the cases have in common, philosophically, strategically and tactically. These elements are analyzed in *Reasons for Success*. We note here that many of the sentences from one chapter could have been lifted out and put into another one without the author who received the sentences even noticing that the wordings were someone else's, so similar are the experiences and ideas being presented. While the contributors come from many backgrounds and disciplines, not to mention countries, they have converged on a set of philosophical principles and pragmatic actions that appear to be effective across a wide range of rural environments.

It is possible for popular self-help movements such as Chipko and Bhoomi Sena in India to emerge without substantial outside assistance. But there is not much evidence that such initiatives have the kind of widespread beneficial impact on people's lives, indeed empowering them as well as making them better off, that are seen here.[2] In a previous analysis of Asian rural development experience, we commented on both the paternalist fallacy and the populist fallacy, finding each misconceived by attributing exclusive wisdom, virtue and efficacy either to the educated elites or to the uneducated masses (Uphoff and Esman 1974, 13–16).

The cases here give examples of where sympathetic but hard-headed leadership, operating from a variety of institutional bases (government, NGO, university) or from none at all could make common cause with rural people, learning with and from them how to make desired and sustainable improvements in their conditions of life. These were not pure bottom-up programs because initiative came from a variety of outsiders. But these outsiders knew how to enter into the conditions and outlooks of rural people, to fashion programs from the inside out, so to speak. They brought to this encounter the advantages of higher education and high-level contacts, but they knew better than to be patronizing or paternalistic. By showing deep respect for the capabilities of the people whose lives they hoped to help improve, and by being persistent as well as patient (being impatiently patient, one might say), they helped fashion solutions to problems that mobilized and used resources of all sorts most effectively.

This relationship, then, was a dialectical one, in which top-down and bottom-up initiatives became fused in interesting new combinations. Some kind of supporting agency was needed to spread and sustain the new technology, the new organization, the new opportunity. An existing agency could be adapted; NIA is the best example of this (Korten and Siy 1988). But often, new organizational vehicles had to be created. Most often these were some kind of nongovernmental organization, for example, the Orangi Pilot Project, BRAC, Six-S, DESEC, CAMPFIRE, and PDA. AMUL and SANASA set up new systems of cooperatives, while Grameen set up a new bank, and Agroforestry Outreach Project put together a coalition of NGOs to carry out its program, circumventing a government that had many debilitating weaknesses.

Somewhat differently, the integrated pest management program in Indonesia got around the limitations of one government ministry by working through the planning agency. Existing government departments were reoriented and given new tasks in the Rajasthan watershed, Gal Oya irrigation, Iringa nutrition, and Malawi self-help water cases. Plan Puebla worked mostly from a university base, with responsibility eventually, and not fully satisfactorily, handed over to government. In the Guatemala case, there was no institutionalization of capabilities, but there is evidence that they were sustained by the communities themselves. In various ways, these new instruments for promoting development, whether governmental or nongovernmental, were hybrid kinds of organization that engaged and retained the cooperation of multiple stakeholders.

A common denominator was the process of institution building from below. What was started as a pilot effort, free of preconception and formalism, led to new formulations for structure and process that became the core innovation and capability of the program: Grameen Bank's borrower groups and group-based lending; the *naam* groups adapted for Six-S objectives with their "son-and-daughter" mills; AMUL's dairy cooperative structure; the farmer-extensionists in San Martin. Institutional innovations pioneered at early stages became standard operating methodologies, not just procedures, in subsequent stages of program development.

One of the most remarkable and important features of these cases is the way that local people utilize various organizational capabilities, once these are created and command confidence, to solve a wide range of problems and meet a variety of needs. This contradicts the assertions of "policy dialogue" proponents who think it sufficient to "get the prices right" and manipulate incentives from olympian national seats of decisionmaking. These programs have instead created many-faceted and evolving capacities at local levels and higher.[3] Practically all of the programs show a remarkable ability and desire to diversify activities so that development, initially sectoral, becomes more encompassing.

THE ROLE OF RURAL PEOPLE

The chapters here give only glimpses of the enthusiasm and energy that such programs elicit, once they become owned by the people for whom they were intended. For example, when visiting Leuwiliang, Indonesia, in June 1995, Uphoff met two farmers who had been through the farmer field school for integrated pest management (IPM) in their subdistrict. They told not only how they increased their rice yields by almost 100 percent over five years by using what they had learned in the school, but how their initial six farmer groups had organized and trained farmers in another twenty-six groups that formed around them. The name they gave their federation of Leuwiliang groups was "Lovers of Peace." They were continuing to spread the methods that they had learned and were continually refining, impelled by a desire that other farmers be able to improve their production similarly.

Several months after the Gal Oya project in Sri Lanka was formally concluded at the end of 1985, Uphoff visited the area to see how the farmer organizations were carrying on. He was pleasantly surprised to find a dozen farmer-representatives meeting in a schoolhouse to decide how best they could present priority farmer concerns to the next District Agricultural Committee meeting. The farmers assembled were proceeding very systematically and thoughtfully, deciding who should speak on what issues, with what arguments, and with what evidence.

Asked by the farmers to say a few words at the end of the meeting, Uphoff said that he was impressed by how seriously they took opportunities that the program had given them to get decisionmakers to heed farmers' needs and ideas. He said that up to that time he had avoided using the word "success" to describe the farmer organization program, knowing how deceptive and fragile success can be. But now that he had seen how intelligently and effectively they were using their organizations to advance farmer interests, he was ready to consider the program a success, and he thanked them for making it one.

The chairman of the group responded by thanking Uphoff and his ARTI and Cornell colleagues for helping them establish farmer organizations. But he said they wanted ARTI and Cornell to know that farmers in Gal Oya would not consider their program a success until all of the other farmers in Sri Lanka like themselves had the same kind of farmer organizations that had done so much to improve their lives; then they could talk about success. This expression of solidarity and satisfaction—from farmers who, only five years before, had been characterized by officials as impossibly uncooperative and conflict-prone—was an indication of organizational commitment and capacity that has been sustained and has grown in the decade since outside assistance was withdrawn.

Shortly after returning to India from two years at Cornell University, Krishna visited the Andheri Deori watershed in Ajmer district of Rajasthan. This was four years after watershed conservation work had started in the area, and two years before the government department expects to withdraw itself from the area. A critical question when the program started was whether local organizations could be established that had enough competence and cohesiveness to enforce use regulations for the common lands being developed. Too often, excellent pastures and plantations have been planted under government programs, only to be destroyed—by negligence or through acts of vandalism—once the program terminated.

Krishna was happy to see that these expectations were being considerably fulfilled in Andheri Deori. The government department's role had been substantially reduced in the past two years, as farmers have taken a growing share of responsibility for program tasks. The users committee has become a force to reckon with. Both in technical and managerial capacity, they are now able to act as consultants to farmers in neighboring areas. Regular elections for committee members, conducted by the farmers themselves, ensure that the office bearers remain accountable to the membership.

When asked what they would do when the department leaves, farmers said that they are formulating a proposal for a follow-up project that they would manage themselves. Given the number of donor agency officials who have visited the area, this seems a reasonably good prospect. The farmers said that they really did not need the government department any more. They were themselves well-versed in the technologies. They had forged an organization that worked quite well for them, and they were sharing their knowledge with friends and relatives in other villages. Another indication of progress and viability was that the three paraveterinarians in this watershed were each making 3,000–4,000 rupees (US$85–115) a month, and two had bought motorcycles to extend their area of operation.

There were, however, signs that the program was being undermined by too rapid growth. Because the program was seen by government and donor staff as "an oasis of success in a desert of failure," more and more money was being poured into watershed development, without comprehending that this undemined the organizational and technical foundations responsible for success. Officials overseeing the program were not disposed to consider how their previous progress would be undone by pushing the pace of expansion faster than effective management capacities could be created and sustained, both within the concerned government agencies and, most important, within the communities involved.

Attention to building and maintaining of institutional capacities distinguishes the successful cases reported in this book. The other feature most clearly and importantly shared in common is the confidence these programs displayed in the willingness and ability of rural people to cooperate with their neighbors to improve their lives, given reasonable, adequate and assured opportunities. Often, a negative legacy of exploitation or broken promises had to be overcome, and people did not immediately rush to adopt new responsibilities or technologies. But program leadership, from highest to lowest levels, appreciated that people with few resources other than their labor, intelligence, creativity and social networks, would be able through increasing self-reliance to achieve improvements in their lives across a range of sectors and areas. Despite the distressing economic, environmental, political and social crises that the people of this world face as the next century arrives, these cases demonstrate that there are still substantial reasons for hope.

NOTES

1. Estimates of the number of deaths in Guatemala resulting from the violence and repression vary, but the figure 50,000 is often cited. Leaders of the San Martin peasant cooperative were being killed by the late 1970s, and several thousand villagers had to abandon their homes for 3–4 years and live as hunters and gatherers in the mountains when the army destroyed their communities in the warfare that raged throughout the region.

2. Chipko, an environmental protection movement, has become a force to be reckoned with by government and politicians, diversifying into income-generating efforts for its members (Guha 1989). Bhoomi Sena was effective in the late 1970s and early 1980s in gaining land rights for the poor in eastern India, but it is currently characterized as "an armed vigilante group" propped up by the Congress(I) party, "traditionally a party of rich peasantry" (*India Today*, August 31, 1995, p. 29).

3. The "Sixteen Decisions" (Table 1.1) formulated by Grameen Bank borrowers exemplify this process. Once they start improving their incomes through savings and loans, they seek to end dowry and child marriage which impoverish them and diminish their children; they pledge to grow and eat vegetables to improve family nutrition; they agree to invest in education and literacy; and they pledge to help each other and resist oppression of the poor.

References

Adamson, Peter. 1982. Ideas in action: The rains. In *The state of the world's children 1982–83*, edited by James Grant. New York: Oxford University Press.

Aluwihare, P. B., and Masao Kikuchi. 1991. *Irrigation investment trends in Sri Lanka: New construction and beyond*. Colombo: International Irrigation Management Institute.

Amsden, Alice H. 1994. Why isn't the whole world experimenting with the East Asian model to develop?: Review of *The East Asian Miracle*. *World Development* 22(4): 627–33.

ARTI. 1982. *1980 year book for Sri Lanka water management research*. Colombo: ARTI.

———. 1986. *The Gal Oya water management project: End-of-project impact assessment*. Colombo: ARTI. Mimeo.

Ashley, Marshall. 1986. *A study of traditional agroforestry systems in Haiti*. Port-au-Prince: USAID/University of Maine Outreach Research Project.

Balzano, Anthony. 1986. *Socio-economic aspects of agroforestry in rural Haiti*. Port-au-Prince: USAID/University of Maine Outreach Project. Mimeo.

———. 1989. Tree-planting in Haiti: Agroforestry and rural development in a local context. Unpublished Ph.D. dissertation, Rutgers University.

Bannister, Michael, and S. J. Josiah. 1993. Agroforestry training and extension: The experience from Haiti. *Agroforestry Systems* 23(2): 239–51.

BAPPENAS. 1990. *Farmers as experts: The Indonesian IPM national program*. Jakarta: BAPPENAS (National Agency for Planning and Development).

Blair, Harry. 1994. Analyzing the performance gap in Bangladesh: Three approaches. In *Puzzles of productivity in public organizations*, edited by N. Uphoff, 17–42. San Francisco: Institute of Contemporary Studies Press.

Brohier, R. L. 1933. *Ancient irrigation works in Ceylon*. 3 vols. Colombo: Government Printer.

Buffum, William. 1986. *Three years of tree planting in a Haitian mountain village*. Port-au-Prince: Pan-American Development Foundation.

Buffum, William, and Wendy King. 1985. *Small farmer decision-making and tree planting: Agroforestry extension recommendations*. Port-au-Prince: Pan-American Development Foundation.

Bunch, Roland. 1982. *Two ears of corn: A guide to people-centered agricultural development*. Oklahoma City, Okla.: World Neighbors.

Bunch, Roland, and Gabino V. Lopez. 1994. Soil recuperation in Central America: Measuring the impact four to forty years after intervention. Paper presented to International Policy Workshop organized by the International Institute for Environment and Development, 28 November–2 December, Bangalore.

CIMMYT. 1969. *The Puebla Project, 1967–69: Progress report of a program to rapidly increase corn yields on small holdings.* El Bataan, Mexico: CIMMYT.

————. 1974. *The Puebla Project: Seven years of experience, 1967–1973.* El Batan, Mexico: CIMMYT.

Chambers, Robert. 1983. *Rural development: Putting the last first.* London: Longman.

Chauhan, Sumi Krishna, et al. 1983. *Who puts the water in the taps: Community participation in third world drinking water, sanitation and health.* London: Earthscan.

Connelly, Matthew, and Paul Kennedy. 1994. Must it be the rest against the west? *The Atlantic Monthly* 274(6): 61ff.

Conway, Frederick. 1986. Agroforestry outreach project in Haiti. *Medioambiente Caribeño* 2(3): 356–61. Santo Domingo: ENDA-Caribe.

Díaz Cisneros, Heliodoro et al. 1995. *El Plan Puebla 1967–1992: Analisis de una estrategia de desarrollo de la agricultura tradicional.* Montecillo, Mexico: Colegio de Postgraduados.

de los Reyes, Romana, and Sylvia Jopillo. 1986. *An evaluation of the Philippine participatory communal irrigation program.* Manila: Institute of Philippine Culture, Ateneo de Manila.

Esman, Milton J., and Norman Uphoff. 1984. *Local institutions: Intermediaries in rural development.* Ithaca, N.Y.: Cornell University Press.

Fernando, E. 1986. Informal credit and savings organisations in Sri Lanka: The Cheetu system. *Savings and Development* 10(3): 253–63.

Glennie, Colin. 1983. *Village water supply in the decade: Lessons from field experience.* New York: John Wiley.

Government of Ceylon. 1971. *Report of the Gal Oya project evaluation committee.* Sessional Paper I-70. Colombo: Government Printer.

Gow, David, et al. 1979. *Local organizations and rural development: A comparative reappraisal.* 2 vols. Washington: Development Alternatives, Inc.

Grosenick, G. 1986. *Final report: An economic analysis of agroforestry systems in Haiti.* Port-au-Prince: USAID.

HABITAT. 1989. *Malawi gravity-fed rural piped-water program: A case study.* Nairobi: HABITAT.

Harrison, Paul. 1987. *The greening of Africa.* New York: Penguin Books.

Headland, Thomas N., Kenneth L. Pike, and Marvin Harris. 1990. *Emics and etics: The insider/outsider debate.* Newbury Park, Calif.: Sage Publications.

Hill, Catherine B., and Katundu M. Mtawali. 1989. Malawi: Lessons from the gravity-fed piped water scheme. In *Successful development in Africa: Case studies of projects, programs and policies*, edited by R. Bheenick et al. EDF Development Policy Case Studies No. 1. Washington D.C.: World Bank.

Hirschman, Albert O. 1995. *Development projects observed*. Washington D.C.: Brookings Institution.

Hulme, David R., R. Montgomery, and D. Bhattacharya. 1994. *Mutual finance and the poor: A study of the federation of thrift and credit cooperatives in Sri Lanka*. IDPM Working Paper No. 11. Manchester: Institute for Development Planning and Management, University of Manchester, with Department of Economics, University of Reading.

Indrapala, K., ed. 1971. *The collapse of the Rajarata civilization in Ceylon and the drift to the South West*. Peradeniya: University of Ceylon.

International Rice Research Institute (IRRI). 1990. *World rice statistics*. Los Baños: IRRI.

International Science and Technology Institute (ISTI). 1985. *Final evaluation of Sri Lanka water management project (No. 383–0057)*. Washington: ISTI.

Jickling, J. L., and T. A. White. 1992. *An economic and institutional analysis of agroforestry in Haiti*. Washington D.C.: World Bank.

Jodha, N. S. 1990. Rural common property resources: Contributions and crisis. *Economic and Political Weekly* 30 June, A65–78. Bombay, India.

Jonsson, Urban, Bjorn Ljungqvist, and Olivia Yambi. 1991. *Mobilization for nutrition in Tanzania*. In The uses and limitations of information in the Iringa nutrition program, by D. L. Pelletier. Tanzania. Ithaca, N.Y.: Cornell University.

Kaplan, Robert D. 1994. The coming anarchy. *The Atlantic Monthly* 273(2): 44ff.

Kiriwandeniya, P. A. 1992. The growth of the SANASA movement in Sri Lanka. In *Making a difference: NGOs and development*, edited by M. Edwards and D. Hulme, 111–17. London: Earthscan.

Korten, David C. 1980. Community organization and rural development: A learning process approach. *Public Administration Review* 40(5): 480–511.

Korten, Frances F. 1982. *Building national capacity to develop water users' associations: Experience from the Philippines*. Staff Working Paper No. 528. Washington: World Bank.

———. 1988. The working group as a catalyst for organizational change. In *Transforming a bureaucracy: The experience of the Philippine National Irrigation Administration*, edited by F. Korten and R. Siy. West Hartford, Conn.: Kumarian Press.

Korten, Frances F., and Robert Y. Siy Jr., eds. 1988. *Transforming a bureaucracy: The experience of the Philippine National Irrigation Administration*. West Hartford, Conn.: Kumarian Press.

Lauraya, Fay M., Antonia Lea Sala, and C. M. Wijayaratna. 1993. Self-assessment of performance by irrigators' association. In *Performance measurement in farmer-managed irrigation systems*. Proceedings of an International Workshop on Farmer-Managed Irrigation Systems, November 1991, Mendoza, Argentina. Colombo: International Irrigation Management Institute.

Lauwerysen, Herman. 1985. *Socio-economic study of two tree-planting communities.* Port-au-Prince: Pan-American Development Foundation.

Lecomte, Bernard J. 1986. *Project aid: Limitations and alternatives.* Paris: OECD Development Center.

Lecomte, Bernard J., and Lédéa Bernard Ouedraogo. 1975. Comment permettre aux jeunes et aux femmes de s'équiper en réalisant des activités collectives de saisons séche. Dakar: ENDA. [Report of Accra conference] Mimeo.

Liebenow, J. Gus. 1981. Malawi: Clean water for the rural poor. *Waterlines* 2:3 (August 1981), part 1, and 3:1 (July 1984), part 2.

Lowenthal, Ira P. 1989. Social soundness analysis of the national program for Agroforestry. DESFIL report prepared for USAID/Haiti.

Lovell, Catherine H. 1992. *Breaking the cycle of poverty: The BRAC strategy.* West Hartford, Conn.: Kumarian Press.

Murray, Gerald. 1979. Terraces, trees, and the Haitian peasant: An assessment of 25 years of erosion control in rural Haiti. Port-au-Prince: USAID. Mimeo.

———. 1984. The wood tree as a peasant cash-crop: An anthropological strategy for the domestication of energy. In *Haiti—Today and tomorrow*, edited by C. R. Foster and A. Valdman, 141–60. Lanham, Md.: University Press of America.

———. 1987. The domestication of wood in Haiti: A case study in applied evolution. In *Anthropological Praxis: Translating Knowledge into Action*, edited by R. M. Wulff and S. J. Fiske, 223–42. Boulder, Colo.: Westview Press.

Murray-Rust, D. Hammond, and M. P. Moore. 1984. *Formal and informal water management systems: Cultivation meeting and water delivery in two Sri Lankan irrigation systems.* Cornell Studies in Irrigation No. 2. Ithaca, N.Y.: Irrigation Studies Group, Cornell University.

Mustamin, M. 1988. Health hazards due to the use of pesticides in Indonesia: Data collection and surveys. Proceedings of Pesticide Management and Integrated Pest Management workshop, 23–27 February, Pattaya, Thailand.

Narayan, Deepa. 1995. *The contribution of people's participation: Evidence from 121 rural water supply projects.* Environmentally Sustainable Development Occasional Paper Series No. 1. Washington, D.C.: World Bank.

Ouedraogo, Lédéa Bernard. 1977. *Les groupeménts pre-cooperatifs au Yatenga.* Paris: Centre de Recherches Cooperatives.

Pelletier, David L. 1991. *The uses and limitations of information in the Iringa nutrition program, Tanzania.* CFNPP Working Paper No. 5. Ithaca, N.Y.: Cornell Food and Nutrition Policy Program, Cornell University.

Pincus, Jonathan. 1991. Farmer field school survey: Impact of IPM training on farmers' pest control behavior. Jakarta: Integrated Pest Management National Program, BAPPENAS.

Pradervand, Pierre. 1989. *Listening to Africa: Developing Africa from the grassroots.* New York, N.Y.: Praeger.

Robertson, Lyndesay H. 1981. The development of self-help gravity piped water projects in Malawi. In *Rural Water Supply in Developing Countries*. Ottawa: International Development Research Centre.

Siy, Robert Y., Jr. 1982. *Community resource management: Lessons from the Zanjera*. Quezon City: University of the Philippines Press.

Smucker, Glenn R. 1982. *Social and organizational conditions for tree planting in the Northwest of Haiti*. Port-au-Prince: USAID.

Smucker, Glenn R., and Joel C. Timyan. 1995. Impact of tree planting in Haiti, 1982–1995. Port-au-Prince: SECID/Auburn Productive Land Use Strategy Project. Mimeo.

Sudarwohadi, Sastrosiswojo. 1993. *Development, implementation and adoption of integrated pest management for major vegetable pests in Indonesia*. Bandung: Lembang Horticultural Research Institute.

Svendsen, M., and C. M. Wijayaratna. 1982. The spatial distribution of irrigation water management and yields on the Gal Oya Left Bank. *Sri Lanka Journal of Agrarian Studies* 3(2): 69–82.

UNICEF. 1993. *We will never go back: Social mobilization in the child survival and development programme in the United Republic of Tanzania*. New York: UNICEF.

Uphoff, Norman. 1986. *Local institutional development: An analytical sourcebook with cases*. West Hartford, Conn.: Kumarian Press.

———. 1988. Assisted self-reliance: Working with, rather than for the poor. In *Strengthening the poor: What have we learned?*, edited by J. P. Lewis, 47–59. New Brunswick, N.J.: Transaction Books.

———. 1990. Paraprojects as new modes of international development assistance. *World Development* 18(10): 1401–11.

———. 1992. *Learning from Gal Oya: Possibilities for participatory development and post-Newtonian social science*. Ithaca, N.Y.: Cornell University Press.

Uphoff, Norman, and Milton J. Esman. 1974. *Local organization for rural development: Analysis of Asian experience*. Ithaca, N.Y.: Rural Development Committee, Cornell University.

Uphoff, Norman, and R. D. Wanigaratne. 1982. Local organization and rural development in Sri Lanka. In *Rural development and local organization in Asia*, edited by N. Uphoff, vol. I, 479–549. New Delhi: Macmillan.

Vincent, Fernand. 1984. Peasant strategies: The case of the Six-S Association. Innovations et Reseaux pour le Developpemént Forum. Geneva: IRED.

Warner, D. B., J. Briscoe, C. Hafner, and Bert Zellner. 1986. *Malawi self-help rural water supply program: Final evaluation*. WASH Field Report No. 186. Washington: USAID.

White, T. A., and J. L. Jickling. 1993. Forestry and soil conservation projects in Haiti: Policy lessons for external aid. Paper for the Department of Forest Resources, University of Minnesota at Minneapolis.

Wijayaratna, C. M. 1982. The spatial pattern of water adequacy and resulting farmer responses in a tank irrigation system irrigation scheme in Sri Lanka. Paper presented to Workshop on Modernization of Tank Irrigation Problems and Issues. Center for Water Resources, University of Technology, Madras.

———. 1986. Assessing irrigation system performance: A methodological study with application to Gal Oya scheme, Sri Lanka. Unpublished Ph.D. dissertation, Department of Agricultural Economics, Cornell University.

World Bank. 1993. *The East Asian miracle: Economic growth and public policy.* Policy Research Report. Washington, D.C.: World Bank.

About the Contributors

F. H. Abed, founder and executive director of the Bangladesh Rural Advancement Committee (BRAC), initially worked in a multinational company in Europe and Canada, and returned to help rehabilitate war refugees coming back from India when Bangladesh won its independence in 1971. His earlier training in architecture and accountancy provided useful skills for building one of the largest nongovernmental organizations in the world, with 14,000 staff reaching 55,000 villages and serving more than one million families. In 1981–82, he was a visiting scholar at the Harvard Institute for International Development and was awarded a doctor of law degree, *Honoris Causa*, by Queen's University in Canada in 1994.

Benjamin U. Bagadion, a former assistant administrator of the National Irrigation Administration (NIA) in the Philippines, initiated the participatory irrigation development program of that agency in 1976 and led its expansion until his retirement from NIA in 1985. Before 1975, while head of NIA's engineering department, he played a key role in putting in place the legal, organizational and financial policy framework for the agency's participatory irrigation program. Since retirement from NIA, he has continued to consult on the agency's program and on efforts in other Asian countries to develop similar programs and capacities.

Roland Bunch has worked in rural development in Latin America for twenty-nine years. During that time, he was the founder of the San Martin Program in Guatemala; the Central American representative of World Neighbors, a nongovernmental organization that promotes sustainable agriculture, natural resource management and human resource development; head of the rural development department of the Panamerican School of Agriculture in Honduras; and a cofounder of COSECHA, an agricultural advisory organization based in Honduras that has worked with programs in some twenty-two nations during its first four years. His book, *Two Ears of Corn: A Guide to People-Centered Agricultural Improvement* (1982), has been translated into nine languages.

A. M. R. Chowdhury has been associated with the Bangladesh Rural Advancement Committee (BRAC) since 1977 and has been director of research since 1992. Over the years he developed BRAC's Research and Development Division into a full-fledged, multidisciplinary unit with over

100 staff members. He has a M.Sc. from the London School of Economics and Political Science and a Ph.D. from the London School of Hygiene and Tropical Medicine. He was a 1992–93 MacArthur Fellow at Harvard University.

Juan Demeure is a Bolivian citizen with a degree in educational sciences from the University of Leuven in Belgium. Since the early 1960s, he has been actively involved in development projects in Bolivia and other Latin American countries. In 1963, along with a group of young professionals, he founded DESEC, a Bolivian NGO specializing in rural development. Besides serving as DESEC's president, Demeure has participated in consulting missions on rural institutions and credit for FAO, UNDP, the Inter-American Development Bank and other international organizations. During 1981–82, he was a Humphrey Fellow at the Massachusetts Institute of Technology.

Heliodoro Díaz Cisneros is currently Program Director for Latin America and the Caribbean for the W. K. Kellogg Foundation. He continues to teach part-time in the Center for Rural Studies of the Postgraduate College of the National School of Agriculture at Chapingo, Mexico, having earned a B.S. in agronomy from that institution and a Ph.D. in development studies from the University of Wisconsin. He joined Plan Puebla as evaluator in 1967 and served later as an extension agent and coordinator for that project. He has written forty professional papers on rural development and evaluation and has authored three books on these subjects.

Milton J. Esman is John S. Knight Professor Emeritus of International Studies and former director of the Center for International Studies at Cornell. A veteran participant, observer and analyst of development policies and programs, he has been particularly interested in the institutional and administrative dimensions of development. His publications include *Management Dimensions of Development* (Kumarian Press, 1991) and, in collaboration with Norman Uphoff, *Local Organizations: Intermediaries in Rural Development* (Cornell University Press, 1984). He served as senior advisor in public administration to the prime minister's office of the government of Malaysia, 1966–68, and taught at the Graduate School of Public and International Affairs at the University of Pittsburgh before coming to Cornell.

Edgar Guardia is a Bolivian economist with degrees from the University of Houston and Arizona State University. Since 1983, he has been general manager of DESEC, a Bolivian NGO supporting development in rural communities and regions. He has done consulting work with local Bolivian institutions and was recently elected to the executive committee of SOLIDARIOS, the Council of American Development Foundations. During 1987-88, he was a Humphrey Fellow at Cornell University.

Leobardo Jiménez Sánchez is an agronomic engineer at the National School of Agriculture at Chapingo, Mexico, with a M.S. and Ph.D. from the University of Wisconsin. He joined the Office of Special Studies for the Ministry of Agriculture and the Rockefeller Foundation's Mexican Agriculture Program in 1958 and the Postgraduate College of Agriculture in 1963, where he continues to teach rural development studies. In 1967 he became the first coordinator of Plan Puebla, and he is still involved in the design, operation and evaluation of regional strategies for rural development projects in Africa, Latin America and Asia.

Urban Jonsson was born in Sweden, and has graduate degrees in chemical engineering, economics, and food science and nutrition. In 1976, he became chief of the nutrition planning section in the Tanzania Food and Nutrition Center in Dar es Salaam, participating in the development of national nutrition policies. After two years with the United Nations University's World Hunger Program, he returned to Tanzania as UNICEF country representative and helped to plan and implement the Iringa nutrition project. He subsequently was appointed UNICEF's chief of nutrition at its New York headquarters. In 1989 he spent a sabbatical at Cornell University, and since 1994 has served as UNICEF's regional director for South Asia.

P. A. Kiriwandeniya is general manager for SANASA, a national federation of savings and loan societies in Sri Lanka, which has grown since 1978 to more than 750,000 members throughout the country. Having previously been involved with NGO activities that he considered too dependent on outside resources, he helped refashion existing savings societies into more modern and inclusive financial institutions. He has been associated with Community Aid Abroad, the OXFAM affiliate in Australia, and has worked with the World Council of Credit Unions to spread cooperative savings programs in other countries.

Akhter Hameed Khan joined the Indian Civil Service in 1935, studying at Cambridge University from 1936 to 1938. The colonial rulers' handling of the Bengal Famine of 1943 led him to resign from the civil service and take up work in a village near Aligarh as a laborer and locksmith. After several years he began teaching in Delhi and then became principal of Victoria College at Comilla, in what is now Bangladesh. He served briefly (1954–55) as director of the government's Village Agricultural and Industrial Development program and spent 1958 at Michigan State University before becoming first director of the Pakistan (now Bangladesh) Academy for Rural Development at Comilla in 1959. For twenty years he gave leadership for rural development experiments in Pakistan and Bangladesh. In 1980, he decided to apply the principles learned from years of work on rural development to the problems of squatters living in a vast colony called Orangi outside Karachi. He has been a visiting professor at Michigan State, Princeton, Harvard and Oxford.

Anirudh Krishna is a member of the Indian Administrative Service, Rajasthan cadre, most recently serving as director of tourism and culture. He was responsible for setting up and directing the Department of Watershed Development in Rajasthan in 1991 which is protecting 400,000 hectares of degraded or deteriorating land and which twice received the Indian Government's National Merit Certificate for best watershed development, involving user committees as well as interdisciplinary teams of technicians and officials. He has master's degrees in economics from the Delhi School of Economics and in international development from Cornell, where he was a Humphrey Fellow during 1993–94.

V. Kurien returned to India in 1949 after completing a master's degree overseas and was assigned to work with a government experimental creamery in the town of Anand in the state of Gujarat. From this began a life-long association with dairy development and farmer cooperatives. The Anand coops, whose district union came to be known as AMUL, became a model for a statewide and then a national network of dairy cooperatives. In 1965, the Government of India created the National Dairy Development Board, which Kurien was asked to head. Thirty-one years later, NDDB member coops cover one-third of India's 500 districts, with nine million households belonging and benefiting. Kurien still serves as the chief executive and honorary chairman of NDDB.

Reggie J. Laird, presently a research professor at the Postgraduate College of Agriculture in Chapingo, Mexico, received a B.S. degree from Mississippi State University, a M.S. from the University of Wisconsin and a Ph.D. from the University of California. In 1952, he joined the Rockefeller Foundation agricultural program in Mexico, where he worked primarily on developing fertilizer recommendations for maize and wheat. In 1966, he moved to the International Maize and Wheat Improvement Center (CIMMYT) and was a cofounder of Plan Puebla. When responsibility for Plan Puebla moved to the Postgraduate College in Chapingo in 1974, he joined the soils department of that institution.

Bernard J. Lecomte was born in France and trained as an engineer. After working for some years in the industrial sector, he participated in several regional planning projects in Senegal, Madagascar and Cameroon between 1958 and 1965. For eight years he headed a cooperative firm for socioeconomic studies (CINAM) in Paris, returning to Africa in 1973 where he worked as a trainer and evaluation specialist in a private institute (CESAO) in Burkina Faso. There he became acquainted with Bernard Lédéa Ouedraogo, and together they founded Six-S, a locally-based, multinational association dedicated to fighting the effects of drought in the Sahel and to ending peasants' social and economic impoverishment. He served as president of Six-S from 1977 to 1990 and has been working as a consultant with numerous organizations trying to change North-South relations.

Wilbald Lorri, managing director of the Tanzania Food and Nutrition Center (TFNC), holds a B.Sc. in biological sciences, a M.Sc. in food science and technology, and a Ph.D. in food science and nutrition. He joined TFNC in early 1977 as a project officer responsible for child nutrition issues and served subsequently as director of the Food Science and Technology Department. He was a member of the group that conceptualized and developed the approach for implementing the Joint Nutrition Support Program in Iringa during 1983 and has published several papers on young child nutrition in journals.

Simon Metcalfe, having grown up in Zimbabwe, spent the 1970s doing urban social and community work in England. He returned to Zimbabwe in 1980 to work on primary health care and community development projects for a British NGO, getting involved with issues of wildlife management and protection in rural areas as they related to alleviating rural poverty. He began working with the Zimbabwe Trust's Institutional Development Unit in 1988 and helped establish the Communal Areas Management Program for Indigenous Resources (CAMPFIRE). During 1991–92, he was a Humphrey Fellow at Cornell University, and he is now ZimTrust's technical advisor for CAMPFIRE as well as an honorary research fellow with the Center for Applied Social Sciences at the University of Zimbabwe.

Gerald F. Murray is a cultural anthropologist who teaches at the University of Florida. Originally trained in linguistics, his anthropological research in rural Haiti led him to propose an alternative to conventional reforestation strategies. He became the first chief of party for the USAID-funded Agroforestry Outreach Project in Haiti in 1981 and served for two years, maintaining contact with the project after returning to teaching. He has been a consultant for USAID, the World Bank, OAS and other agencies on agricultural and forestry projects in the Caribbean, Central and South America, East and West Africa and the Indian Ocean region.

Ida Nyoman Oka received his first degree in Indonesia, then was trained in entomology at Cornell University. After completing his Ph.D. in 1977, he joined the Indonesian ministry of agriculture, becoming head of its directorate of agricultural quarantine. From 1978 to 1986 he served as a member of FAO's panel of experts on rice IPM (Integrated Pest Management) and during the mid-1980s he helped establish Indonesia's national IPM program for rice protection. He was chairman of the program's working group from 1991 until 1994, when he retired from government service to serve as senior technical advisor of the national IPM program. The government of

Indonesia has awarded him several medals for his leadership and service for integrated pest management.

Lindesay H. Robertson served as a military engineer in the British Army, having attended the Royal Military Academy at Sandhurst and Cambridge University, before a mountaineering accident ended this career in 1953. Six years later, he went to Malawi (then Nyasaland) and worked for almost ten years with village cooperatives as a Presbyterian missionary. In 1968, he joined the department of community development as a water engineer and in this capacity worked with villagers, local administrators and other technical personnel to develop a participatory program for self-help rural water supplies. He retired from the Malawi government service in 1986 and returned to his native Scotland.

Antonio Turrent Fernández is currently leader for maize research at the National Institute of Agriculture, Forestry and Animal Husbandry (INIFAP) as well as a professor in agronomic engineering at the Postgraduate College of Agriculture in Chapingo, Mexico. He has a master's degree from the Postgraduate College and a Ph.D. from Iowa State University. His research and teaching activities address soil, crop and labor productivity and soil and water conservation for traditional farming. He is a member of scientific committees for the National Council of Science and Technology (CONACYT) and the National System for Scientists (SNI) in Mexico.

Norman Uphoff has been a professor of government at Cornell University since 1970. In 1990 he was appointed director of the Cornell International Institute for Food, Agriculture and Development (CIIFAD), an interdisciplinary program dedicated to sustainable agricultural and rural development. Before that he chaired the Rural Development Committee at Cornell and directed its Rural Development Participation Project under a cooperative agreement with USAID from 1977 to 1982. During 1978–79 he spent a sabbatical year in Sri Lanka at the Agrarian Research and Training Institute and then worked with ARTI colleagues on the Gal Oya irrigation water management project from 1980 to 1985, making follow-up visits through 1989. He also helped introduce participatory irrigation management in Nepal between 1986 and 1989.

Mechai Viravaidya, chairman of the Population and Community Development Association (PDA), was educated in Australia before joining the National Economic and Social Development Board in his home country, Thailand. He established the Community-Based Family Planning Services in 1974, which eventually built a network covering over 16,000 villages in 158 districts, reaching about 16 million people. He has served as a deputy minister of industry (1985–86) and cabinet spokesman (1986–88). His awards include the Margaret Sanger Award (1985) by the U.S. Planned Parenthood Federation and the Ramon Magsaysay Award for Public

Service. He was director of his country's National AIDS Prevention Committee and a member of WHO's Global Commission on AIDS. He serves on numerous boards of directors including the National Environmental Board and the National Cultural Commission.

C. M. Wijayaratna has headed the Sri Lanka national program of the International Irrigation Management Institute (IIMI) and is currently responsible for a participatory watershed management project in Sri Lanka implemented by IIMI. He is an agricultural economist with a master's degree from Leeds University and a Ph.D. from Cornell University. He was head of the irrigation, water management and agrarian relations division of the Agrarian Research and Training Institute in Sri Lanka during the early 1980s when the Gal Oya project started. He has worked as a rural settlement specialist for the U.N. High Commission for Refugees in Somalia and as an agricultural economist for FAO/UNDP. Before heading IIMI's program in Sri Lanka, he served as head of its program in the Philippines.

Muhammad Yunus is the founder and managing director of Grameen Bank, which currently operates 1,055 branches providing credit to over two million poor people residing in 36,000 villages in Bangladesh. He originated the concept of a bank that lends without collateral to the poorest of the poor in 1976 while teaching economics at Chittagong University as an action research project. He earned a Ph.D. from Vanderbilt University and taught economics at Middle Tennessee State University before joining the faculty at Chittagong in 1972. A member of many commissions and advisory groups, including the Global Commission on Women's Health (WHO) and the Advisory Council for Sustainable Development (World Bank), he has received numerous awards including the Magsaysay Award (1984) and the World Food Prize (1994).

Index

Institutions/organizations given in text by their abbreviations are listed this way here.

Of Related Interest
from Kumarian Press

Promises Not Kept

The Betrayal of Social Change in the Third World, Third Edition

John Isbister
UNIVERSITY OF CALIFORNIA, SANTA CRUZ

Industrialized countries and leaders of Third World nations made promises that were never kept. One result of these broken promises is that social change has often been effectively blocked. In the third edition, the author looks at some of the success stories that have taken place in East Asia and asks why such experiences have not been more widespread.

Third World Studies / Area Studies / Cultural Anthropology / Sociology / Geography / Political Science / International Studies

When Corporations Rule the World

David C. Korten
AUTHOR, *GETTING TO THE 21ST CENTURY*
PRESIDENT, PEOPLE-CENTERED DEVELOPMENT FORUM

In the minds of many, "globalization," "free trade" and the hope for rapid economic development in the Third World have become synonymous. The consequences—the growing gap between rich and poor within the developed nations as well as between the developed and Third World, the devastating impact on the environment and the high price that developing countries must pay—are often overlooked. Fortunately, the author provides alternatives to what is becoming a less and less attractive option. Korten has played major roles within the establishment he critically examines and we all gain from this opportunity to view these issues from his unique and penetrating perspective.

Political Science / Economics / International Business / International Development Studies / Environmental Studies

Achieving Broad-Based Sustainable Development

Governance, Environment, and Growth with Equity

James H. Weaver and Kenneth Kusterer
THE AMERICAN UNIVERSITY

Michael T. Rock
WINROCK INTERNATIONAL

Economic growth can lead to terrible consequences if the political, social, and environmental results are ignored. The authors provide a model that looks at growth wholistically by extending the usual economic considerations into the social, political, and environmental arenas. They then show what governments can do to achieve broad-based sustainable development—which is the kind of development most worth having.

Economics / International Economics / Political Economy / Third World Studies / Sociology / Environmental Studies

The Immigration Debate
Remaking America

John Isbister
UNIVERSITY OF CALIFORNIA, SANTA CRUZ

There is a lot being said today about immigration and the most recent immigrants. John Isbister separates the truth from the popular fiction in a balanced presentation that provides the information needed to come to informed conclusions.

Contents include the history of immigration into the United States, the structure of current immigration, the changing legal framework, the economic as well as the demographic impact of immigration on the population and the impact of immigration on American society in general.

> *Public Policy / Demography / Immigration / Ethnic Studies / Ethics / Political Science / Sociology / Economics*

Multi-Track Diplomacy
A Systems Approach to Peace, Third Edition

Louise Diamond
EXECUTIVE DIRECTOR

Ambassador John McDonald
CHAIRMAN
INSTITUTE FOR MULTI-TRACK DIPLOMACY

Peace making takes more than governments. This work delineates how nine tracks within the peace making process are interlinked.

The nine tracks are: government ... professional ... business ... the private citizen ... research, training and education ... activism ... religion ... funding ... and communications and the media

> *Conflict Resolution / Peace Studies / Political Science / International Relations / Sociology*

GAZA
*Legacy of Occupation—
A Photographer's Journey*

Dick Doughty
EDITOR, ARAMCO WORLD

Mohammed El Aydi
UNITED NATIONS COMMUNITY DEVELOPMENT OFFICER

Gaza and the PLO-Israeli peace process are continually in the news but the conditions under which the Palestinians in refugee camps are living are often overlooked. This is a very personal portrait of daily life in Gaza's camps during these changing times.

> *Current Affairs / Middle East Studies / Arab Studies / Ethnic Studies / Visual Anthropology*

Call or write us
for a complete catalog.

Kumarian Press, Inc.
14 Oakwood Avenue
West Hardford, CT 06119-2127
U.S.A.

800-289-2664 / order toll free
860-233-5895 / inquiries
860-233-6072 / fax
kpbooks@aol.com / e-mail